ROMAN POLITICAI

MW00654323

What can the Romans teach us about politics? This thematic introduction to Roman political thought shows how the Roman world
developed political ideas of lasting significance, from the consequen-
tial constitutional notions of the separation of powers, political legitimacy, and individual rights to key concepts in international relations,
such as imperialism, just war theory, and cosmopolitanism. Jed Atkins
relates these and many other important ideas to Roman republicanism, traces their evolution across all major periods of Roman history,
and describes Christianity's important contributions to their development. Using the politics and political thought of the United States as
a case study, he argues that the relevance of Roman political thought
for modern liberal democracies lies in the profound mixture of ideas
both familiar and foreign to us that shaped and enlivened Roman
republicanism. Accessible to students and non-specialists, this book
provides an invaluable guide to Roman political thought and its
enduring legacies.

JED W. ATKINS is an Assistant Professor of Classical Studies at
Duke University. His research focuses on Greek, Roman, and early
Christian moral and political thought. In addition, he works on the
modern reception of ancient political thought. He is the author of
Cicero on Politics and the Limits of Reason: The Republic and Laws
(Cambridge, 2013) and is co-editing (with Thomas Bénatouïl) the
forthcoming *Cambridge Companion to Cicero's Philosophy.*

KEY THEMES IN ANCIENT HISTORY

EDITORS

P. A. Cartledge
Clare College, Cambridge

P. D. A. Garnsey
Jesus College, Cambridge

Key Themes in Ancient History aims to provide readable, informed and original studies of various basic topics, designed in the first instance for students and teachers of Classics and Ancient History, but also for those engaged in related disciplines. Each volume is devoted to a general theme in Greek, Roman, or where appropriate, Graeco-Roman history, or to some salient aspect or aspects of it. Besides indicating the state of current research in the relevant area, authors seek to show how the theme is significant for our own as well as ancient culture and society. It is hoped that these original, thematic volumes will encourage and stimulate promising new developments in teaching and research in ancient history.

Other books in the series

Death-ritual and social structure in classical antiquity, by Ian Morris
978 0 521 37465 1 (hardback) 978 0 521 37611 2 (paperback)

Literacy and orality in ancient Greece, by Rosalind Thomas
978 0 521 37346 3 (hardback) 978 0 521 37742 3 (paperback)

Slavery and society at Rome, by Keith Bradley
978 0 521 37287 9 (hardback) 978 0 521 37887 1 (paperback)

Law, violence, and community in classical Athens, by David Cohen
978 0 521 38167 3 (hardback) 978 0 521 38837 5 (paperback)

Public order in ancient Rome, by Wilfried Nippel
978 0 521 38327 1 (hardback) 978 0 521 38749 1 (paperback)

Friendship in the classical world, by David Konstan
978 0 521 45402 5 (hardback) 978 0 521 45998 3 (paperback)

Sport and society in ancient Greece, by Mark Golden
978 0 521 49698 8 (hardback) 978 0 521 49790 9 (paperback)

Food and society in classical antiquity, by Peter Garnsey
978 0 521 64182 1 (hardback) 978 0 521 64588 1 (paperback)

Banking and business in the Roman world, by Jean Andreau
978 0 521 38031 7 (hardback) 978 0 521 38932 7 (paperback)

Roman law in context, by David Johnston
978 0 521 63046 7 (hardback) 978 0 521 63961 3 (paperback)

Religions of the ancient Greeks, by Simon Price
978 0 521 38201 4 (hardback) 978 0 521 38867 2 (paperback)

Christianity and Roman society, by Gillian Clark
978 0 521 63310 9 (hardback) 978 0 521 63386 4 (paperback)

Trade in classical antiquity, by Neville Morley
978 0 521 63279 9 (hardback) 978 0 521 63416 8 (paperback)

Technology and culture in Greek and Roman antiquity, by Serafina Cuomo
978 0 521 81073 9 (hardback) 978 0 521 00903 4 (paperback)

Law and crime in the Roman world, by Jill Harries
978 0 521 82820 8 (hardback) 978 0 521 53532 8 (paperback)

The social history of Roman art, by Peter Stewart
978 0 521 81632 8 (hardback) 978 0 52101659 9 (paperback)

Ancient Greek political thought in practice, by Paul Cartledge
978 0 521 45455 1 (hardback) 978 0 521 45595 4 (paperback)

Asceticism in the Graeco-Roman world, by Richard Finn OP
978 0 521 86281 3 (hardback) 978 0 521 68154 4 (paperback)

Domestic space and social organisation in classical antiquity, by Lisa C. Nevett
978 0 521 78336 1 (hardback) 978 0 521 78945 5 (paperback)

Money in classical antiquity, by Sitta von Reden
978 0 521 45337 0 (hardback) 978 0 521 45952 5 (paperback)

Geography in classical antiquity, by Daniela Dueck and Kai Brodersen
978 0 521 19788 5 (hardback) 978 0 521 12025 8 (paperback)

Space and society in the Greek and Roman worlds, by Michael Scott
978 1 107 00915 8 (hardback) 978 1 107 40150 1 (paperback)

Studying gender in classical antiquity, by Lin Foxhall
978 0 521 55318 6 (hardback) 978 0 521 55739 9 (paperback)

The ancient Jews from Alexander to Muhammad, by Seth Schwartz
978 1 107 04127 1 (hardback) 978 1 107 66929 1 (paperback)

Language and society in the Greek and Roman worlds, by James Clackson
978 0 521 19235 4 (hardback) 978 0 521 14066 9 (paperback)

The ancient city, by Arjan Zuiderhoek
978 0 521 19835 6 (hardback) 978 0 521 16601 0 (paperback)

Science writing in Greco-Roman antiquity, by Liba Taub
978 0 521 11370 0 (hardback) 978 0 521 13063 9 (paperback)

Politics in the Roman Republic, by Henrik Mouritsen
978 1 07 03188 3 (hardback) 978 1 107 65133 3 (paperback)

Roman political thought, by Jed W. Atkins
978 1 107 10700 7 (hardback) 978 1 107 51455 3 (paperback)

ROMAN POLITICAL THOUGHT

JED W. ATKINS
Duke University, Durham, North Carolina

CAMBRIDGE
UNIVERSITY PRESS

CAMBRIDGE
UNIVERSITY PRESS

University Printing House, Cambridge CB2 8BS, United Kingdom

One Liberty Plaza, 20th Floor, New York, NY 10006, USA

477 Williamstown Road, Port Melbourne, VIC 3207, Australia

314-321, 3rd Floor, Plot 3, Splendor Forum, Jasola District Centre, New Delhi - 110025, India

79 Anson Road, #06-04/06, Singapore 079906

Cambridge University Press is part of the University of Cambridge.

It furthers the University's mission by disseminating knowledge in the pursuit of
education, learning and research at the highest international levels of excellence.

www.cambridge.org
Information on this title: www.cambridge.org/9781107107007
DOI: 10.1017/9781316227404

© Jed W. Atkins 2018

First published 2018

A catalogue record for this publication is available from the British Library

Library of Congress Cataloging in Publication data
Names: Atkins, Jed W., author.
Title: Roman political thought / Jed W. Atkins, Duke University, North Carolina.
Description: Cambridge, United Kingdom; New York, NY, USA:
Cambridge University Press, 2018. | Series: Key themes in ancient history |
Includes bibliographical references and index.
Identifiers: LCCN 2017057300 | ISBN 9781107107007 (hardback) |
ISBN 9781107514553 (paperback)
Subjects: LCSH: Rome – Politics and government. |
Republicanism – Rome. | Political culture – Rome.
Classification: LCC JC83.A84 2018 | DDC 320.0937–dc23
LC record available at https://lccn.loc.gov/2017057300

ISBN 978-1-107-10700-7 Hardback
ISBN 978-1-107-51455-3 Paperback

Contents

Preface		*page* ix
Timeline		xii
Texts, Translations, and Abbreviations		xvi
	Introduction	I
I	The Roman Constitution in Theory and Practice	II
2	Liberty and Related Concepts	37
3	Citizenship and Civic Virtue	63
4	Political Passions and Civic Corruption	91
5	Rhetoric, Deliberation, and Judgment	II2
6	Civil Religion	136
7	Imperialism, Just War Theory, and Cosmopolitanism	166
	Conclusion	192
Bibliographical Essay		200
Bibliography		205
Index		226

Preface

This book is intended to be a first word on Roman political thought. Not first chronologically, for a number of important works have appeared in recent years on the topic by scholars working in the fields of ancient history, ancient philosophy, the history of political thought, and political theory. Rather, I hope that this book will be a first port of call for those interested in Roman political thought, including (and especially) undergraduate and graduate students as well as teachers and scholars in disciplines such as history, classics, political science, religion, and philosophy.

The book is a product of teaching. Its basic methodology of combining the analysis of texts and concepts finds a distant antecedent in a Cambridge undergraduate history course, "History of Political Thought to c. 1700," for which I offered supervisions during my graduate studies. But above all, the structure and content of this book arose from teaching Greek and Roman political thought at Duke University in a variety of contexts ranging from first-year seminars to large undergraduate lecture courses to graduate research seminars.

My students come to Roman political thought with a variety of expectations and interests: some are interested primarily in contemporary politics or political theory; others, in Roman history or early Christianity or the history of political thought. Hardly any arrive with a preexisting interest in Roman political thought. This is to be expected. In undergraduate and graduate courses on ancient political thought, the Romans typically receive far less attention than the Greeks, if they are taught at all. Yet Roman political thought is perhaps even less accessible than Greek political thought to students and non-specialists. The most fruitful work on Roman political thought takes an integrative approach, combining careful attention to a wide range of texts within their social and intellectual contexts, the consideration of topics of perennial interest in the history of political thought, and the awareness of current trends in political theory. To appreciate what

Roman political thinkers have to offer, then, requires familiarity with a number of different subjects – all undergirded by a great deal of scholarly literature, some of which is highly specialist in nature.

My foremost goal in writing this book is to equip students and teachers to appreciate the character and enduring relevance of Roman political thought by inviting them to consider the fruits of one such attempt at the integrative approach described above. As in teaching, I have aimed above all to make the ideas accessible and relevant – even if, as I shall argue, Roman political thought is most relevant when we take proper account of its "foreign" elements. As a first word, I hope to engage, move, and provoke readers to consider the topic at greater length. Thus, while my first concern is to engage with the ancient texts and ideas themselves, I have also sought to direct readers interested in further enquiry to helpful works within the massive literature.

During the course of writing this book, I have incurred many debts. The first is to my students. I first tried organizing a political theory course thematically with "Democracy: Ancient and Modern," an introductory lecture course analyzing Athenian and American democracy. Undergraduate and graduate seminars on Roman political thought followed the content and structure of this book. Finally, I tried out drafts of chapters 1 and 2 as well as material from chapters 6 and 7 in my first-year seminar on liberty and equality in Greek, Roman, and American political thought. The discussions of the National Archives in the introduction to chapter 1 and the Vietnam Veterans' Memorial in the conclusion to chapter 4 were inspired by the annual field trip that this class takes to Washington, D.C. as part of the Visions of Freedom Focus cluster led by Michael Gillespie.

A number of colleagues and friends helped at various stages of the project. Malcolm Schofield, Benjamin Keim, and Keegan Callanan offered advice and feedback on my initial proposal for this project, which also benefited from comments by an anonymous referee for Cambridge University Press. Others read early drafts of portions of the manuscript and graciously offered comments. These include William Altman, Tolly Boatwright, Bob Connor, Luca Grillo, Daniel Kapust, Sean McConnell, Kavin Rowe, and Catherine Steel. Ted Graham helped compile the timeline. I am grateful to the editors of the Key Themes in Ancient History series, Paul Cartlege and Peter Garnsey, and to Michael Sharp at Cambridge University Press for the invitation to contribute and for sound advice at every step of the process. I am also indebted to Peter and Paul for extremely helpful comments on two earlier drafts of the manuscript. Kate Mertes compiled the index.

Chapter 2 draws on material from J. W. Atkins forthcoming d, and chapter 6, from J. W. Atkins 2017. These publications arose from conferences at London and Tübingen. I am grateful to Arena Valentina and Otfried Höffe for invitations to participate. Chapter 7 adapts material to be published (in Chinese) in J. W. Atkins forthcoming a.

Finally, I am grateful to my family: Claire, William, and Caroline. This book is dedicated to the three of you, with love.

Timeline

(Some dates are traditional or approximate. The names and dates of the major periods of Roman history are printed in bold.)

753 BCE	**Foundation of Rome**
753–509	**Roman Monarchy**
?510	Rape of Lucretia
509–27	**Roman Republican Era**
509	First Valerian law, establishing right of appeal
494–287	The Struggle of the Orders
451/450	Codification of the Twelve Tables
445	Canuleian plebiscite abolishing ban on marriage between plebeians and patricians
300	*Lex Ogulnia*, opening priesthoods to plebeians
287–146	**Middle Republic**
286	*Lex Aquilia*, protecting against loss of property
280–275	War with Pyrrhus
264–241	First Punic War
234	Birth of Cato the Elder
221–201	Second Punic War
216	Battle of Cannae
?200	Birth of Polybius
199	First Porcian law, expanding rights of the Valerian law
195	Second Porcian law
186	Reform of the Bacchanalia
184	Third Porcian law
167	Polybius is brought to Rome
155	Carneades in Rome
149–146	Third Punic War
149	Death of Cato the Elder
146–27	**Late Republic**

133–121	Reforms of the Gracchi brothers
?118	Death of Polybius
116	Birth of Varro
111–105	War with Jugurtha
108	Birth of Pompey
107	First consulship of Marius
106	Birth of Cicero
104–100	Second through sixth consulships of Marius
100	Birth of Caesar
?99	Birth of Lucretius
95	Birth of Cato the Younger
91–88	Social War
?87	Cicero's *De inventione*
86	Birth of Sallust; seventh consulship of Marius
?86–82	*Rhetorica ad Herennium*
82–81	Dictatorship of Sulla
73–63	Third Mithridatic War
73–71	Third Servile War; revolt of Spartacus
65/4	Quintus Cicero's *Commentariolum*
63	Consulship of Cicero; conspiracy of Catiline; birth of Augustus
59–53	First Triumvirate (Caesar, Pompey, Crassus)
59	Birth of Livy
55	Cicero's *De oratore*; death of Lucretius?; circulation of *De rerum natura*
56–51	Cicero's *De republica* and *De legibus*
49–45	Civil War
49	Caesar crosses the Rubicon, invading Italy
46	Death of Cato the Younger; Cicero's *Brutus*
46–44	Dictatorship of Caesar
44	Assassination of Caesar on the Ides of March; Cicero's *De officiis*
43–33	Second Triumvirate (Octavian, Mark Antony, Lepidus)
43	Death of Cicero
42/1	Sallust's *War of Catiline*
41/40	Sallust's *Jugurthine War*
?40–35	Sallust's *Histories*
31	Battle of Actium
?30–14 CE	Livy's *Ab urbe condita*
35	Death of Sallust

27	Death of Varro
27 BCE–476 CE	**Roman Imperial Era**
27 BCE–284 CE	**Principate**
27 BCE–14 CE	Reign of Augustus
19	Publication of the *Aeneid*
4	Birth of Seneca; birth of Jesus
5 CE	Birth of St. Paul
14	Death of Augustus; inscription of *Res Gestae Divi Augusti*; abolition of *contio*
17	Death of Livy
23/4	Birth of Pliny the Elder
30	Death of Jesus
37	Birth of Nero
?40–?50	Birth of Dio Chrysostom
45–58	Missionary journeys of St. Paul
?50	Birth of Plutarch
54–68	Reign of Nero
54–62	Seneca's tutelage of Nero
55	Birth of Epictetus
55/6	Seneca's *De clementia*
56	Birth of Tacitus
56–64	Seneca's *De beneficiis*
61	Birth of Pliny the Younger
64	Great Fire of Rome, for which the Christians were blamed
65	Death of Seneca
?67	Death of St. Paul
68	Death of Nero
70	Destruction of Temple in Jerusalem by Titus
77–84	Agricola's campaign in Britain
79	Eruption of Vesuvius; death of Pliny the Elder
81–96	Reign of Domitian
?95	Quintilian's *Institutio oratoria*
96–98	Reign of Nerva
98	Tacitus' *Agricola* and *Germania*
98–117	Reign of Trajan
100	Pliny's *Panegyricus*
101/2	Tacitus' *Dialogus*
109/10	Tacitus' *Histories*
113	Death of Pliny the Younger

?114–?120	Tacitus' *Annales*
?115	Death of Dio Chrysostom
117–138	Reign of Hadrian
?119	Death of Tacitus
?120	Death of Plutarch
135	Death of Epictetus
155	Birth of Tertullian
161–180	Reign of Marcus Aurelius
170–180	Publication of Marcus Aurelius' *Meditations*
200	Birth of Cyprian
212	Antonine Constitution
239–284	Crisis of the Third Century
240	Birth of Lactantius; death of Tertullian
250	Decree of Decius
258	Cyprian martyred
284–476	**Dominate**
284–305	Reign of Diocletian
312	Conversion of Constantine
313	"Edict of Milan"
320	Death of Lactantius
330–1453	**Byzantine Era**
330	Foundation of Constantinople
354	Birth of St. Augustine
380	Edict of Thessalonica
386	St. Augustine's conversion to Christianity
410	Visigothic sack of Rome
426	St. Augustine's *City of God*
430	Death of St. Augustine
476	Traditional Fall of Western Empire
482	Birth of Justinian
527–565	Reign of Justinian
530–533	Justinian's *Digest*
565	Death of Justinian

Texts, Translations, and Abbreviations

Translations are either my own or taken from widely available English translations. When using the translations of others, I have indicated the last name of the translator in parentheses following the translation; I have followed a similar practice to indicate the edition of the Greek or Latin text where relevant. Please note the following editions:

> *M. Catonis praeter librum De re rustica quae exstant*, H. Jordan (ed.), Leipzig, 1860.
>
> *M. Tulli Ciceronis, De re publica, De legibus, Cato Maior de senectute, Laelius De amicitia*, J. G. F. Powell (ed.), Oxford, 2006.
>
> *Oratorum Romanorum fragmenta liberae rei publicae*, E. Malcovati (ed.), Turin, 1953.

Abbreviations for classical names and titles of works follow Lidell-Scott-Jones and the Oxford Latin Dictionary. The first appearance of an author or work is unabbreviated. Please note the following abbreviations for classical periodicals and series:

AJPh	*American Journal of Philology*
ANRW	H. Temporini et al. (eds.), *Aufstieg und Niedergang der römischen Welt*. Berlin, 1972–.
BICS	*Bulletin of the Institute of Classical Studies*
CJ	*The Classical Journal*
ClAnt	*Classical Antiquity*
CPh	*Classical Philology*
CQ	*Classical Quarterly*
G&R	*Greece and Rome*
GRBS	*Greek, Roman, and Byzantine Studies*
HPT	*History of Political Thought*

JRS	*The Journal of Roman Studies*
MEFRA	*Mélanges de l'École française de Rome. Antiquité.*
REA	*Revue des études anciennes*
TAPhS	*Transactions of the American Philosophical Society*

Introduction

In 64 BCE, during a time of great political unrest at Rome, Marcus Tullius Cicero ran for consul, the highest political office in the land. Born into a wealthy family from the small town of Arpinum about 60 miles south of Rome, Cicero had received a first-rate education. As a young man at Rome, he learned rhetoric from Lucius Crassus, a most accomplished orator and former consul, and philosophy from the head of Plato's Academy, Philo of Larissa, who taught Cicero to argue on all sides of a given issue. He supplemented this foundation by studying abroad in Greece from 79 to 77 BCE, where he continued his study in philosophy and rhetoric. After he returned to Rome, Cicero found great success as an advocate and established himself as the most acclaimed orator in Rome. He also launched his political career, progressing swiftly through the traditional order of political offices known as the *cursus honorum* until only the consulship remained.

Despite his considerable past success and formidable intellectual and political talent, Cicero's campaign for the consulship faced long odds. Since the end of monarchical rule at Rome in 509 BCE, the highest offices had been dominated by a limited number of aristocratic families (*nobiles*). This period of Rome's history, known as the Republic (509–27 BCE), saw a prolonged struggle between the elite and plebeians, which resulted (among other reforms) in lower magistracies opening up to "new men," political outsiders who lacked senatorial ancestors. But it was still rare for new men, whose ambitions were scorned and derided by the *nobiles*, to attain the consulship. Cicero was a "new man" (*homo novus*).

Cicero clearly needed all the help he could get, so his brother, Quintus, wrote a handbook advising him on how to win the upcoming election. Quintus' *Commentariolum petitionis* provides a snapshot of the practical workings of Roman politics during the Republic. It offers practical advice about what a candidate should do to run a successful campaign that results in the Roman people voting to entrust him with Rome's highest office.

Cicero must utilize political alliances (*amicitiae*) among the elite and display the virtues used to cement these alliances, such as generosity and gratitude. Rhetoric and skillful public speaking are paramount. He should understand the power of emotions like fear and hope in politics. Ideally he could broaden his base by threading the needle of presenting himself as a politician concerned with the non-aristocratic people's welfare (a *popularis*) and as someone devoted to strengthening the influence of the senate (an *optimas*). But above all, he must stay focused. "Every day as you go down to the Forum, tell yourself: 'I am a new man. I seek the consulship. This is Rome.'"[1]

Several of the political practices, institutions, emotions, and virtues described by Quintus in such pragmatic and realistic terms appear in the writings of Cicero, Polybius, Sallust, Livy, and Tacitus, where they contribute to an ideology that has come to be known as republicanism.[2] This ideology has several important defining characteristics. Rome is conceived as a commonwealth or *res publica* (literally, "the public matter"). It has a constitution that recognizes "popular sovereignty" and the rule of law. Republicanism stresses the importance of civic virtue and citizenship, and the danger of civic corruption. Essential too are oratory as an instrument of political decision-making, devotion to Rome and its gods, and a commitment to Rome's standing and glory in both domestic and international contexts. Although ancient Latin contained no word for "republicanism," Romans and non-Roman observers wrote at length on the basic elements of republicanism and on Rome's political culture, which held them together.[3]

Like many concepts, Roman republicanism can be better understood by clarifying what it is not. It does not necessarily correspond to the historical time period known as the Republic: some of the most important treatments of republican themes are found in historians, such as Livy and Tacitus, writing after the Republic had been transformed into a monarchy. Moreover, to speak of Roman republicanism as an ideology is not to suggest that all of the thinkers who engaged with its primary themes agreed with one another or even saw themselves as working within an

---

[1] For Republican elections and electioneering (including discussion of Q. Cic. *Pet.*), see Yakobson 1999 and Feig Vishnia 2012 (introductory level overview). Feig Vishnia 2012 also provides an overview of the scholarly debate over the authorship of the *Commentariolum petitionis* (108–10). For our purposes it makes little difference whether Quintus Cicero is its author.
[2] Republicanism as conceived by the later tradition: Pocock 1975; Skinner 1978; Rahe 1992. Roman republicanism: Connolly 2015. For Polybius, Sallust, Livy, and Tacitus as republican thinkers, see Balot 2010 (Polybius); Kapust 2011b (Sallust, Livy, and Tacitus); Vasaly 2015 (Livy).
[3] For *res publica*, see now Hodgson 2017.

identifiable tradition of thought; indeed, "republican" thinkers diverged on their conceptions of some of republicanism's central concepts. Nor does the republican ideology necessarily correspond to practical everyday political realities. In fact, Roman republicanism may be described as projecting a "realistic utopia" in which historical and current political practices, institutions, and values become ideals designed to hold the commonwealth together.[4]

The current book offers an introduction to Roman political thought that places at its center this ideological notion of Roman republicanism. In the pages to follow, we will investigate how the basic elements of republican thought were articulated and defended in the Republic, and then transformed or rejected later in Roman history. Roman republicanism, then, is presented here as an entrée into the much broader subject of Roman political thought. This broader category requires definition. Let's take the three terms in reverse order.

First, "thought." As opposed to political philosophy, which consists of the systematic and theoretical treatment of politics usually written by an author working within a philosophical tradition, political thought designates a much broader field, encompassing any and all thinking about politics (C. J. Rowe 2000: 1–2; Cartledge 2009). Political thought may be conveyed through a broad range of media and literary forms, from poetry to historiography to inscriptions to philosophical treatises and dialogues. I have sought to employ as great a range of this literary evidence as the subject and space allow.

Second, "political." The term "political" comes to us from Greece, not Rome. So in a sense by speaking of Roman *political* thought, we are already using conceptual language that is foreign to Rome. However, in doing so we are following much earlier observers of Roman history. Writers such as Polybius, Cicero, Dionysius of Halicarnassus, Josephus, and Cassius Dio used the key Greek political concept of *politeia* to describe Roman political society and culture. Often translated in English as "constitution" or "regime," the term *politeia* in Greek political thought is a multivalent concept, encompassing the arrangement of offices and institutions in a political society as well as its political culture or way of life, that is, fundamental social values and principles comprising and determining citizenship, laws, religion, ethical norms, military organization, education, art, music, the economy, international relations, and more (J. W. Atkins forthcoming e). Latin lacks any simple equivalent to *politeia*. When Latin

---

[4] Roman republicanism as an ideology: Wilkinson 2012: 7–17.

writers needed to translate the Greek word, they often turned to the equally multivalent *res publica*. However, as Cicero indicates in his *De republica*, whose very title offers a Latin version of Plato's *Politeia* (*Republic*), no less central than the formal institutions of the *res publica* were the laws, practices, and customs that shaped its citizens. Indeed, the Roman "constitution" is composed of the laws, rights, and customs that shaped the Roman way of life over time (see chapter 1). Accordingly, the analysis of virtually every chapter of this book turns on the rich interplay between the formal political institutions and political culture that characterized Roman political thought.

Roman social and political culture was highly competitive. All Roman citizens, regardless of class, were concerned with standing and esteem in the eyes of others. For plebeians, this standing separated them from slaves; for elites, standing was maintained and enhanced by successfully receiving public honors, by enjoying military success, and by holding political office. Citizens' lives were highly regulated by perceptions of honor and shame, which directed all aspects of their public and private lives. In addition to citizens' social behavior, Roman political culture regulated public institutions, such as criminal and public law, state religion, the military, and domestic and foreign policy (Hölkeskamp 2010: 17–18). Both ancient proponents and critics of Roman republicanism engaged Roman political culture in their analyses. Important terms for Rome's political culture include *honor, gloria, decus, virtus, nobilitas, dignitas, auctoritas, imperium, pietas, religio, ius, lex, mos, aequalitas, libertas,* and *mos maiorum*. The meanings and significance of these terms for Roman political thought will be discussed throughout this book.[5]

It is important here to note that many of the terms I have identified as comprising Roman political culture more precisely reflect Rome's elite culture as portrayed by such self-styled defenders of the senatorial aristocracy (*optimates*) as Cicero, whose writings disproportionately shape our view of the Roman Republic. A number of important works in recent years have attempted to dive beneath the predominating aristocratic ideology to disclose a suppressed but potent Roman crowd with their own egalitarian, "democratic" ideology and political culture. While a political culture shaped by an aristocratic "honor code" lies near the heart of Roman republicanism as it is disclosed in our most significant surviving texts dealing with political themes, these same works sometimes challenge and critique

---

[5] Roman political culture: Hölkeskamp 2010; Blits 2014; Arena and Prag forthcoming. Roman honor: Lendon 1997; Barton 2001; Kaster 2005.

the predominant ideology, whether from perspectives working from inside (e.g., Sallust) or outside (e.g., Lucretius) of republicanism. This too is part of the story of republicanism and (more broadly) of Roman political thought.[6]

Third, "Roman." My conception of the political means that *Roman* political thought includes that which is prompted by reflection on the Roman *politeia*. Consequently, this book includes analysis not only by Roman citizens, including those such as Plutarch and Dio Chrysostom who wrote in Greek and employed Greek concepts, but also by foreign observers of the Roman *politeia* such as Polybius. Even though Rome was traditionally founded in 753 BCE, due to my focus on republicanism, the nature of our textual evidence (such evidence was thin before the second century BCE), and the constraints of space, I concentrate especially on the first century BCE and first two centuries CE, periods known as the late Republic (146–27 BCE) and Principate (27 BCE–CE 284). Space unfortunately prohibits a thorough treatment of early Christian political thought, even though many Christians too were Romans. Still, we will explore several significant ways in which Christianity transformed or challenged Roman republicanism.

The contents of this book are organized thematically: each chapter takes one or more key concepts pertaining to Roman republicanism and traces them across relevant periods of Roman history. Featured concepts include the following: the Roman constitution, sovereignty, and legitimacy; liberty and such related topics as slavery, equality, rights, and property; citizenship and civic virtue; political passions and civic corruption; rhetoric, political deliberation, and judgment; civil religion and religious toleration; and imperialism, just war theory, and cosmopolitanism. The movement within each chapter is diachronic, though chapters are not comprehensive in their chronological scope. The movement across chapters begins with a chapter on the institutional components of the Roman *politeia* as it develops from the dawn of the Republic to the beginning of the Byzantine era. This chapter also doubles as a sketch of Roman political and institutional history. Chapters 2 through 7 deal with fundamental analyses of aspects of Roman political culture, beginning with liberty, which according to Cicero "is natural to the Roman people" (*Philippics* 6.19), and concluding with the idea

---

[6] Roman crowd and popular politics: Millar 1984; 1986; 1998; Morstein-Marx 2004; Wiseman 2009. Connolly 2015 takes a literary approach to Roman republicanism focusing on subversive elements existing in texts by Cicero, Sallust, and Horace alongside the predominant principles of the Roman regime. Honor code and ideology: Hölkeskamp 1993; Long 1995.

of cosmopolitanism, which considers Rome in light of a notional world community.

The structure of this book integrates individual texts and arguments with a political concept's broader history at Rome. This approach has a number of advantages. Readers can trace the transformation of ideas over time or "listen in" on debates about concepts within and beyond the republican tradition. The thematic approach also facilitates bringing Roman political thought into conversation with alternative analyses of fundamental political concepts by other voices in the history of political thought and by contemporary political theorists.

A short, introductory book must be selective. My primary consideration for deciding which texts should be discussed in each chapter was what would facilitate an accessible and stimulating treatment of the concept or concepts under discussion. While I aimed to cover a broad range of authors and texts over the course of the book, I did not hesitate to use authors or works in multiple chapters if they contributed to multiple concepts. Cicero appears in every chapter, a decision made both to reflect the significance of his own contributions to the concepts explored in this book and to provide a consistent reference point for viewing the contributions of others. Polybius, Sallust, Livy, Seneca, Tacitus, and St. Augustine also make significant appearances in multiple chapters. Other writers and texts make major contributions to a single chapter (e.g., Lucretius, Plutarch, Quintilian, Tertullian), and many others show up briefly in one or more places throughout the book. At appropriate points, I have provided some very basic introductory remarks to help orient readers to the most significant writers and texts, but in every case such treatments are subordinate to the concept(s) investigated in the chapter. I have similarly been selective in citing modern scholarship, both because of space constraints and because we are relatively well served by reference works in this area.[7]

As Aristotle saw when he completed his study of 158 *politeiai*, the concept of *politeia* provides a handy analytical lens for the comparison of different political societies. Three comparisons in particular concern us in this book. Let's take them in ascending order of the importance given them. The first is the relationship between Roman republicanism and Athenian democracy. Over the past three decades, scholars have debated to what extent Republican Rome was democratic (see chapter 1). Several chapters (1, 2, 3, 5, 6) touch on this question, often through brief comparisons with

---

[7] Important works include C. J. Rowe and Schofield 2000; Balot 2009; Hammer 2014. See bibliographical essay for details.

democratic Athens. The political culture of Roman republicanism generally suppressed the sort of full civic participation theoretically promoted by democratic Athens. But no less an important transmitter of republicanism than Cicero argued that popular sovereignty was essential for the legitimacy of the *res publica* and that respect for popular judgment was necessary for legitimate oratory (see chapters 1 and 5). Since it is impossible within the scope of this volume to pursue comparisons with Athens at any length, the interested reader should consult the comparative analyses of democratic Athens and Republican Rome provided by the team of scholars in Hammer (2015) and the discussion in Cartledge (2016).

Democratic Athens of the fifth and fourth centuries BCE gave birth to political theory. Greek, and especially classical Athenian, political thought has claimed a far greater share of modern-day political theorists' attention than that of the Romans. In fact, for much of the twentieth century, Roman political thought was frequently ignored or dismissed as derivative of Greek thought by political theorists (Hammer 2008: ch. 1). In contrast, recent scholarship on Roman political thought has turned to comparisons with the Greeks in order to highlight original Roman contributions. At appropriate points, I draw brief comparisons with Greek political thinkers such as Thucydides, Plato, and Aristotle, as well as with the philosophies of Stoicism and Epicureanism that originally flourished in Athens. In this book, I am less interested in the question "Why Roman instead of Greek political thought?" than in the more general question "Why Roman political thought?" However, the former question is not difficult to answer. Consider just some of the ideas or issues pursued in this book that one could not explore to the same extent, if at all, through a study of Athenian political thought:[8]

- Political legitimacy
- The separation of "constitutional" powers
- Individual, protected, "constitutional" rights
- The extension of citizens' rights to non-citizens
- Arguments for religious toleration
- The tension between universal (or "cosmopolitan") principles and the particular values that shape and define citizens' relationships to their particular polities
- Just war theory

---

[8] Original Roman contributions via comparison with Greek political thought: see, e.g., E. M. Atkins 1990; Schofield 1995; Lintott 1997; J. W. Atkins 2013; Straumann 2016; Remer 2017. Why the Romans?: Hammer 2008; 2014; Connolly 2015.

- The creative contributions to political thought resulting from the rise of Christianity
- How the transition from a republic to monarchy impacts topics such as liberty, citizenship, civic virtue, law, frank speech, political decision-making, civil religion, and religious toleration
- The relationship between "republicanism" and "empire."

The second major comparison of regimes is facilitated by Rome's transformation from a republic to a form of monarchy under the Empire. Throughout this book we will look at just what points the crucial changes occurred that transformed republican rule to monarchy, changes initially introduced in the name of restoring the Republic. In many cases we find that the transformation of Roman institutions and political culture was comparatively small and gradual, even if the net effect from the point of view of a committed republican like Cicero would have been astonishing. While some changes like the abolition of popular assemblies in 14 CE were blatantly conspicuous, the majority came from altering the mixture of the ingredients that composed republicanism – increasingly emphasizing law and order at the expense of conflict and disagreement (chapters 1, 5, 7); bolstering the republican notion of freedom as absence of another's control at the expense of the complementary republican notion of freedom as related to status, agency, and participation (chapter 2); expanding the juridical notion of citizenship as a bundle of protections and rights from citizenship's "core and heart" (Gardner 1993: 2) under the Republic to encompass almost the whole of the concept under the Principate (chapter 3); removing the virtue of justice from its preeminent position as the chief virtue for citizens and assigning its administration solely to the emperor (chapters 2, 3); and the redrawing of the public and private spheres, transforming the *res publica* ("the people's property") in significant ways into the emperor's *res privata* ("private property"; chapters 1, 2, 6).

The third and final comparison of regimes is between Roman republicanism and modern liberal democracy. The question of Roman republicanism's relationship to, and relevance for, modern liberal democracy has fascinated scholars since Benjamin Constant's nineteenth-century essay "The Liberty of the Ancients Compared with that of the Moderns" stressed that Rome, like Athens, was by and large irrelevant and dangerous for modern regimes (see chapter 2). Subsequent scholarship has both affirmed and challenged Constant's conclusion. In particular, a number of important recent works have argued that Roman republicanism contributed to or anticipated important aspects of our modern liberal-democratic situation, such as individual liberty, constitutionalism, and concerns with economic inequality. However, to approach Roman republicanism in order to discern its contemporary relevance invites the danger of focusing on those aspects that appear to some degree compatible with liberal democracy at the expense of those that are less savory but no less important. And predictably studies concerned with the contemporary relevance of Roman republicanism have given liberty, constitutionalism, and rhetoric far more attention than civil religion or imperialism.[9]

It is in fact impossible to neatly cleave the (from our perspective) more palatable parts of Roman republicanism from the unsavory or antiquated. Almost all of the concepts discussed in this book emanate from the common core of Rome's illiberal political culture. As we shall see, one can no more understand republican liberty than republican imperialism without noting the vital importance of Rome's honor code. Hence, this book invites readers to return to republicanism's origins in a status-driven, hierarchical, slave-owning world with a very different set of values from those prevailing in western liberal democracies. The elite Romans that bequeathed to us republicanism "knew nothing of capitalism or globally interrelated markets; they had no interest in modern subjectivities and autonomies; they assumed the necessity of empire; and they pursued military and political life within an ethical framework characterized by canons of nobility, aristocratic excellence, and traditional moral virtues" (Balot 2010: 486). Consequently, the study of Roman political thought enables us to approach republicanism afresh by providing critical distance from the modern ideas of capitalism, individual autonomy, the nation-state, and liberal-democratic constitutions that are often taken for granted in accounts of republicanism based largely on the modern republican tradition.[10]

I am strongly convinced of the relevance of Roman political thought for contemporary liberal-democratic readers. In fact, I have self-consciously written this book as a citizen of one such liberal-democratic regime and have not hesitated to draw comparisons to American political history, institutions, culture, and practices. As will become clear, I think that we must work hard to highlight the familiar concepts in Roman political thought, especially given the historical myopia of our own age. However,

---

[9] Individual liberty: Pettit 1997; Skinner 1998. Constitutionalism: Straumann 2016. Economic inequality: Connolly 2015. Rhetoric: Connolly 2007; Kapust 2011b; Remer 2017.

[10] For this criticism, see Balot 2010: 486 and the conclusion of this book. Republicanism based on the modern tradition: Pettit 1997; 2012; Viroli 2002; cf. Skinner 1998.

relevance may be found in what from our perspective is strange, jarring, or distasteful as well as in those aspects that strike a more familiar or comforting chord. Throughout this book, I will try to show that it is precisely this deep mixture of the familiar and the foreign that makes Roman political thought especially interesting and relevant. In the conclusion, I reflect on how this may be so.

CHAPTER I

The Roman Constitution in Theory and Practice

The Roman Constitution

Each year millions of visitors travel to Washington, D.C. to see the original United States Constitution, Bill of Rights, and Declaration of Independence in the National Archives Museum. When Americans think of a constitution, they naturally think of the historic document containing the nation's supreme laws, which organize and regulate state power. They are not alone. With the exception of the United Kingdom, almost all contemporary nations have a written constitution.

The Romans did not. The Roman "constitution" is not found in a single codified document, or even in a set of laws and treaties. In fact, there was no single Latin word for the idea of a constitution. *Constitutio*, from which we get our English word "constitution," was commonly used during the Roman Imperial era to indicate an emperor's enactment or decree. The Romans described what modern historians refer to as the "Roman constitution" with a variety of Latin words for custom (*institutum, mos, consuetudo*), statute (*lex*), and customary law (*ius*; Lintott 1999: 4).

In order to appreciate how this conglomeration of concepts formed a "constitution," we might consider a rare occasion on which the word *constitutio* does refer to the Roman "constitution." In his work *De republica* (*On the Republic*), Cicero (106–43 BCE) adapts a general meaning of the word *constitutio* (an arrangement, an order, or a set of defining principles or characteristics) to refer to the order or defining principles of Roman political society. According to Cicero, the defining principles of the Roman order developed over time (*Rep.* 2.37) and were reflected in law (*lex, ius*), rights (*iura*), and the established social, legal, and political customs (*mos, institutum, consuetudo*) that shape the Roman way of life. Thus, in his account of the "constitution (*constitutio*) of the republic" in book 2 of *De republica* (2.37; see also 1.41, 69), Cicero touches on citizenship, law, citizens' rights, religion, national character, military action, and sources of wealth as well as the form, function, and development of various political institutions and offices. Rome's political and social institutions were embedded in and arranged according to a larger social order, which we may call political culture.

Like Cicero, some modern historians emphasize that the institutional and legal aspects of the Roman "constitution" were deeply embedded in and regulated by Rome's political culture (Hölkeskamp 2010). This political culture consisted of concepts like *auctoritas* (authority, influence, guidance), *dignitas* (standing or esteem), *honos* (honor), *gloria* (glory), *gratia* (favor), *virtus* (virtue), and the conglomeration of time-tested principles, models, and standards of personal, social, and political behavior grouped under the heading *mos maiorum* (ancestral custom). Thus, just as the Greek idea of "constitution" or *politeia* included a community's way of life (*bios*), so the Roman conception of their "constitution" has as much to do with the Roman way of life as with political institutions, magistracies, and procedures (see introduction).

Despite their common integration of political institutions and culture, the Romans more clearly than the Greeks approached the modern idea of a constitution, as Benjamin Straumann has argued in a recent book. According to Straumann (2016), modern constitutionalism requires the existence of deeply entrenched rules that govern the institutions through which political power is exercised. These rules are harder to change than common legislation. Such higher-order legal norms circumscribe institutional power and limit the type of legislation that an assembly may pass. In particular, Roman customs (*mores*) gave special weight to certain political institutions and customary citizens' rights (*iura*), such as the right to a trial or to possess private property. As in modern thought, these citizens' rights, which are antecedent to rather than conferred by any particular rulers or assembly, "serve as trumps or limitations on the actions of rulers" (J. W. Atkins 2013: 141). We will examine the most important of these citizens' rights in the next chapter, where we will also consider in detail whether the Romans shared our modern notion of rights.

What accounts for the special status of these rights and institutions? The first and most traditional source is customs that were especially longstanding and politically important in Roman history (J. W. Atkins 2013: 141–44). The second-century CE jurist Ulpian nicely relates why these customs carried such force. Echoing the formulation of the first-century BCE linguist and polymath Varro, Ulpian identifies customs (*mores*) as "the tacit consent of the people, which has been consolidated with time through long habit" (Ulp. *Regulae* 1.4, quoted in Arena 2015: 224).[1] If customs represent

---

[1] Cf. Varro's definition of *mos* at Servius, *In Vergilium commentarius* 7.601.

popular consent ratified over time, then they possess substantial power to direct, guide, and restrain political behavior.

A second potential source is nature. As Straumann (2016) argues, Cicero attempts in his *De legibus* (*On the Laws*) to use natural law to justify as higher-order norms basic institutions and magistracies of a modified version of the Republican "constitution."

In sum, there are both important similarities and differences between the ways Romans conceived of their "constitution" and the typical modern notion of a constitution. So long as we keep this in mind, we can follow convention and use the term "constitution" (without scare quotes) when discussing Rome's fundamental political institutions and procedures.

What are the basic institutions, magistracies, and procedures of the Roman Republican constitution? We will review the most important of these in this chapter. After examining the analyses of the Republican constitution by Polybius and Cicero, the chapter traces how the Roman constitution changed under the Principate and Empire. Along the way, we will listen to ancient observers reflecting on Rome's changing constitution, yielding powerful accounts of enduring political ideas such as the mixed constitution, sovereignty, and legitimacy.

Polybius on the Republican Constitution

The Roman Republican constitution was conceived in violence. According to the traditional Roman account, kings ruled at Rome from its founding in 753 BCE until 509 BCE. The historian Livy (c. 59 BCE–CE 17) describes the event that precipitated the end of the monarchy at the close of the first book of his history, *Ab urbe condita* (*From the Foundation of the City*). Sextus Tarquinius, the son of the seventh and final king, Tarquinius Superbus, raped Lucretia, the wife of an aristocrat. After Lucretia committed suicide, Brutus – a friend of Lucretia's husband and nephew of the king – rallied the people to drive the Tarquins from Rome and abolish the monarchy. In its place the Romans established two annually elected magistrates called consuls (Livy 2.1–2).

Many of the details of the early years of the Republic are hazy, since they are provided by historians such as Livy writing hundreds of years after the fact. The evidence is better for the "middle" (287–146 BCE) and "late" Republic (146–27 BCE). Our earliest and perhaps best account of the Roman Republican constitution comes from an outsider, the Greek historian Polybius.[2] Born into the governing class in Megalopolis in the

---

[2] Polybius' account of the Roman constitution as "best": Millar 1984; Lintott 1999.

Peloponnese around 200 BCE, Polybius served as a cavalry commander before being taken as a hostage to Rome in 167 BCE; he would stay among the Romans for seventeen years. During this time, Polybius became acquainted with some of Rome's leading families. Thus, he acquired a close-up look at the Roman political system in practice. According to Polybius' *Histories*, Rome's constitution accounted for its rise from Italian power to world superpower. Because of its constitution, Rome achieved world dominance despite extreme reversals of fortune, such as the disastrous defeat at Cannae in 216 BCE, when more than 60,000 Roman soldiers died on the battlefield at the hands of Hannibal and the Carthaginians.

Polybius' account of the Roman Republican constitution is found in the fragmentary sixth book of his *Histories*. The Greek word he uses for "constitution" is *politeia*. As one would expect given the typical meaning of this term, Polybius' account covers both Rome's formal political institutions and broader aspects of its political culture, such as religion, patriotism, civic virtues, honor, and the funeral oration. Hence much as Cicero's, Polybius' conception of a constitution involves far more than the institutions and deeply entrenched juridical rules covered by the modern concept.

Polybius analyzes the Roman constitution using the categories of rule by one, the few, and the many familiar from Greek political thought, with a lineage going back at least to the historian Herodotus writing in the fifth century BCE. According to Polybius, the Roman constitution combines all three categories of rule so thoroughly that not even Romans can tell definitively whether their constitution is a monarchy, aristocracy, or democracy (6.11.11). Each part of the constitution, when examined on its own, provides a clear example of rule characteristic of these different constitutions (6.11.12). He illustrates this claim by taking his readers on a tour of the Roman constitution. We will follow Polybius on this tour, at some points supplementing his account with details that he omitted or with later constitutional developments. At the conclusion, we will answer two important questions: Is Polybius an accurate guide to the Roman constitution? What is the significance of Polybius' account as a work of political theory, irrespective of its historical accuracy?[3]

Polybius begins with rule by one, or monarchy (6.12). Despite the fact that two consuls were elected annually, Polybius found a monarchical element in the consulship, Rome's highest magistracy, by virtue of the consuls holding the greatest *imperium* (power of command) both at home and

---

[3] Rule by one, the few, and the many as guiding principles of Greek political thought: Cartledge 2009.

abroad. Consuls had the authority to command troops and to preside over the senate and the popular assemblies (with the exception of the assembly of the plebs; see below). From the fourth century BCE, the office was open to plebeians as well as patricians, and from 367 at least one of the two consuls had to be a plebeian. By early in the second century BCE, a minimum age of forty-two and previous occupancy of the second highest office (praetor) were established as prerequisites for the consulship.[4] The consulship is the main magistracy discussed by Polybius. The other magistracies on the *cursus honorum* are either mentioned in passing or omitted altogether.

Next Polybius considers the Roman constitution from the perspective of rule by the few and turns to the senate (6.13). The senate was the main advisory council for magistrates and consisted mainly of ex-magistrates, who were members for life (though senators could be expelled by a special magistracy known as the censor, usually held by ex-consuls). While the senate technically was a guiding and advising rather than a legislative body, in practice its authority was vast and extended to a wide range of matters of public policy, from warfare, to religion, to finance. As Polybius points out, the senate has power over revenue, crimes in Italy requiring a public investigation (such as treason, poisoning, and assassination), the declaration of war, and the reception of foreign embassies (6.13). The senate was also the main forum for political debate (see chapter 5). In the late Republic, one automatically gained entrance to the senate after becoming quaestor, a junior magistracy (the minimum age requirement was thirty) on the traditional *cursus honorum*. For admission to and continued membership in the senate during the late Republic, senators also had to meet a minimum wealth requirement of 400,000 sesterces – a significant amount but one that was attainable by (and indeed required of) members of the second-highest class, the equestrians. (The emperor Augustus would later increase the senatorial wealth requirement to 1,000,000 sesterces – a huge amount within reach of only a few hundred families – to draw a sharper distinction between the senatorial and equestrian orders.)

Finally, Polybius moves to rule by the many and to the power of the people (6.14). The people are "sovereign" (*kurios*) over "honors and punishments," that is, over the elections of the magistrates and the law courts (6.14.4). Though certain practical details would change (see below), during the Republic popular assemblies possessed the sole power to pass

---

[4] For the consul, see Pina Polo 2011a. For additional magistracies, see Lintott 1999 and the various summaries of Roman Republican institutions provided by Rawson 1983: 232–35; Brennan 2004: 61–65; North 2006; Mouritsen 2015. These were among the sources I consulted in supplementing Polybius' account of Roman institutions.

legislation and, through elections, alone could entrust to magistrates the power of command (*imperium*) crucial to the legitimacy of their use of force (cf. 6.14.9–10). For these reasons, many modern scholars agree with Polybius and identify the people as Rome's sovereign authority – an issue to which we shall soon return. In the realm of international relations, the people decide questions of war and peace; they have power to ratify or reject treaties put to them by the senate (6.14.10–11).[5]

What Polybius refers to as the "people" (*dêmos*) requires substantial elaboration. The Latin word for "people," *populus*, was used in two senses. Sometimes it referred to the entire citizen body regardless of class; at other times, it indicated the lower class, the plebs, in contrast to the elite (Schofield 2015: 115–16). Roman popular assemblies, which Polybius indiscriminately lumps together when describing the powers of the "people," mirrored these two uses of the term. The people as a whole, including both patricians and plebeians but excluding slaves, women, and children, assembled in three forms, which received the following names: Curiate Assembly (*comitia curiata*), Centuriate Assembly (*comitia centuriata*), and Tribal Assembly (*comitia tributa populi*). There was also the assembly of the plebs (*concilium plebis*).

The Curiate Assembly, the oldest Roman assembly, held only formal power by the late Republic. Divided by wards (*curiae*), this assembly's main function was to ratify the powers of command (*imperium*) of the highest elected magistrates.

More important in the late Republic was the Centuriate Assembly, which began as a military assembly (*centuriae* were military units). The Centuriate Assembly, typically presided over by a consul, elected such higher magistrates as consuls, praetors, and censors. Earlier in the Republic it dealt with crimes of treason, capital cases, and passed legislation binding on the people. However, it declined in use in both its legislative and its judicial capacities in the late Republic. The Centuriate Assembly was divided according to wealth into five classes, which were further subdivided into centuries. There were 193 centuries in total. All of those owning little or no property (*proletarii* and *capite censi*) were placed within a single century. Decisions were determined by a majority of centuries rather than by a majority of individual votes.

The last type of assembly of the whole people, the Tribal Assembly (*comitia tributa*), was one of the most commonly used during the late

---

[5] The people as Rome's sovereign authority: Nicolet 1980: 224; Millar 1995; 1998; Ando 2011; Hammer 2014: 9–10.

Republic. It met and voted by tribes (thirty-five in all by the first century BCE), a majority of which carried the vote. This assembly elected junior magistrates (quaestors, aediles, military tribunes), passed legislation, and handled popular trials concerning non-capital offenses. As with the Centuriate Assembly, in the late Republic the responsibility for criminal cases moved from the Tribal Assembly to standing criminal courts (*quaestiones perpetuae*). Presided over by a magistrate (normally a praetor) who also appointed jurors (from the propertied class), the trial involved opportunities for speeches on behalf of the prosecution and the defendant, the presentation of witnesses, and a majority vote by the jury (Alexander 2006: 244–45).

The assemblies of the plebeians (*concilia plebis*) were created during the so-called conflict of the orders, a period early in the history of the Republic (494–287 BCE) in which the plebs struggled to achieve important protections and freedoms against the patricians (see chapter 2). The first secession of the plebs in 494 BCE resulted in the creation of the *concilium plebis*. Originally its laws were binding only on the plebs; however, the *Lex Hortensia* of 287 BCE extended the legislation to all citizens, after which time the *concilium plebis* passed most of the routine legislation at Rome. It both elected, and was presided over by, the tribunes of the plebs, another important popular institution arising out of the conflict of the orders. (The tribunate was instituted in 494–493; the first tribunes of the plebs were the spokesmen for the plebs in their negotiations with the patricians.) Tribunes (eventually ten served annually) were supposed to defend the interests of the plebs, that is, the vast majority of the Roman *populus*. To this end, they had the power to veto legislation by popular assemblies or decrees of the senate. Tribunes were sacrosanct: any person committing acts of physical violence against a tribune was accursed and liable to death. An extension of a tribune's sacrosanctity was his veto power, which also included the capacity to grant "help" (*auxilium*) to citizens against magistrates in response to a formal appeal (*appellatio*; see chapter 2).

One final type of popular "assembly" deserves to be mentioned. The non-decision-making meeting known as the *contio* was an important popular institution that has received increased attention in recent years from historians (Pina Polo 1996; Millar 1998; Morstein-Marx 2004). Only a magistrate may convene a *contio*. Magistrates might call a *contio* to propose legislation before the people at least three successive market days (seventeen to twenty-five days) before it is due to be put to the vote in a *comitium* (Morstein-Marx 2004: 8). They might also convene an ad hoc *contio* in order to address the people directly, occasions to which Cicero attributed great influence and unpredictability (*Pro Flacco* 57). While the *contio* was not a decisive deliberative assembly, it played a crucial role in supporting the ideological notion that the *res publica* was "the people's business." By serving as the primary means by which politicians consulted, informed, "polled," and rallied "the people," "the *contio* embodied the fundamental principles of the free *res publica*, founded on *libertas* [liberty] and popular 'sovereignty'" (Mouritsen 2017: 80; for more on the *contio*, see chapter 5).

As this brief survey indicates, popular assemblies at Rome took complex forms, and their powers were ordered and limited by a number of institutional, class, and ideological factors. For Polybius to group them all indiscriminately under the power of "the people" would be a bit like giving an account of "popular power" in the American political system by lumping together town-hall meetings, the state legislatures, both branches of Congress, and local, state, and national elections, and then calling it all "democracy."[6] As we shall see, the level of generality with which Polybius treats the role of the people in the Roman constitution has important implications for his account.

Polybius concludes his analysis by describing the interaction between these different parts of the constitution (6.15–18). The powers possessed by any one group, however considerable, require the support of other parts to carry out significant public policies. Take the case of a consul holding absolute *imperium* over a large army in the field. The consul is dependent upon the senate for military provisions, extending his command to allow him to finish expeditions of more than a year, and awarding him the important honor of a triumph upon his return. Finally, at the end of his time in office, the consul will give an account to the people for his actions. Due to the distribution of powers among the consuls, the senate, and people, each governing organ has the ability to cooperate with or obstruct the other.

How well does Polybius capture the character of the Roman constitution? As scholars frequently note, while Polybius is certainly right to note the difficulty of classifying the Roman constitution, his one-few-many schema hardly does justice to its details. In particular, he omits important details from his accounts of the magistracies and popular assemblies to give the false impression that the Roman constitution contained three separate sets of internally unified and functionally equal legal powers.[7]

---

[6] I have adapted this metaphor from McGing 2010: 184.
[7] Greek theory distorts Polybius' account: Von Fritz 1954; Walbank 1998; Cartledge 2016: 249–63; Mouritsen 2017: 7–13. For a more positive assessment of Polybius' sensitivity to Roman reality, see Lintott 1997; 1999: 24–25.

Consider monarchy. In order to find "rule by one" at Rome, Polybius needed to ignore the fact that executive power at Rome was divided between two consuls, both of whom equally possessed the highest *imperium*. He also downplayed the fact that *imperium* had been dispersed through other magistracies, such as the praetor, dictator, and *magister equitum* (leader of the cavalry; see Beck 2011). Similarly, Polybius does not mention the fact that consuls were members of the senate before, during, and after their consulship, and shared common economic and political concerns with fellow members of the ruling class. These and other considerations undercut Polybius' case for a unified "monarchical" power within the consulship, and few scholars take seriously Polybius' claim to locate a monarchical element in the Roman constitution.

Democracy is a different matter. Following Polybius' emphasis on the "sovereignty" of the people to legislate and to elect offices – crucial for validating the decisions of the political community – scholars such as Fergus Millar have argued that Rome was in fact a type of democracy.[8] This raises two issues that bear on Polybius' treatment of "the people" at Rome: whether the people are sovereign and whether popular sovereignty at Rome implies that the popular element in the Roman constitution was democratic.

First, sovereignty. The idea that "the people" validate the decisions of the political community is deeply engrained within Roman republican ideology. This notion reflected political reality in Republican Rome to the extent that popular consent, provided by the various voting assemblies, was a necessary condition for the validity of laws and of the senior magistrates' *imperium*. By indiscriminately classifying all of the popular assemblies as "the people," Polybius effectively conveys this republican conception of popular sovereignty in which the various assemblies comprised of smaller groups of citizens stand for the approval of "the people" as a whole.

However, Polybius' vague treatment of popular power fails to account for several important limits to the Roman republican conception of sovereignty, the character of which can be better appreciated by comparing it to the modern notion of sovereignty. For modern political philosophers, beginning with Jean Bodin in the sixteenth century and Thomas Hobbes in the seventeenth, sovereignty entails supreme authority, the

---

[8] Rome as a democracy: Millar 1984; 1986; 1995; 1998; 2002b; qualified by North 1990. Millar is reacting against the predominant twentieth-century view of Rome as an oligarchy dominated by elites through political alliances and patronage with poorer clients (see, e.g., Syme 1939; Badian 1958; Gelzer 1969).

unquestionable right to command and to be obeyed by others within a political community (Philpott 2011). Roman republican sovereignty does not fully meet this definition. First, it is not clear that the people possessed, even in a formal sense, supreme authority. Cicero (*Rep.* 2.56) notes that the votes of the Centuriate Assembly required ratification by the *auctoritas* of the senators (*auctoritas patrum*). Even if only a formality, this procedure implies that the people's will was not the supreme authority inasmuch as it required, at least symbolically, the validation of the Roman aristocratic council (Mouritsen 2017: 20). Moreover, the people at Rome do not possess the unquestionable right to command obedience, at least not without important qualifications. For instance, the people cannot assemble themselves without the initiative of a magistrate or tribune. And once assembled, attendees at a *comitia* do not have the power to debate, modify, or introduce new legislation but only to vote "yes" or "no" on legislation put to them. What is more, as we shall see in chapter 6, popular legislation could be annulled by a priest called an augur, a power that Cicero presents as an important instrument for limiting the popular will (Cic. *Leg.* 2.31; 3.27). None of these limits to popular sovereignty are factored into Polybius' account.

One final important point about sovereignty: the modern notion of popular sovereignty entails a corresponding notion of political legitimacy. To hold that the people retain the fundamental right to command entails that legitimate political rule must be conducted on behalf of, and with the consent of, the people. This requires an account of the people as a body of rights-holders and an abstract notion of "government" as something to be validated or invalidated by these rights. Both of these requirements are absent in the account of Polybius, who consequently (and in line with classical Greek political thought) had no such conception of political legitimacy.[9]

What about democracy? Polybius' general and unified account of popular power, with no attention to class and other limiting features, allows him to exaggerate the influence of the "democratic" element by drawing a false equivalence between the Roman *populus* and the *dêmos* in a Greek democracy (Cartledge 2016: 257). The limitations of Rome's democratic element become clear when compared with Athens, the democratic

---

[9] For a helpful discussion of sovereignty at Rome to which my own discussion in the previous two paragraphs is indebted, see Mouritsen 2017: 19–25. Sovereignty and legitimacy: Philpott 2011: 561. Criteria for legitimacy: Schofield 1995; J. W. Atkins 2013: 140–44.

gold standard (Mouritsen 2001: 35–36, 93–94; Hölkeskamp 2010: 20–21; Cartledge 2016: 247–63).

Let's begin with the process of passing legislation and voting within the assemblies. In ancient assemblies and modern legislatures alike, there are few powers greater than the power to frame legislation and set the agenda, to determine what can be voted on, what may be discussed, who may speak, and for how long (Garsten 2006: 1–2). At Rome, these powers did not reside with the people. Unlike in democratic Athens, Roman popular assemblies could vote only on proposals recommended by magistrates; citizens had no right to speak freely in the assemblies. While Athenians voted according to the principle of "one-man, one-vote," the Romans voted in blocks. This ensured that not all votes counted equally. For example, since the Centuriate Assembly voted in blocks according to wealth, and the vote ended as soon as the requisite number of candidates received a majority of votes, elections for Rome's highest offices may have been decided before the centuries from the poorest classes had a chance to vote. (Historians debate to what extent this happened; perhaps this system placed the deciding votes in the hands of the poor.) Finally, within the Roman electoral system there was no provision for the democratic mechanism of the lottery, the means of selecting members of the Athenian council of 500 (the steering committee for the people's assembly) and the people's law courts. Given these features of the Roman voting system, Cicero, a critic of democracy, sharply distinguished it from a democratic system like that at Athens (*Flac.* 15–16).

Next, there is the crucial issue of political participation, which received little emphasis in Republican Rome in comparison to Athens. Mouritsen (2001: ch. 2) estimates that only 3 percent of citizens voted during the late Republic, and fewer participated in the non-voting assemblies. While participation at Athens fluctuated, it was considered important, at least in theory; for example, in c. 392 BCE Athens introduced remuneration to encourage a higher turnout at assemblies by making it possible for poorer citizens to attend, who otherwise would not have been able to afford to do so. Political equality, the defining principle of the democratic Athenian regime, gained little traction within the prevailing Roman republican ideology (see chapter 2).

This brings us to a final key factor differentiating Republican Rome from democratic Athens: the former's aristocratic political culture, which Polybius discusses at the conclusion to book 6 when he turns to consider Rome's "customs and laws" (6.47.1). Polybius places religion at the heart of Roman political culture. Roman religion is "the greatest difference contributing to the superiority of the Roman constitution (*politeia*)" and "what holds together the Romans' public affairs" (6.56.6–7). Revealing his own aristocratic biases, Polybius argues that since the "multitude" is "always fickle and full of lawless desires, irrational anger, and violent passion," the elite must "check" them with the "invisible fears" of religion (6.56.11). To Polybius' mind, this method of aristocratic social control, which fundamentally shaped the Roman *politeia*, preserved the predominance of the senate, thereby contributing to Rome's superiority over its more democratic rival, Carthage (see chapter 7).

Why did Polybius, who found much in Rome's aristocratic political culture that agrees with his own anti-democratic biases, exaggerate the popular role in Rome's constitution? The answer requires us to step back and place Polybius' treatment of the Roman constitution within the historian's broader concerns with chance, causality, and prognostication. Since at least the time of Herodotus, Greek historians and philosophers had noticed that a finite number of forms of political rule – constitutions – shaped human political life (J. W. Atkins forthcoming e). Polybius' own classification of these forms of rule depended upon the number of rulers and whether the form of rule was good or corrupt. Moving from the rule by one person to rule by the many, Polybius pairs good forms of constitutions (kingship, aristocracy, and democracy) and their corrupt opposites (tyranny, oligarchy, and mob rule). In the thought of Plato and Aristotle, ideal forms of rule were dependent in part upon chance, a force that, as Polybius observed, played a powerful role in human affairs. However, Polybius argued that constitutions did not change by chance. Instead, their movements followed a fundamental "law of nature" (6.9.10), which produced a cyclical pattern of constitutional change – Polybius' well-known theory of *anakuklôsis* (Trompft 1979). If statesmen can understand this law, they will have the ability to predict the future direction of a polity's constitution and plan accordingly (6.9.11).[10]

Polybius' "law of nature" is based on a particular view of human nature and social psychology (Hahm 1995). Human beings are by nature rational, self-interested creatures moved by fear and sympathy from shared suffering to live together and cooperate in political society. So long as the fear of harm is present due to a real or imagined danger, human beings will cooperate with one another and the political society will remain stable. Civil strife and revolution occur when secure conditions remove from

---

[10] Polybius' anti-democratic bias: Lintott: 1999: 23–24; Cartledge 2016: 257–58. Chance and causation: Brouwer 2011 (with bibliography). Prognostication: Brink and Walbank 1954.

some members (especially the ruling class) the imaginative capacity to put themselves in the position of other members; hence, they have no qualms about increasing their own advantage at the expense of others. The recipients of these injustices revolt and establish a different form of constitution, with a different number of rulers exemplifying different values than those of their predecessors (6.5–9).

This account of constitutional instability suggests a solution: the institutionalization of fear so that it is distributed among all who share in the constitution. Polybius identified just such a mechanism in the mixed constitution of Lycurgus, the famous Spartan lawgiver (6.3.8), who achieved political equilibrium by carefully counterbalancing the monarchical, aristocratic, and popular elements of Sparta's constitution. Similar principles, in Polybius' view, accounted for the success of the Romans, who "arrived at the same end as Lycurgus – the best form of constitution in our day" (6.10.14). Thus, in his analysis of the success of Rome's constitution, Polybius brings into play his earlier account of human psychology (see esp. 6.18). The actors that comprise each part of the constitution are, like all human beings, fundamentally self-interested, driven to increase their own power, standing, and honor; but they are also responsive to fear, in particular, the fear that other parts of the constitution will interfere with their power. In times of war, the "competition" between the parts of the constitution to do the most to save the republic ensures that nothing is left undone. In times of peace, this same competitive and self-interested attitude keeps any one individual or part from growing too powerful.

It is likely that the requirements of Polybius' theory of constitutional change led him to distort the Roman constitution. Given his model, Polybius needs to construe the Roman constitution as composed of monarchical, aristocratic, and democratic components, each possessing its own well-defined legal powers that are strong enough to counterbalance the powers of the others. This also partially accounts for his divergences from prior Greek models of the "mixed constitution." Thucydides' and Aristotle's versions of the "mixed constitution," in which oligarchic and democratic values were blended or "fused" together within the constitution, would not have yielded distinct and separate powers. And while Aristotle's predecessor, Plato, at one place introduced the language of "curbing" into his discussion of the mixed constitution, his predominant metaphor was the mixing and blending of principles (Hahm 2009). More importantly, Plato did not include anything approximating Polybius' idea of the separation of powers, a concept that is analytically distinct from that of the mixed constitution (J. W. Atkins 2013: 92). It is this notion

of the separation of powers, which flows from his scientific account of
regime change with its promises for political prognostication and institutional design, that constitutes Polybius' enduring contribution to political
thought (see conclusion).[11]

One final point. It would be misleading to portray Polybius' constitutional theory as informed completely by Greek theory at the expense of
Roman constitutional reality. Polybius suggests that Rome's constitution
developed over many generations "through many struggles" (6.10.14), and
it is reasonable to suppose that this idea comes from his observation of the
present Roman agonistic political culture and his historical awareness that
essential constitutional provisions arose from conflicts between the plebeians and patricians (Lintott 1997: 80; 1999: 24; cf. Cicero, *Rep.* book 2).
If so, it was Polybius' contact with Rome that enabled him to transform
the fundamental goal of Greek constitutional thought. For Polybius, the
goal of politics is no longer the harmony or unanimity (*homonoia*) sought
by Plato, Aristotle, and much of classical Greek political thinking. Rather
than eliminate conflict, Polybius shows how it may be made productive
by a well-designed constitution. By linking the agonistic desire for power,
honor, and status that defines Roman political culture with the common
good or advantage of the broader political community, Rome conquered
the world in less than fifty-three years (220–167 BCE).[12]

Cicero on the Roman Constitution

The Roman constitution's capacity to make conflict productive, which
Polybius praised in theory in the second century BCE, would be challenged
in practice in the first, a century filled with a series of civil wars. The first
civil war began in 88 when, in an unprecedented act, one of Rome's consuls, Sulla, marched on Rome. Following a second march on Rome in 82,
Sulla assumed the dictatorship (a dictator was a magistrate with supreme
imperium appointed for a short term to deal with a specific military or
civil emergency), changed the constitution by weakening the powers of the
tribunes, and proscribed his political enemies. In 63 Catiline, recent loser
of the consular election to Cicero, led an army against Rome. The 50s saw
the establishment of an uneasy political alliance between three military

---

[11] Mixed constitutions of Thucydides and Aristotle: Hahm 2009; Aristotle's mixed constitution as a
"fusion": Lintott 1997: 72. Separation of powers as the defining feature of Polybius' constitutional
thought: J. W. Atkins 2013: 92–93; Straumann 2016: 152–53 (stresses legal nature of power).

[12] Link between agonistic desire for status and the common good: Erskine 2013. The account of
Polybius in this section draws on J. W. Atkins 2013: 85–93.

and political heavyweights, Marcus Licinius Crassus, Pompey the Great, and Julius Caesar, which gave way to outright civil war in the early 40s after Caesar crossed the Rubicon in 49. Within a year, Caesar had defeated Pompey and held the first of a series of dictatorships, which ended with his assassination on the Ides of March, 44 BCE.

In the midst of this instability, in the late 50s, Cicero wrote what in his estimation was his greatest work of political philosophy, *De republica*. The work showcases a dialogue set in 129 BCE in the aftermath of the tumultuous attempt by the tribune Tiberius Gracchus to redistribute public land to landless citizens. The legislation, though having substantial popular appeal, brought Gracchus into conflict with the majority of the senate: the law passed the assembly only after another tribune, who attempted to veto the legislation, was removed from office. In spite of being a tribune, which implied sacrosanctity, Gracchus was ultimately killed in a riot led by Scipio Nasica, a former consul from a family of patrician descent. The dialogue's main character, the general and consul Scipio Africanus, was Scipio Nasica's cousin. The work's conversation begins when one of the characters, referring to the turmoil brought by Gracchus' death, asks why there are now "two senates and almost two peoples" (1.31).[13]

Thus, as with Polybius' earlier account of the Roman constitution, the resolution of political conflict is a central theme of Cicero's work. Like Polybius, Cicero is concerned with constitutional change (*Rep.* 1.45, 64–68; 2.45); he too suggests that a constitution incorporating democratic, aristocratic, and monarchical elements is the most resistant to change (1.45, 69; 2.42), and he identifies the Roman constitution as a mixed constitution that developed over time.

Because of these similarities, scholars frequently assimilate Cicero and Polybius to a single tradition of thinking about the mixed constitution. However, there are important differences, beginning with the historical perspective from which each writer approached the constitution: Polybius tries to explain Rome's unparalleled success, whereas Cicero, in light of recent political turbulence, tries to restore the constitution, which he describes as a beautiful painting faded over time (5.2). There are at least six other theoretically significant differences.

The first difference concerns human nature. Whereas in Polybius human beings are driven into society "due to the weakness of their nature" (6.5.7), for Cicero the "first cause of their coming together is not so much weakness as a certain natural herding together of human beings" (1.39). Moreover,

---

[13] For the political context evoked by the dramatic setting of *De republica*, see Zetzel 1995: 6–8.

human beings are a complex mix of passions and reason (2.67; J. W. Atkins 2013: 104); human nature is neither as transparent, predictable, or controllable as Polybius supposed. In Scipio's accounts of constitutional degeneration in books 1 (1.64–68) and 2 (2.45–51), Polybius' socio-psychological insights are conspicuously not applied. Indeed, the latter passage, which treats the degeneration of monarchy into tyranny at Rome, portrays fear as the catalyst rather than the restrainer of the ruler's unjust behavior (see especially 2.45).

Second, and following from the first, Cicero's account denies that there is any single fixed pattern of constitutional change; rather, the simple regimes pass power between them randomly, as if playing a game of ball (1.68).

Third, whereas Polybius is concerned with "pragmatic history" – with deeds rather than with ideal regimes like Plato's *Republic* (6.47.7–8) – Cicero remains very interested in images of ideal, rational rule. His treatment of monarchy represents one model (1.58–60); the ideal state of Plato's *Republic*, another (2.21–22, 52); and the picture of the heavenly order in the concluding Dream of Scipio in book 6, a third (see esp. 6.21 Powell = 6.17 Zetzel, with J. W. Atkins 2013: ch. 2). Given that it is responsive to the irrationality and contingency that drives human affairs (2.57), the Roman mixed constitution of Cicero's *Republic* is not the best constitution absolutely but the best constitution possible. Most accurately, inasmuch as Carthage and Sparta are also mixed constitutions, Rome is the best exemplification of the best possible constitution (2.42, 66). In presenting the mixed constitution as the best practical constitutional form, Cicero follows Plato and Aristotle, who introduced their own versions of the mixed constitution in response to non-ideal political conditions.[14]

Fourth, whereas Polybius had emphasized the people's sovereignty over laws and elections as an important element in his account of Rome's constitution, Cicero goes further and makes popular sovereignty fundamental to the very notion of a commonwealth (*res publica*), which he defines as the "property of the people" (*res populi*), evoking the idea of property ownership from Roman law (1.39; Schofield 1995). The people in a sense own the commonwealth. By "people" (*populus*) Cicero means the citizen body as a whole. In order for a citizen body to exist (rather than a mere "crowd," *multitudo*), a sufficiently large group of people must be brought together

---

[14] For the mixed constitution in Plato, see *Laws* 3.693c–e. Aristotle says that the polity, a mixture of democracy and oligarchy, is the best practical alternative for most Greek city-states. For discussion, see J. W. Atkins 2013: ch. 3, esp. 81–83.

by agreement about justice (*ius*) – later unpacked at 1.49 as entailing equal rights under law – and common advantage (1.39). Government of the *res publica* is carried out by magistrates on behalf of the Roman people, who entrust themselves to the magistrates' care (1.51). To betray this trust by ruling the *res publica* as if it belonged to one individual or one part of the people does not indicate the existence of an inferior constitution; rather, such rulers cannot legitimately claim to rule a commonwealth at all. Likewise, if a mob should subvert the rule of law, the commonwealth does not have a bad constitution (Polybius' mob rule), but no constitution, for once the laws and rights that bind the people together are removed, no citizen body (*populus*) remains (3.35 Powell = 3.43–45 Zetzel).[15]

Cicero's discussion of citizens' rights and political legitimacy sets him apart not only from the thought of Polybius but also from that of Plato and Aristotle. Fred Miller, Jr. has argued (controversially) that individual rights were essential to Aristotle's account of political justice. Even so, Aristotle lacks Cicero's conception of a citizen body as the holder of a priori rights (in Cicero's case, grounded in Roman tradition) that place limitations on how magistrates may rule and against which they must justify their legitimate authority. With his analysis of the concept of *res publica*, Cicero supplements the question of the best form of constitution (think of it as a ceiling or upper limit) that was the guiding principle of the political thought of Plato and Aristotle with the question of what counts as a legitimate form of rule (think of it as a floor, or lower limit), which became a central question in the thought of John Locke and his followers in the liberal tradition.[16]

Fifth, though like Polybius, Cicero occasionally employs the language of "balancing" and "checking" powers, *De republica*'s account of the Roman constitution goes well beyond the balance of powers emphasized in Polybius' model. This is most apparent in one of the few passages where Cicero utilizes balancing language. There must be a balance of "power (*potestas*) in the magistracies, authority (*auctoritas*) in the deliberation of the aristocrats, and liberty (*libertas*) in the people" (2.57). What is important is not the senate's formal power, but its *auctoritas*, its influence. *Auctoritas* means precisely not to have power (*potestas*) or command (*imperium*); it is an advising and educative capacity rooted in the senate's ties to Roman

---

[15] Sovereignty in Cic. *Rep.*: Schofield 1995; Arena 2016 argues for a "quasi-alienation" of popular sovereignty in Cicero's sequel, *De legibus*.

[16] Cicero's definition: Schofield 1995; Asmis 2004; J. W. Atkins 2013: ch. 4. Legitimacy: Schofield 1995. Rights in Aristotle: Miller 1995. Aristotle and Cicero compared on rights and legitimacy: J. W. Atkins 2013: 144–48.

tradition and its lack of formal legal power (Oakeshott 2006: 226; Arendt 2006: 171–206). As Dio Cassius notes (55.3.5), *auctoritas* has no equivalent in Greek thought; thus, it is unsurprising that it played no significant role in Polybius' account.

More generally, whereas Polybius had innovated with his account of the separation of powers, Cicero returns to a view of the mixed constitution closer to Aristotle's model, which stresses the blending of the principles and interests of different socio-economic classes (Lintott 1999: 220–25). As a consequence of this different approach, Scipio, unlike Polybius, recognizes that class dynamics come into play within the different elements of the Roman constitution. Thus, in his account of the development of the Centuriate Assembly, Scipio illustrates in some detail the arrangements that enabled the wealthy aristocracy, though in the minority, to have the greatest power (2.39). For Scipio the "popular" element of the Roman constitution is not truly "democratic"; in fact, he argues approvingly that the development of the popular element of Rome's constitution denies the principle, at the heart of Athenian democracy, that "the greatest number should have the greatest power" (2.39). As for the mixture between the different classes, Scipio emphasizes that the mixture must be "fair" or "equitable" (2.57) rather than "equal," and the version of the Roman constitution that he presents and approves favors the aristocracy. (See further chapter 2 for Cicero's discussion of democratic equality.)

Sixth, and finally, there is Cicero's treatment of political conflict. As Joy Connolly has recently argued (2015: ch. 1), conflict between the plebeians and patricians shapes the development of the Republican constitution outlined in the second book of Cicero's *De republica*. Given Cicero's belief that the struggle for glory and *imperium* is essential for aristocratic liberty (see chapter 2), it is doubtful that he would approve of any regime that completely eliminated these agonistic desires in the name of complete order and absolute rational control (J. W. Atkins 2013). Nevertheless, the statesman's most important duty is vividly portrayed as ensuring harmony and concord among the different political orders, a harmony facilitated by justice (2.69). By self-observation and education, the statesman offers himself as a mirror to other citizens (2.69). Republican institutions that channel conflict are not enough if a republic lacks justice, consensus, and concord – and virtuous statesmen who can bring them about through education and persuasion.[17]

---

[17] Cicero and Polybius: Ferrary 1984; Asmis 2005; J. W. Atkins 2013: ch. 3; Straumann 2016: ch. 4. Cicero's ideal statesman: Zarecki 2014 (links the ideal statesman to Cicero's acceptance of the

The Roman Constitution: From Republic to Monarchy

By December 43 BCE Cicero was dead, a victim of proscriptions by the triumvirate of Mark Antony, Marcus Lepidus, and Gaius Octavius, who had successfully filled the power vacuum left by the death of Octavius' great uncle, Julius Caesar. This arrangement was short-lived. Lepidus soon lost influence, and Octavius and Antony engaged in a power struggle that ended with the defeat of Antony and the Egyptian pharaoh Cleopatra at Actium in 31 BCE. Exhausted from two decades of civil war, the Romans permitted the victor, Octavius, to rule for the next forty-five years. (Fifty-seven years in all, from the date of the formation of the triumvirate in 43 BCE to his death in 14 CE.) Thus, from the Romans' own perspective the Republic ended as it had begun: with violence. Just as the rape of Lucretia triggered its beginning, so civil war led to its demise.

Octavius did not openly overthrow the Republic. In fact, in his *Res Gestae* (*Deeds Accomplished*), he goes out of his way to present himself as the Republic's liberator and restorer. Yet despite his emphasis on the perpetuation of republican institutions, laws, customs, and magistracies, there were important changes. In 27 BCE, Octavius was granted the title of Augustus – a name that according to the historian Cassius Dio (53.16.8) implied that he was more than human – and that of *princeps* (first citizen). He would hold the consulship continuously for several more years in violation of the annual rotation of the office that, according to the historian Livy (2.1.1), had first distinguished the Republic from a monarchy. In 23 BCE Augustus, without being elected to the office, received a lifetime entitlement to the full powers of the tribune of the plebs, including the rights to introduce legislation, to call the people's assembly and senate into session, and to exercise veto power to block other magistrates – all of this despite not officially holding the office. Although after 23 BCE Augustus no longer held one of the two consulships, he received "greater proconsular power" and perhaps also, in 19 BCE, consular power for life.[18] His proconsular power gave him command over the armies and ensured that only he would enjoy the honor of a triumph for victories abroad. Thus, Augustus

---

inevitability of monarchy at Rome); Nicgorski 2016: ch. 5 (describes a "Socratic" ideal statesman who exercises prudence in changing circumstances).

[18] Historians disagree about whether Augustus received lifetime consular powers in 19 BCE. The chief source for this view is Dio 54.10.5.

enjoyed *imperium* both within Rome (consular *imperium*) and outside of Rome (proconsular *imperium*).[19]

Despite Augustus' insistence that he had "transferred the *res publica* from [his] power into the dominion of the senate and Roman people," and that all magistracies were equal in power (*Res Gestae* 34), from the vantage point of a Republican observer, the changes would have been significant. By consolidating the *imperium* of several magistracies in his hands and by obtaining the powers of the tribunate, Augustus greatly reduced the public space previously available for elites to participate in politics. In the process, he detached his various powers from the traditional constraints of offices to which they were attached.

In 2 BCE, Augustus had the senate, which he had "packed" with his own supporters, confer upon him the name "father of the fatherland" (*Res Gestae* 35). It did not escape the notice of ancient observers that the *princeps* and Roman "republic" were becoming increasingly intertwined. As the poet Ovid once put it, "Caesar is the *res publica*" (*Tristia* 4.4.15).[20] There is a sense, as the historian Tacitus, writing in the early second century, observes, that by "throwing off equality" Augustus transformed the public concern, *res publica*, into his own private *domus*, with himself as the *paterfamilias*. The constitution (*status civitatis*) had been transformed; the old *mores*, lost (*Annals* 1.4). Later in the *Annals*, when recounting Augustus' funeral, Tacitus imagines a debate about the *princeps*'s rule, which gives the final word to his detractors (1.9–10). Augustus' famed devotion to the Republic was a mask for his lust for mastery; his famed peace was bloody. Beyond the façade of old names and magistracies, it became apparent that Augustus would suffer neither check nor balance to his power (Wallace-Hadrill 1993).

From other vantage points, constitutional changes did not seem so stark under the Principate – what modern historians call the period from 27 BCE to 284 CE. For example, Roman jurists continued to emphasize the twin elements of popular sovereignty – the people's power to pass legislation (*Digesta* 1.3.1; *Dig.* 1.3.32.1; Gaius, *Institutes* 1.3) and to confer *imperium* on magistrates, including the *princeps* (*Dig.* 1.4.1.pr), even if such "sovereignty" in reality was no more than "the vestiges of a Republican myth" (Johnston 2000: 624). Magistrates' powers and jurisdictions were strictly determined and circumscribed by law. Failure to exercise power within

---

[19] Augustus' tribunician powers and proconsular *imperium*: see, e.g., Syme 1939: 336–37; Adcock 1959: 75–78; Cartledge 2016: 267.

[20] See Hodgson 2017: ch. 7.

these limits resulted in acts that were null and void. Yet despite all the talk of conferred and limited powers by the jurists under the Principate – what Johnston (2000: 630) refers to as the "idea of the constitutional state" – the head of the state, the *princeps*, remains largely and ominously absent from their treatment of public law.

But the *princeps* would not elude treatment by others. He is eloquently addressed in the first book of *De clementia* (*On Mercy*) by Seneca the Younger (c. 4 BCE–65 CE). Seneca was an adherent of Stoicism, a philosophical school that began in Greece during the Hellenistic Age that followed Alexander the Great's death in 323 BCE; his literary output includes a dozen philosophical essays, 124 letters on ethical topics, and nine tragedies. Seneca also served as political advisor to Nero (ruled 54–68), and it is to Nero that *De clementia* is addressed. Written shortly after the emperor assumed power in 54 at the age of seventeen, the work advises the new *princeps*. The first book praises Nero and reminds him of his duties as *princeps*, an exercise that draws on Greek kingship treatises and Latin panegyric or praise speech (Braund 2009). Seneca uses terms central to republican conceptions of the constitution to theorize about kingship, a term that he is not shy about using interchangeably with *princeps* (1.4.3).

First, consider the republican conception of a "citizen body" (*populus*). In contrast to Cicero, who had argued that the "bond of law," justice (*ius*), and common advantage transformed a mere crowd (*multitudo*) into a body of citizens (*populus*; *Rep.* 1.39, 49), Seneca suggests that the crowd (*multitudo*) is dependent only on the yoke (1.1.1) or bond (1.4.1) of the *princeps*. He further strengthens the necessary association between *princeps* and citizen body by exploiting the metaphor of a body: "you [Nero] are the mind of your *res publica*; it is your body" (1.5.1).

Once again, comparison with Cicero is illuminating. In his *Pro Marcello*, a speech delivered in 46 BCE, Cicero had praised Julius Caesar for his clemency and had highlighted the Republic's deep dependency on the life (*anima*) of one man (22–23). Revisiting the interdependence between Caesar and the Republic two years later under very different political circumstances, Cicero exploited the body metaphor to justify the dictator's assassination – like a gangrenous limb, tyrants must be amputated before they destroy the entire body (*De officiis* 3.32). Seneca diffuses Cicero's argument for tyrannicide by recasting the relationship of *princeps* to citizen body in the terms of *Pro Marcello*. To remove the *princeps* is to remove the animating principle from the citizen body; thus, Caesar's assassination resulted in the death of the *res publica* (1.4.3). In the metaphor the ailing limbs are now disobedient citizens, and mercy (*clementia*) is the virtue that should guide the *princeps* when surgery is necessary. Without the *princeps* there is no citizen body.

Seneca similarly exploits the republican (and more particularly Ciceronian) notion of government as a matter of trust (*fides*) undertaken by a guardian (*tutela*; Cic. *Rep.* 1.51; *Off.* 1.85), notions that for Cicero were incompatible with monarchy (*Off.* 1.26; Stacey 2014: 139). Now this power has been entrusted to the *princeps*, not by the people but by the gods, who have selected him to be their representative and as such to exercise the powers of life and death for the world (1.1.2). It is to the gods that the *princeps* must give an account (1.1.4). Nevertheless, he is bound by the obligation imposed by responsibilities to the people and the greatness of his position. Rule (*imperium*) is therefore a "noble slavery" (1.8.1) imposed on the emperor, a condition that he shares with the gods (1.8.3). He must conduct his rule rationally according to natural law (1.19.1).

Accountable only to the gods, the *princeps*'s behavior is regulated by his own conscience rather than by the republican devices of law and popular accountability after leaving office. The *princeps* watches over himself *as if* he were going to have to give an account before the laws (1.1.4; Griffin 2000: 537). One of the goals of *De clementia* itself is to facilitate this self-watching: "I have set out to write about mercy, Nero Caesar, to act in a way as a mirror and show you to yourself" (1.1.1). By exercising conscience, Nero should develop an appropriate *persona* or role (1.1.6) – not a false "mask" (*persona* is a theatrical term) that is at odds with one's true "character" (*natura*). Like other Stoics, Seneca argues that the true role for the *princeps* is that which agrees with the station nature has assigned him (Brunt 2013: 275–309). This involves exercising magnanimity, enabling one to stand above petty issues that would provoke anger in most private citizens, as well as mercy – a prudential decision to apply a penalty less than what could justifiably be imposed under law. As the "father of the fatherland," he should rule in a paternalistic manner that promotes peace, trust, justice, and security among his children; in short, he should subordinate his own interests to theirs (1.14.1). This paternal, rational care that instills goodwill in his subjects is what separates the king from the tyrant (1.13.1–5). It also wins the love of his citizens, the *princeps*'s only impregnable defense (1.19.6). To argue that the *princeps* should supplement love with fear, as Machiavelli later would do in chapter 17 of *The Prince*, is to overestimate the psychological reciprocity that flows from the mutual dependence of *princeps* and people (1.19.5), the torments of conscience (1.13.3), and the power of fear to motivate as well as to enervate one's enemies (1.12.4–5).

All this adds up to a defense of monarchy in light of the seemingly irreparable failure of the Republican constitution. In another work (*De beneficiis* 2.20), Seneca had criticized Brutus, one of Caesar's assassins, because he had falsely supposed that "liberty," "equality of civic rights," and the rule of law (for which, see chapter 2) could be maintained once the *mores* that had sustained the Republican constitution had been lost. Given the current incapacity of the people for self-government, the *princeps* is presented as simply indispensable. The only alternative is "the license to self-destruct" (*Cl.* 1.1.8; trans. Braund).

Several of the themes represented in Seneca's complex and brilliant *De clementia* would be appropriated in speeches presented to the emperor Trajan (ruled 98–117 CE) by his advisors Pliny the Younger (61–c. 113 CE) and Dio Chrysostom (c. 40–115 CE). Pliny's *Panegyricus*, delivered to the emperor before the senate on September 1, 100 CE, is a classic eulogy of the *princeps*'s virtues (see chapter 3). However, from the perspective of theoretical analysis of the institution of the Principate, more interesting are the speeches of Dio Chrysostom – a talented orator (Chrysostom means "golden mouth") and eclectic Greek philosopher from Prusa in Bithynia (now northwestern Turkey).

Towards the beginning of Trajan's reign, Dio delivered four orations on kingship to the *princeps*. Like Polybius, Dio divides constitutions (*politeiai*) by the number of rule into three simple good types and their degenerate opposites (3.45–50). However, for Dio there is a clear hierarchy among the good types (democracy is the worst), and the best form is not a mixed constitution but kingship (3.50). As in Seneca, and in kingship treatises in general, Dio extols the virtues of the good king, in particular, the classic cardinal virtues of wisdom, justice, courage, and self-control (3.58–60). Pushing a version of the Stoic thesis that only the wise (i.e., the completely virtuous person) is really king, Dio argues that even if a man should secure the constitutional position of king, and even if, like Alexander the Great, he should conquer the world, he will still never be king if his character is "slavish, illiberal, and vicious" (4.75). A king's greatest threat to his rule comes from himself rather than from another world superpower (4.55–58). What makes a ruler a legitimate king is not so much his constitutional position as his moral character.

Like Seneca, Dio emphasizes that the good king is guided by natural law (1.42–44). Indeed, the king should realize that the universe itself is a type of city; its citizens include all human beings and the gods; it is ruled by reason (*logos*), which is the "only strong and indissoluble principle of fellowship and justice" (36.31). This is the Stoic idea of the cosmic city, which will be explored in greater detail in chapter 7. Such an idea of a city (*polis*) has critical capacity. Traditional regimes like tyrannies, democracies, and oligarchies are not worthy of the name "city," marked as they are with constant strife, division, and conflict (*stasis*) over political rule. Rather, the city that is worthy of the name is "kingship according to law with complete friendship and agreement (*homonoia*)" (36.31). Concord and friendship were key characteristics attributed to the city by early Stoic thinkers, who, influenced by Cynic anti-conventionalism, leveraged their revised conception of the city to challenge conventional regimes (Schofield 1999a; J. W. Atkins 2015). Dio's treatment of monarchy thus carries critical potential.

One way of lending perspective to Dio's analysis of monarchy would be to compare it with Cicero's republican thinking about the constitution in which the legitimacy of a ruling authority depended on the existence of a law-bound sovereign citizenry that has entrusted *imperium* to magistrates who rule in their interest. On Dio's conception, the legitimacy of a regime depends on the sovereign self-control of a monarch who rules according to the rational and lawful administration of divine reason that regulates the universe. Still, despite the critical potential that these ideas had for critiquing regimes, Dio, like Seneca and Pliny, seems to have been more concerned with directing and challenging the current *princeps* than in advocating radical revisions to political and social institutions (Gill 2000; Brunt 2013: 151–79).

Political Legitimacy and Residual Republican Constitutionalism in the Empire

The Principate ended in 284 CE with the advent of Diocletian's reign, which marked what historians called the "Dominate" after the new title of address adopted and imposed by emperors: *dominus* (lord or master). Two years later, Diocletian shared his rule with another emperor in the eastern part of the empire; both men appointed sub-emperors, leading to what historians refer to as the tetrarchy (rule by four). This system came to an end in 313 CE, when Constantine defeated his rivals to become sole emperor in the western part of the empire; in 324, Constantine became sole ruler over both halves of the empire. After the death of Theodosius I in 395, the split between east and west became more pronounced for the next century or so. The western empire traditionally ended in 476, when Emperor Romulus Augustulus was forced to abdicate power. After this episode, there was only one legitimate emperor ruling from Constantinople in Turkey until the city fell to the Ottoman Empire in 1453.

More important than the institutional changes during this time was the rise in importance of Christianity. In 313, following his own conversion to Christianity the year before, Constantine issued the "Edict of Milan," which extended toleration to Christians (for toleration, see chapter 6). In a 380 edict, Theodosius expressed his will that all Roman citizens embrace their emperor's own version of Trinitarian Christianity.

Even under the Roman Empire, with the Republic long in the rear-view mirror, concerns raised by Republican analyses of the constitution were not completely irrelevant. Consider examples from two authors who, in light of concerns of their own times, found it useful to revisit Cicero's Republican account of legitimacy. The first is St. Augustine (354–430), whom we will discuss in greater detail in future chapters. Defending Christians against the charge that Christianity had led to the sack of Rome by the Germanic Visigoths in 410, Augustine in his monumental *City of God* exploits Cicero's definition of a *res publica* to argue that pagan republican government before the advent of Christianity had a legitimacy problem. On Augustine's account, Roman history shows that there was never the type of consensus on justice that Cicero's definition required for a genuine citizen body. If justice is absent, what separates a citizen body from a gang of robbers, and the *imperium* of its magistrates from the violence of thieves? The Roman Republic, Augustine suggests, fails Cicero's own criterion for legitimacy (*De civitate Dei* 2.21; 4.4; 19.21). Augustine himself attempts to save Cicero's definition by suggesting that common objects of love characterize a people rather than a shared commitment to justice; thus, even an unjust political society may be recognized as legitimate (19.24). Love provides a criterion for ranking polities: the better the objects of the loves that bind them, the better the people.

The second example is from an anonymous *Dialogue on Political Science*, written during the reign of Justinian I (ruled 527–65) at the doorstep of the Byzantine period. Justinian's famous legal reforms led to the compilation of the *Corpus Iuris Civilis*, which includes the *Digest*, the principal source legal historians use to reconstruct Roman law between 31 BCE and 235 CE (Johnston 1999: 14). However, this period also featured constant strife and warfare, which may have led to questions about Justinian's legitimacy. This would explain why the *Dialogue* delineates a notion of imperial legitimacy with uncommon clarity for the Imperial period. Legitimate imperial authority is both lawful (*nomimos*) and just (*dikaios*; 5.46–49). Legitimacy requires rulers to imitate the goodness, wisdom, power, and justice of God – a deeply Platonic idea (O'Meara 2002: 57) – and for regimes to embed God's justice in public law. But a lawful regime also involves the republican idea that power to rule must be offered by the citizens (5.46–47). And, as in Cicero, whose *De republica* the author frequently cites, justice requires a notionally mixed constitution in which monarchical powers were granted "with the assent of the subjects" and "the deliberation of the *optimates* [i.e., the aristocracy]" (5.49; trans. Bell). By exploiting ideas from both Plato and Cicero, the author argues that a legitimate monarchy should be something like a constitutional monarchy, with sovereign authority grounded in the rule of law, which also provides scope for political involvement among the citizens (at least the aristocracy).[21]

Conclusion

The Roman Republican constitution has proven a remarkable stimulant to constitutional thought, aided by the powerful accounts of its earliest observers. Romans and observers of Rome living under very different circumstances, from the height of the Republic to the twilight of the Roman Empire, offered different conceptions of sovereignty, legitimacy, and the mixed constitution. The most fundamental text for these ideas in the ancient world, Cicero's *De republica*, was lost from about the seventh century until the nineteenth century.

However, the Roman constitution's earliest analyst has a more modern legacy; indeed, the key elements of Polybius' theory of the mixed constitution are shared by the man sometimes credited with founding modern political science, Machiavelli (J. W. Atkins 2013: 83–85). The power of Polybius' suggestion that institutional design could channel selfish passions, thereby making conflict productive, was well understood in the eighteenth century by Montesquieu, who also further developed Polybius' notion of the separation and balance of powers (Pangle 1973: 120–21). These ideas were also central to the political philosophy of the eighteenth-century framers of the American constitution, who knew their Polybius well (Bederman 2008: 59–85). While we must keep in mind that for the framers ancient republics served in many respects more as "antimodels" than models (see *Federalist* 9), we should not overlook the debt to the unwritten Roman constitution incurred by the written one on display in Washington, D.C.[22]

---

[21] This paragraph is much indebted to Bell 2009. "God" refers to the Christian God given scriptural allusions, which (among other factors) point to an origin in Alexandrian Christian NeoPlatonism (MacCoull 2006).

[22] "Antimodels": Richard 1994: ch. 4.

CHAPTER 2

Liberty and Related Concepts

Liberty: Ancient and Modern

"We hold these Truths to be self-evident, that all Men are created equal, that they are endowed by their Creator with certain unalienable Rights, that among these are Life, Liberty and the Pursuit of Happiness – That to secure these Rights, Governments are instituted among Men, deriving their just Powers from the Consent of the Governed." With these words, the Declaration of Independence sets forth several principles that Americans have come to associate with a free society: the recognition of natural equality, inalienable individual rights, and government by the consent of the governed.[1] Similarly, the Preamble to the Universal Declaration of Human Rights, adopted by the United Nations General Assembly in 1948, begins by asserting that the "equal and inalienable rights of all members of the human family is the foundation of freedom, justice and peace in the world." Protecting fundamental human rights and freedoms by the rule of law is essential to protecting against "tyranny and oppression." These familiar documents attest to the modern liberal-democratic creed that a free society is one that protects and promotes individual liberty through the recognition of individual rights.

Despite the universalizing language of these declarations, their principles are far from universally accepted. For the overwhelming majority of societies in world history, these principles were demonstrably false rather than "self-evident." One way of explaining the relative historical uniqueness of these documents is to place them within a broader historical context in which important modern social and economic developments transform how liberty is understood. This is the basic argument of Benjamin Constant in his famous 1819 lecture "The Liberty of the Ancients

---

[1] Allen 2014 offers a close reading of the Declaration that suggests the document's argument about equality undergirds its treatment of liberty.

Compared with that of the Moderns" (see Fontana 1988). According to Constant, the liberty of the Greeks and Romans was characterized by the lack of individual rights and by the subordination of the private to the public, and of the citizen to the polity. What mattered were free societies. Citizens were free insofar as they participated in public affairs; private actions were strictly monitored. Ancient liberty, aided by slavery, warfare, and small, relatively homogeneous societies, sounds much like oppression to citizens living in large, modern, pluralistic, ethnically diverse, commercial nation-states.

Two further analyses of liberty dominate modern scholarship. The first is by a later admirer of Constant, Oxford political theorist Isaiah Berlin (1909–97). In a famous essay based on a 1958 lecture entitled "Two Concepts of Liberty," Berlin (1969: 118–72) distinguished between two types of liberty, negative and positive. Negative liberty ("freedom from") he defined as the absence of external constraints or interference. This view of freedom runs from Hobbes through Locke and the subsequent liberal tradition of political thought. While Berlin leaves open the possibility that ancient societies may have enjoyed some negative liberties in practice, the Greeks and Romans did not possess the concept as a "conscious political ideal" since they lacked the notion of individual rights (129). Positive liberty ("freedom to"), on the other hand, Berlin defines as the capacity to act in such a way as to realize one's potential.

It is tempting (as Berlin himself invites by mentioning Constant) to map Berlin's "positive" and "negative" liberty onto Constant's "ancient" and "modern" liberty. From a political perspective, both men share the same concern – protecting individual private liberties from collective political projects. However, whereas Constant identifies the liberty of the ancients as political liberty, that is, political or patriotic activity, on Berlin's account political activity only counts as positive liberty if it is joined to the notion that in pursuing such civic activity we are fulfilling our human potential – a view endorsed by modern proponents of classical republicanism such as Hannah Arendt (1958; 1968; 1973; 2006). Thus, to tie political participation to liberty is not automatically to hold to a positive view of liberty; after all, there are many reasons to participate in politics without supposing that by doing so one is fulfilling one's nature as a human being.

The second analysis of liberty, which I will call "neo-republican" to distinguish it from the classical republican view associated with thinkers like Aristotle and Arendt, understands freedom as the absence of dependence or domination; it is associated above all with the work of Quentin Skinner (see, e.g., 1998; 2002) and Philip Pettit (1997), who trace the concept back to the Romans. Often presented as a third concept of liberty alongside positive and negative liberty, the neo-republican version is attractive to some modern theorists insofar as it is even more demanding and emancipatory than Berlin's notion of negative liberty (Viroli 2002). As Berlin admitted (1969: 129), on his account of negative liberty, one can be free under despotic rule so long as the despot generally does not interfere with one's actions. The neo-republican view, construing freedom as the absence of domination, and domination as subjection to a master's arbitrary will, offers a different analysis of the benevolent despot. On this account, one is unfree under any and every kind of despotism – even if the despot is liberal-minded and laissez faire, since at any time this "master" could coerce his subjects to do something according to his whim. In other words, under such a despotism, even though your actions are not generally interfered with, you are still dependent upon the whim of another and hence unfree. For neo-republicans, the key question is not "to what extent is my activity generally being impeded?," but "am I currently in a condition where I am subject to another's arbitrary will?" Are conditions being met to guard against such mastery or domination?

In the view of its supporters, the neo-republican conception of freedom avoids the deficiencies of both the liberal tradition, with its negative conception of liberty, and the classical republican tradition, with its positive conception of liberty. As with liberalism, the neo-republican view avoids tying liberty to any thick account of human nature and of the human good, thereby avoiding the worries that accompany positive views of liberty that promote a single account of human flourishing in modern, pluralistic societies. At the same time, like classical republicanism, it expands the conditions for freedom beyond the non-interference of one's actions, thereby answering critics of liberalism who believe that negative liberty insufficiently describes freedom. Consequently, the neo-republican theorists offer a very different view of what the Romans have to offer to the modern world than Constant supposed. The Romans have bequeathed a tradition of freedom that, far from being oppressive and dangerous for modern society, promises to emancipate even more people than the liberal version championed by Constant and Berlin.

As we will see, Constant's influential account uses too blunt an instrument in cleaving apart ancient and modern liberty. Lumping Greece and Rome on one side of the ancient–modern divide artificially obscures both Rome's differences from classical Athens and its similarities to modern regimes – unfortunately, since Roman conceptions of liberty share both similarities and differences with Athenian as well as with modern thought.

Indicating where these differences and similarities lie is the primary goal of this chapter, which focuses on liberty and such related concepts as equality, property, rights, and slavery in Roman thought. In this chapter as much as any other, we moderns find the mix of the familiar and foreign that makes Roman political thought so interesting and instructive.

In keeping with the primary theme of this book, republicanism, we will focus our attention on the most important sources for this ideology: the jurists, Cicero, Sallust, and Livy. At the heart of the Roman Republican idea of freedom are two sets of notions that still concern us today – ownership/control and involvement/participation. For the predominant Roman Republican ideology, political participation primarily meant participation by the elite, motivated by (what is from our modern, liberal vantage point) an illiberal honor code. In fact, as our discussion of political equality will reveal, republican thinking of liberty in terms of ownership may be used to thwart arguments for a more widespread, democratic participation in politics. Roman republicanism thus does not serve as a model for liberal-democratic emancipatory projects in any straightforward way.

Liberty, Slavery, and Domination in the Roman Law of Persons

There is no more conspicuous indicator of the differences between Roman and contemporary discussions of freedom than their foundations. The Romans built their views of liberty, not on presocial, abstract consider-ations of inalienable human rights or human dignity, but on the social and concrete institution of slavery (see Buckland 1908). Slavery was part of Roman society from the earliest period of the Republic; it is already assumed to be a fundamental part of Roman society in Rome's first writ-ten law code, The Twelve Tables, codified in 451/450 BCE. As to the exact number of slaves, historians differ. Walter Scheidel (2011: 289) estimates the percentage of the total population of Italy represented by slaves at 15–25 percent in the late Republic, though estimates have ranged as high as 40 percent under Augustus (Bradley 2011: 251). All told, over 100 mil-lion people were seized and sold as slaves throughout the Roman world between the fifth century BCE and fifth century CE (Scheidel 2011: 309). Regardless of the exact number, slaves, employed both in agriculture and in domestic service in wealthy households, became an important part of Roman society and economy.

Given the degree to which slavery was embedded in Roman society, it is unsurprising to find that Romans fundamentally conceived of liberty as the absence of slavery (Brunt 1988: 283; Roller 2001: 220–33). Roman law divided all persons between "slave" (*servus*) and "free" (*liber*; see further Buckland 1908; Watson 1987). Near the beginning of the chapter in the *Digest* on human status, we read: "Certainly, the great divide in the law of persons is this: all human beings are either free (*liberi*) or slaves (*servi*)" (*Dig.* 1.5.3). Slaves are those who are in the power of another (*alieni iuris*; *in aliena potestate*), whereas free persons are those who are under their own power or jurisdiction (*sui iuris*; *Dig.* 1.6. titulus and 1.6.1). The master (*dominus*) had power over his slaves, who were in many respects property. Under Roman law, they could be owned, bought, sold, given away, made to work, punished, put to death – all at their master's whim. A slave is subject to the ownership and control of another who has the capacity to treat his property as he wishes.

According to the *Digest* (1.5.4), "freedom is one's natural power of doing what one pleases, save insofar as it is ruled out either by coercion (*vis*) or by law (*ius*). Slavery is an institution of the law of nations (*ius gentium*), whereby someone is against nature made subject to the ownership of another" (trans. Watson, modified). The terminology here requires explanation. The jurists distinguished between types of law (*ius*). The *ius civile*, "civil law," is law particular to various polities (e.g., Rome, Athens, Sparta). The law of nations (*ius gentium*) is law common to all human beings regardless of polity. Sometimes the jurists also spoke of natural law (*ius naturale*) as a third distinct type of law common to all animals (*Dig.* 1.1.1.3; but cf. Gaius, *Inst.* 1.3). Thus, slavery, as a product of the *ius gentium*, might be regarded as a human institution and not as a natural condition for any human being (cf. *Institutes of Justinian* 1.2.2). However, unlike both Cicero's natural law theory outlined in *De legibus* books 1–2 and later versions such as that of Thomas Aquinas, for the jurists human law, not natural law, was most authoritative (J. W. Atkins 2013: 224–26). There is no evidence that the jurists saw nature as invalidating the provisions of Roman law (*ius civile*). Consequently, there were for the jurists no natural or human rights, though Tony Honoré (2002) has credited human rights to the Severan age lawyer Ulpian (193–235 CE).

Roman law regulated slavery just as it did the ownership of other property (Gaius, *Inst.* 1.52–53). Although slaves were their master's property, there were limits to how masters may use or abuse their slaves. Of course, masters could choose to be even more lenient; indeed, the lax master who gives his slave free rein is a motif of Roman comedy. This phenomenon is significant for understanding the predominant Roman tradition of thinking about freedom. If a slave still maintains his slave status even though his actions are not interfered with, then the simple non-interference of his actions is insufficient to constitute freedom. What makes a slave unfree is the fact that he is owned by his master, who at any time could exercise his authority arbitrarily against his slaves. This notion, as well as the legal texts from which it is derived, is fundamental for the (neo-) republican notion of freedom (Skinner 1998; Arena 2012).

The Roman law of persons contains some complications to the simple binary between "slave" as under another's power and "free" as under one's own power. Free citizens remained "in the power" of their father as long as he lived; a free woman remained under the guardianship of a male relative who had oversight over her financial and legal affairs (*Dig.* 1.6.3, 4; Just. *Inst.* 1.13.pr, 1.55; Buckland 1963: 142). Roman law and custom did provide for the emancipation of children from their father's power (*Dig.* 1.7). But until special legal action was taken, adult children continued to be under the control of their living fathers; they could not own property or benefit from a will. As Clifford Ando notes (2010: 194), this aspect of the law of persons suggests an important contrast with the way modern liberal democracies view the liberties of citizens. In modern democracies, the norm is for individual citizens to be regarded as independent, atomized bearers of rights and possessed of legal personality. However, for the Romans, the norm was for the family, represented by the oldest male relation, to be the legal personality subject to rights and freedoms. Individuals within the family tended not to have legal personality and the attendant rights and freedoms unless and until special legal action was taken.

The Romans themselves recognized the power of the paterfamilias as extraordinary and compared it to the power of a master over his slave (Gaius, *Inst.* 1.55). However, the father's power over his son is concentrated in the private sphere of the household, which involves property, marriage, and children; paternal power over adult sons did not extend to public life (*Dig.* 1.6.9; 36.1.14). A father cannot, for example, stop an adult son from seeking election to a magistracy, nor can he tell his son what to do in official matters related to the conduct of his office. Hence, the field of domination matters – a Roman citizen is more readily dominated in the private realm than in the public sphere (Arena 2012: 25–26).

The legal understanding of liberty as freedom from mastery or domination was fundamental for Roman conceptions of political freedom. Political societies like individuals could be described as free (*sui iuris ac mancipi*) or unfree (*in potestate*) – under the ownership of another state (Cic. *Ad Brutum* 1.16.4; Livy 35.32.11). And just as in the domestic sphere the slave of a lax master still remains in a condition of servitude by virtue of being subject to his master's arbitrary will, so too in the political sphere "many things are altogether lacking for a people who is under a king, especially liberty (*libertas*). For liberty does not consist in yielding to a just master (*dominus*) but no master" (Cic. *Rep.* 2.43). A people cannot be free under a master, even if he turns out to be a "most just and wise king," for they are "ruled by the nod and will of one person" (*Rep.* 1.43).

This conception of freedom as independence from the control of a master's arbitrary will foregrounds a particular set of problems in politics: ownership and control (Markell 2008). To be unfree is to be *owned* by another and *controlled* by their arbitrary will. The Romans utilized a number of Latin words to capture just this aspect of control involved in mastery: *obnoxius* (subservient), *licentia* (license, lawlessness), *libido* (desire, inordinate desire, willfulness), *vis* (force, power, violence), *coercere* (to coerce, control, restrain), *dominari/dominatio/dominatus* (to dominate, mastery), *nutus* (the nod of a master), *cupido* (desire), and *superbia* (a master's unrestrained arrogance). These terms are central to the discussions of the loss of liberty by writers such as Cicero, Sallust, Livy, and Tacitus. Freedom, then, would be enabled inasmuch as one is able to find ways to limit this control.[2] Questions of control and ownership will remain central to our discussion of liberty throughout the chapter.

Property, Individual Liberties, and Citizens' Rights

If liberty involves (at least in part) for Roman republicanism a question of ownership, then it should not be surprising to find that liberty is related to property in Roman thought. Slaves were, after all, a type of property, and the same Latin word – *dominus* – is the usual word for the master of a slave as well as for the owner of property (Roller 2001: 225).

There are several parallels between the Roman treatment of slavery and property. As those of slavery, provisions for the ownership and protection of private property go back to the Twelve Tables. Protection of private property was further established by the *Lex Aquilia* of c. 286 BCE, which provided means by which a property owner could recover damages for injured or lost property (Johnston 1999: 55). Second, just as the Romans had no natural right to liberty, so too they could claim no natural right to property, such as that later famously articulated by John Locke (but cf. Straumann 2016: ch. 4). As Cicero observed, "there is no private property

---

[2] For a more extensive treatment of the vocabulary of mastery, see J. W. Atkins forthcoming d.

by nature." Rather, "each person's own is made of what had been common by nature" (*Off.* 1.21). Cicero suggests that "long occupation" (among
other devices) establishes claims to private property, so that each person
should hold on to his own property. If someone seeks another's property
for himself, he will violate the human fellowship.

Later in *De officiis* (*On Duties*), Cicero argues that it is the "proper function of citizenship and the city to guarantee to each person the free and
undisturbed control of his property" (*Off.* 2.78; cf. 2.73). On balance Cicero
likely does not believe that private property rights are entirely beyond the
considerations of social justice (Barlow 2012; but cf. Wood 1988); nevertheless, one's rights as a citizen should mean that one's possessions cannot
arbitrarily be confiscated by magistrates or private citizens. One of the
marks of a free city is the right of citizens not to have their property confiscated without legal process – a point that Cicero argued forcefully in his
speech *De domo sua*, which addressed the confiscation and destruction of
his own property by his political enemy Clodius, who drove him into exile
in 58 BCE (see *Dom.* 33).

The consideration of property rights leads to the larger question of rights,
and onto slippery terrain. The type of rights discussed in the Declaration
of Independence or Universal Declaration of Human Rights – rights that
one possesses by virtue of one's humanity and are for this reason inalienable – was not a concept actively deployed by Roman political thinkers.[3]
This does not mean that there was no potential space for such a concept in
Roman thought. For instance, in book 3 (3.27) of *De officiis*, Cicero argues
that we have a duty to refrain from violence against other human beings
precisely because they are human beings. If human beings have a duty not
to harm other human beings, then correlatively we might say that human
beings have a right not to be harmed. We might. But Cicero doesn't. His
focus here is on the *duty* of justice, on what is just or right, to be construed in terms of an objective right order based on natural law that unites
human beings into a community of rational beings with one another and
with the gods. Thus, even if we find room for natural or human "rights"
within the structure of Cicero's thought, as some enlightenment thinkers
did (J. W. Atkins 2014; Straumann 2015), these "rights" would only make
sense alongside correlative duties to other human beings, to one's country,
to the gods – duties supported by a framework that the modern world has
largely jettisoned.[4]

[3] For a different perspective on human rights at Rome, see Bauman 2000.
[4] Community of gods and men: Cf. Cic. *Rep.* 3.27 Powell = 3.33 Zetzel; *Leg.* 1.23, 33. In *Off.* the
    emphasis is on the community of men, but the gods come into the picture at 1.153 and 3.28. In *De*

While scholars such as Alasdair MacIntyre (1984), Michel Villey (1946; 1964), and Leo Strauss (1965) argue rightly that the ancient Greeks and Romans did not think in terms of *human* or *natural* rights, the Romans did have the concept of and language for individual rights based on civil law and customary practices.[5] Peter Garnsey (2007; 2017) has persuasively argued that the use of rights language was widespread in Roman property law and the law of persons. That rights language was used prevalently in relationship to property is unsurprising when one thinks analytically about a right. Rights, as modern legal philosophers frequently define them, are justified claims to a certain good or action (Hohfeld 1919). Ownership is one form of status that is commonly taken to entail such claims. If I own a piece of property, then I will be said to hold the rights to it, and thus the power to dispose of my property as I wish. Furthermore, I will have the freedom in my action over it from others' interference or control – unless, of the course, there is some stipulation limiting the extent to which I may exercise my right. Similarly in Roman law we find that the idea of a right is linked closely with the ideas of ownership and control. "Right," *ius*, is frequently paired with "power," *potestas*, to indicate the power or control that one has over one's property or over another person (Gaius, *Inst.* 1.52–53; Just. *Inst.* 1.13.1). The expression *ius potestasque*, "right and power," appears to have been used as a formula for the concept of rights (J. W. Atkins 2013: 126–28).[6]

If liberty consists in the absence of ownership or control by another, then rights may serve as one way to demarcate limits of this ownership and control; they designate the limits within which one may "do as one pleases" unimpeded, to borrow a formulation from Roman law (*Dig.* 1.5.4), or in Berlin's words, "an area in which I am not frustrated" (1969: 161). Along with the fair and equal application of the rule of law, rights allow citizens to be free by protecting their actions from the arbitrary interference and coercion of magistrates or other citizens (Arena 2012: 48, 67; see further discussion below).

Consequently, a person who is rightless is in danger of losing his liberty. As Cicero argues, when magistrates rule as kings, Roman citizens find all

---

legibus Cicero attempts to use natural law's objective, right order to defend the institutions and rights of the Roman constitution (cf. J. W. Atkins 2013: chs. 5–6 and Straumann 2016: ch. 4; see further chapter 6).

[5] Human and natural rights: see further the discussion of Tertullian in chapter 6. If Tertullian did articulate the concept of natural or human rights, he is the exception that proves the rule that the Greeks and Romans did not think in terms of such rights.

[6] For the concepts of ownership and property (and their limits) in Roman political thought, see Garnsey 2017.

of their "rights, powers, and liberties removed" (Cic. *De lege agraria* 2.29).
An even more striking connection between the loss of rights and mastery is
found in a speech attributed by the historian Sallust to C. Licinius Macer,
tribune of the plebs in 73 BCE. Addressing the plebs in the wake of legislation that weakened the office of tribune of the plebs by Sulla, two-time
consul and dictator in 81 BCE, Macer, in the words of Sallust, argued that
the other tribunes were no longer protecting "your rights." As a result,

> all have now yielded to the tyranny of the few (*in paucorum dominatio-
> nem*) … they have plundered you and made a stronghold of spoils. In the
> meantime you hand yourself over like cattle, a herd of men to be owned
> and enjoyed by individual masters stripped of all that your ancestors left
> you, except that through the ballot now you yourselves choose your own
> masters (*dominos*), as before you chose your defenders. (Sallust, *Histories*
> 3.48.6; trans. Batstone)

Macer here connects the loss of rights with metaphors from slavery
(*dominus*) and property law. ("Enjoyed" evokes a usufruct, a right that
allows one to enjoy the fruits of another's property.) The plebs, having lost
the protection of their rights, are now reduced to property, freely exploited
by their owners like cattle. In order "to recover their freedom," they should
look to history and follow the plebs whose succession in 494 BCE led to
the creation of the tribunes of the plebs, "the defenders of all their rights"
(*vindices … omnis iuris sui*; 3.48.1; trans. Batstone).

As Macer's historical reference suggests, the acquisition of citizens' rights
and their protection by the tribune were important for freedom. These
rights belonged to all citizens, though sources such as Cicero, Sallust, and
Livy present their acquisition as particularly important for securing the
freedoms of the plebs in their struggles against the patricians during the
conflict of the orders. Our earliest source for this period is Cicero's *De
republica* book 2, but the most extensive treatment is found in the early
books of Livy's *Ab urbe condita*, a 142-book masterpiece relating the history
of Rome from its founding under kings, through the Republic, and ending
with his own lifetime under the Augustan Principate (c. 753 BCE–9 CE).
Modern historians question the historical accuracy of Livy's early books,
but these books were invaluable for the later republican tradition – most
obviously, for Machiavelli's *Discourses on the First Decade of Livy*.[7]

Livy's narrative of the early Republic begins in book 2, which picks up
the history of Rome immediately following the expulsion of the kings.

---

[7] Livy's political thought: Hammer 2008: ch. 3; Hammer 2014: ch. 5; Vasaly 2015.

Livy begins the book by announcing "from this point I will be relating the deeds of a free Roman people" (2.1.1). The problem of freedom throughout these early books is posed in terms of ownership and control by another's will. At the very outset of the Roman Republic, Livy explains how liberty was nearly lost when young associates of the deposed Tarquin monarchy pined for the arbitrary will – *licentia* – of a king who, unbound by "law" and "equal rights," could grant whatever request he wished (2.3.3). Ownership and control resurface later in the book: should the patricians be under the control of the people (*in populi … potestate*; 2.56.16)?; in whose hands (*in manu*) did the republic belong (2.57.3)? The tyrannical exertion of coercion (*coercere*) is vividly displayed in the person of Appius Claudius, who unlawfully abducted a plebeian girl – a master (*dominus*) taking a slave (*mancipium*; 3.48.3) that for Livy evoked the rape of Lucretia that led to the end of monarchy and the beginning of republican liberty.

What measures are put into place to defend citizens against domination? Livy focuses on two devices with good republican credentials. The first is the rule of law. The rule of law guards the people against "the whim and license (*libidinem ac licentiam*)" of magistrates (3.9.5). If part of the *res publica* is to avoid falling into the mastery of another part, the rule of law must apply evenly to all citizens regardless of class (3.34.3). Livy gives expression to the republican ideal that the accountability of even the most powerful citizens to the law (*lex*) is essential "for equalizing liberty" (38.50.8). The alternative to the equitable application of law (*ius*) is violence (*vis*; 38.50.9) and mastery (*dominatio*; 4.5.1). The image of the rule of law as the alternative to violence, coercion, and mastery that emerges in Livy is familiar to readers of Cicero, where it receives frequent expression (see, e.g., *Pro Sestio* 92; *Pro Cluentio* 146–47).

Livy's second device, citizens' rights, also enjoys the republican imprimatur of Cicero. According to Cicero, citizenship (*civitas*) is a right (*ius*) that preserves freedom (*libertas*) against violence (*vis*) by magistrates and other citizens (Cic. *Dom.* 80). Livy's narrative of the development of the Roman Republic isolates four citizens' rights that are particularly central for liberty – *provocatio* (right of appeal), *appellatio* (right to ask tribunes for help or *auxilium*), *conubium* (right to marry), and *suffragium* (right to vote). Perhaps the two most important concepts for Livy's account of citizens' rights and liberties are *auxilium* and *provocatio* – "the two bastions for protecting liberty," as they are called at one point (3.45.8). *Auxilium* is introduced at 2.33.1, along with the creation of the tribunate, as the right of the tribunes to choose to assist citizens who appeal to them for help against magistrates (Lintott 1999: 121–28). This right protected citizens, plebs and patricians alike, from the arbitrary coercion of magistrates. As for *provocatio*, this right protected citizens from the arbitrary punishments of magistrates by giving them the ability to appeal a magistrate's use of force to a Roman popular assembly (Lintott 1972; Harries 2007: 14–16). Both Livy and Cicero indicate that the creation of a magistracy not subject to the right of appeal was tyranny (Cic. *Rep.* 2.53–54; Livy 3.55.4–5; 10.9.4). Appius Claudius, the tyrannical head of the decemvirs, upon prosecution demanded the right of appeal on the grounds that as a Roman citizen he should exercise "the common right of citizenship" (*communi iure civitatis*; Livy 3.56.10).

The board of decemvirs was charged with creating a code of laws (what became known as the Twelve Tables) that "made rights equal (*iura aequasse*) for all – the highest and the lowest" (Livy 3.34.3). Equal rights before the law, also presented as essential for protecting citizens from domination by Cicero at *De officiis* 2.41, are a frequent theme in the early books of Livy. This concept is especially prominent at the beginning of book 4, when the tribune Canuleius proposes to remove the ban on intermarriage between plebs and patricians and to allow plebs to be elected to the consulship. The marriage ban was eventually lifted, and the citizens attained *ius conubii*, the civil right to marry.

As for the opening up of the consulship to plebs, the argument here is especially interesting. Canuleius argues that plebs should have access to the consulship by the extension of the fundamental right of *suffragium*. (Indeed, Cicero says that the loss of this right is tantamount to tyranny at *Rep.* 2.39.) Thus, Canuleius claims (4.3.5), "we are reclaiming and seeking to exercise a right belonging to the people (*id quod populi est repetimus atque usurpamus*), that the Roman people entrust offices to whomever they wish (*velit*)." Canuleius appeals to the idea of ownership, in which one asserts possession by exercising one's right (*usurpamus*), which in turn allows one to exercise one's will (*velit*; 4.3.5). This language is used again at Livy 5.12.8–9, where we find that the exercising of one's right to vote (*usurpandi iuris causa*) is a means to establish liberty (*stabiliendae libertatis*). The civil right to vote in a popular assembly – the capacity to elect magistrates for office, or to enact or reject legislative proposals by the tribunes – establishes liberty understood in terms of non-domination. By guarding against dependence on another's will, the free exercise of *suffragium* allowed the people to express their will, thereby enabling them to live according to their own will (see Livy 4.3.7). For this reason, in the first century BCE, champions of the people (*populares*) argued against their more aristocratic opponents (*optimates*) that liberty demanded that votes should proceed by secret ballot, a mechanism that would protect against the influence of the aristocracy (Cic. *Sest.* 103; Wirszubski 1950: 50). *Suffragium*, then, is a civil right that provides freedom from arbitrary control as well as a degree of participation in politics (Brunt 1988: 297; Arena 2012: 54; for the development of *suffragium* in Roman history, see de Ste. Croix 1954).

These four citizens' rights combine with the property rights discussed above to provide Roman citizens with a menu of rights that protect their liberty from interference from magistrates and from other citizens. Such citizens' rights, the "bulwark of our citizenship and freedom," Cicero argued, were part of the *mos maiorum* and should trump the power of magistrates and "even the authority of the whole Roman people" (Cic. *Dom.* 80). With the partial exception of *suffragium*, these rights are fundamentally defensive in nature – "a shield rather than a sword," to borrow the description of liberty based on equal civil rights (*iure aequo*) advocated by the consuls in Livy's narration of the second secession of the plebs (3.53.9–10).[8]

This notion of protective, individual citizens' rights separates Rome from classical Athens. Historians disagree about whether Athens valued individual liberties or was an "illiberal democracy" focused on upholding the values and freedom of the *polis* as a whole at the expense of individual liberties. Similarly, scholars debate whether the Athenians possessed the notion of rights in some form. What we do not find in Athens is precisely the phenomenon we have been observing in Roman thought: the notion of rights working to protect individual freedom. While scholars continue to argue for Constant's basic position that the concept of rights protecting individual liberties is a "very modern concept" (D. Carter 2013: 84), the evidence shows that the Romans viewed the notion of individual protective rights as an important part of ensuring freedom. The language of individual rights in political thought originated not in an egalitarian, modern, commercial republic but in the hierarchical, slave-owning Roman Republic.[9]

Liberty and Equality

Like Constant, contemporary political theorists frequently assume that citizens' full political participation lies at the core of classical republican

---

[8] Liberty and rights as fundamentally defensive: Kapust 2004; Raaflaub 1984; 2004; 2005.

[9] Athens as valuing individual liberties: Hansen 1999; Wallace 2009; Cartledge and Edge 2009. Athens as an "illiberal democracy": Rahe 1992: ch. 7. Did the Athenians possess rights? Yes: Miller 1995; D. Carter 2013; no: Ostwald 1996; Hansen 1999: 327; Edge and Cartledge 2009; maybe so: Ober 2000: 27–61.

thought. Quentin Skinner (1998) has argued that some writers in the later republican tradition offered a participatory solution to the problem of domination. Matt Edge (2009) has attributed a similar position to democratic Athenians. According to Edge, democratic partisans at Athens argued that political equality or *isonomia* – that is, the equal capacity of citizens to share and participate in political rule and decision-making (Hansen 1999: 396) – was the prerequisite for freedom. For unless the citizens ruled equally according to their own will, they would necessarily be subservient to the will of another, and hence, unfree (cf. Aristotle, *Politics* 6.2 and Edge 2009).

What about the Romans? We have already observed that the citizens' right of *suffragium* ensured at least a minimal degree of participation. How far did this participation extend? Did at least some Roman republicans construe "equal rights" or (to use another phrase to which we shall return) "equal liberty" to include, like the democratic Athenian conception of *isonomia*, equal political rights to participate fully in rule? These questions have gained increased traction due to the trend, noted in the last chapter, among some ancient historians to emphasize the popular or "democratic" nature of the Roman Republican constitution. They raise the question of the relationship between liberty and equality. Consider three examples from the texts of Livy and Cicero that showcase conflict over liberty and equality.

The first example, from Livy 34, concerns debates over the *Lex Oppia* of 215 BCE, the first in a series of sumptuary laws that restricted both a women's wealth and her display of that wealth. Noble women opposed the laws, which they say represent slavery, as the result of unwelcome interference in affairs that should remain under the control of their husbands or fathers, not the law (34.7.13). They cannot bear the external imposition of equality that eradicates social differences (34.4.14). An equality that eradicates distinctions is seen to interfere with freedom inasmuch as it restrains an individual's capacity to excel or stand out. On the other hand, Cato the Elder (234–149 BCE) defends the legislation in the name of freedom. Making an argument similar to some current critics of Berlin (Skinner 2002), Cato argues that the women's essentially negative conception of liberty as freedom from constraint overlooks a constraint even more fundamental than law, the internal constraint of passions like greed. One can be controlled by passions as well as by law, and in this case, Cato argues, it is precisely law that liberates from the internal constraints of passion. Second, Cato suggests that such legislation will serve the important social purpose of enforcing harmony by eradicating distinctions that cause rivalry destructive to the *res publica* (Livy 34.2.14, 7.5).[10]

The debate over the sumptuary laws focused on the ways in which achieving equality by removing *social* distinctions impacted liberty. The next two examples raise the connection between liberty and *political* equality in arguments for greater political participation in the name of "equal liberty."

Let's return to the tribune Canuleius, whom we met in the last section (Livy 4.5). Canuleius describes both the right to marry and the right to vote for plebeian candidates for the consulship in terms of enacting equal liberty for all (*omnibus aequa libertas*) instead of mastery (*dominatio*). For the plebs to be granted a share "in the partnership of government" as a mark "of equal liberty" (*aequae libertatis*), they should be permitted "in turn both to obey and to govern the annual magistracies" (4.5.5). He concludes: "No one is going to contend for arrogant masters (*pro superbis dominis*) with whom there is a share neither of offices in the *res publica* nor of marriage in private life" (4.5.6).

Canuleius argues for opening up the consulship to the plebs on the grounds of "equal liberty" (*aequa libertas*). Elsewhere in Livy *aequa libertas* means equality before the law rather than equal political participation (Livy 3.31.7; 4.5.1; 38.50.8). Canuleius' argument for "equal liberty" suggests that a degree of popular political participation is necessary. However, here too Livy has in mind something far short of the equal political participation in the sense of ruling and being ruled in turn that Aristotle attributes to democratic Athens. As Ann Vasaly (2015: 119–21) observes, it is important to note Livy's explanation of the plebs' subsequent decision to elect all patricians to office in the immediate aftermath of the debate (4.6.11–12). By securing the *possibility* of electing plebs to the magistracies, Canuleius achieved his goal: the capacity to "elect whomever they wished" (4.3.7). His concern is therefore more closely related to the question of popular sovereignty than to the question of popular participation in political office. The people's "equal liberty" is attained when the patricians recognize that the plebs "own" the republic (to use Cicero's language; see chapter 1 and below) in the sense that their will is the ultimate and unfettered source of the *imperium* wielded by magistrates (Vasaly 2015: 120). Thus, in line with the rest of the first five books of Livy, the primary concern is with political ownership and control rather than with equal political participation.

[10] This paragraph is indebted to Arena 2011.

The question of equal political participation clearly *is* at issue in our third text, an argument for democracy aired by one of the characters in book 1 of Cicero's *De republica* (1.47–50). In this book, Scipio (the dialogue's main character, whom we met in chapter 1) presents arguments over the proper constitution of a free republic from the perspective of partisans of democracy, aristocracy, and monarchy. The democratic argument begins at 1.47 by claiming that the only state in which "*libertas* has any home" is one in which the people have the power (*potestas*). In order to avoid slavery (*servitus*), one must enjoy "equal liberty" (*aequa libertas*) – the same term we encountered in Livy. However, whereas in Canuleius' speech the term was used to argue for popular sovereignty (and elsewhere in Livy it indicated equality before the law), here the term clearly means equal political participation: the two examples provided of free regimes, democratic Athens and Rhodes, feature the regular rotation of offices that (in theory) provide all citizens with the opportunity to participate directly in rule. What does not suffice is a regime that sounds much like Republican Rome – one in which citizens vote and entrust rule and magistracies to others but have themselves no share in rule (*imperium*) or deliberation. The people are not free to live as they wish but find that they must sometimes give what they don't wish (*nolint*; 1.47).

In keeping with the preceding analysis of liberty in *De republica* (1.43–44, 47), this democratic argument for equal political participation is anchored in the conception of a free people as one that is not dependent on a master's arbitrary will. Alluding to Scipio's earlier definition of a *res publica* as "the property of the people" (1.39; see chapter 1), the democrats contend that full and equal political participation is an essential ingredient in ensuring that the citizens live according to their own will and exercise control as owners or masters (*domini*) over the *res publica* (1.48). By managing their affairs directly, the people can avoid becoming subservient to individuals or factions eager for mastery (*dominandi cupidum*; 1.50). The problem of mastery is solved by the people becoming their own masters.

Crucial to the democratic argument is the contention that citizens must have equal standing and rights before the law. Consider the following passage in which the democratic argument continues to interpret Scipio's earlier definition of *res publica* (1.39), which had portrayed the people as a "partnership" (*societas*) united by an agreement about justice (*ius*):

> Therefore, since law (*lex*) is the bond of the civic partnership, and justice under law is equal (*ius ... legis aequale*), by what justice (*quo iure*) can the association of citizens (*societas civium*) be held together when the status of

citizens is not equal? For if it is not agreeable to equalize wealth, if the innate abilities of all cannot be equal, then certainly rights (*iura*) ought to be equal among those who are citizens of the same commonwealth. (1.49)

To speak of notions like "equal justice under the law" and "equal rights" within the context of a debate over the superiority of direct democracy is to invite controversy, especially given the Athenian precedent evoked earlier in the argument. In democratic Athens, *isonomia* (equality under the law) was a vague enough term to be appropriated by both democrats and aristocrats. The former construed it as implying a numerical (or arithmetic) equality, in which every citizen, being counted the same, has equal capacity to put forward legislation in the assembly or serve on the council that prepared the assembly's business and ran the day-to-day affairs of the city; the latter saw it as being consistent with a proportional (or geometric) equality that incorporated relevant differences in status or merit into considerations of political rule (Cartledge 2009: 6–10). Similarly, within the Roman context of the argument in *De republica*, there is sufficient ambiguity in the democratic call for "equal rights" to allow even aristocrats to affirm this language (Zetzel 1995: 139; Schofield 2015: 121). However, whereas the aristocrats would limit these rights to the protective, largely defensive, legal and civic rights reviewed in the last section, the democratic advocates presumably understand "equal rights" as requiring not only Roman Republican civic and legal rights – without which the majority too could rule tyrannically by whim (1.44; 3.35 Powell = 3.45 Zetzel) – but also the equal opportunity for full participation in assemblies and offices by all citizens.

In this dispute over participation, the terms of debate favor the aristocrats. If freedom is (as the democratic argument agrees) primarily a matter of protection against the ownership and control by a master's arbitrary will, then on this definition one must admit one is free if the will of the ruler can be regularized by laws and limited by rights. To take an example from the modern university classroom, the clear grading policies on a course syllabus restrain and regularize the professor's (otherwise) arbitrary will even if the students had no active role in devising these policies and merely consent to them and to the professor's authority by choosing to remain enrolled in the course. Thus, if democracy's opponents can establish that laws and rights effectively deal with the problem of arbitrary control, and that the franchise secures popular consent to rulers and laws, then, according to the concept of freedom as non-domination, the republic should be free even though citizens do not have equal opportunity to share in rule.

Book two of Cicero's *De republica* attempts to support the aristocratic perspective by providing evidence that the conditions for non-domination were met in Roman history, as the people gradually acquired key rights during the Republic. These include the right of suffrage, which ensured that rulers governed by "the will and consent of citizens" (2.38; cf. 2.39), and the right of *provocatio* (2.53–55, 61–63). Given that these conditions for non-domination have been met, the idea of freedom as "non-domination" furnishes democrats with no compelling counter-argument to Scipio's suggestion that the "free people" should "entrust itself" (1.51) to the care of a manager and caregiver, even at the expense of their own immediate political involvement.

Did this democratic argument for full political participation, aired by aristocrats in a fictional conversation in a philosophical dialogue, reflect an actual political position in Republican Rome? Even if, for reasons discussed in the previous chapter, we might suppose that late Republican Rome fell short of a participatory democracy like Athens in both prevailing political ideology and practice, perhaps, as Valentina Arena (2012) has argued, the democratic argument represents a suppressed popular tradition that construed liberty in terms of "non-domination" as requiring a radical political equality. The case is far from conclusive. But if such an argument were advanced at Rome, the debate in Cicero's *De republica* shows why, even setting ideology aside, it likely would have encountered stiff intellectual opposition. It is difficult to anchor an argument for democratic participation in an account of non-domination given the availability of laws and rights to effectively deal with a master's arbitrary will.[11]

Liberty, Participation, and Political Culture

As important as laws and rights were for securing freedom in Roman republican thought, this is only part of the story. Romans generally enjoyed freedom from magistrates interfering in areas such as philosophy, religious practice, economic life, and speech (for toleration, see chapter 6). Apart from the narrow menu of citizens' rights explored earlier in the chapter, freedom from interference by magistrates in citizens' lives was determined not by rights but by Rome's political culture (Brunt 1988: 300–308).

The Roman way of life was directed by a highly ritualized and intuitive script, which guided all aspects of life: how the Romans walked; talked;

---

[11] For a more detailed analysis and defense of this interpretation of the democratic argument in *De republica* I, see J. W. Atkins forthcoming d.

decorated their homes; treated superiors, inferiors, other private citizens, magistrates, spouses, children, slaves, and foreigners; performed music; entertained themselves; spent money; exercised; and chose a career. All this and more was regulated by "custom and civic codes of behavior," which according to Cicero "are themselves rules for living" (*Off.* 1.148). Citizens' lives were highly regulated by honor and a sense of public shame (*pudicitia*), notions associated with *libertas* (Wallace 2009).

Rome's honor code encouraged practices that modern liberals find deeply inimical to liberty. For all the Romans' concern with political and civic domination, magistrates *could choose* to intervene in many aspects of a Roman's private life. For instance, in the censors' capacity as upholders of traditional mores, they examined all aspects of a Roman citizen's life (Astin 1988). According to Dionysius of Halicarnassus, as opposed to the Athenians (and Spartans) who were not concerned with how citizens lived within their own homes, "the Romans, throwing open every house and extending the authority of the censors even to the bedroom, made that office the overseer and guardian of everything that took place in the home" (20.13.3; trans. Cary, Loeb; modified). For the Romans there was no right to privacy. Barton (2001: 23) exaggerates only slightly when she colorfully observes, "the Roman way demanded a degree of mutual surveillance and inhibition that modern Americans might find only in an Orwellian nightmare or a maximum-security prison."

When they explicitly addressed the relationship between liberty and the honor code, Roman republicans differed in their assessments. For instance, in the second century BCE, Cato the Elder contrasted "liberty," which he grouped with "right," "law," and "commonwealth" as shared goods, with "glory" and "honor" as goods differentiated according to individual merit (Malcovati, *ORF* 252). Cicero makes a similar contrast over a century later during the Republic's death throes (Cic. *Phil.* 1.34). While these formulations offer a juridical conception of liberty achieved by common rights and laws, others extended their notion of freedom to encompass one's social status. On these accounts, to be free is to have a certain status or standing in the eyes of others – *dignitas* (cf. Vasaly 2015: 120). To lose freedom is to lose standing: "slaves," Cicero reminds his brother, Quintus, "are able to have no *dignitas*" (Cic. *Ad Quintum fratrem* 1.2.3). As P. A. Brunt points out (1988: 288–89), "even the humblest citizen had his own social esteem and rank (*dignitas*), which set him at least above the slaves."

Dignitas was an important elite value, and a number of passages by elite Republicans link their standing and liberty to their capacity to participate in politics. Cicero bemoans his lack of freedom under the triumvirate of

Crassus, Pompey, and Caesar. In blocking him from the "highest offices," Cicero complains that the triumvirate removed "the *dignitas* in speaking my opinion and the *libertas* in taking part in public affairs" (*Epistulae ad familiares* 1.8.3; cf. *Fam.* 4.14.1, which describes Cicero's later lack of standing under Caesar). Along similar lines, the following quotation is attributed to the second-century BCE general and statesman Scipio Africanus: "From integrity is born standing (*dignitas*); from standing, public recognition (*honor*); from public recognition, political or military rule (*imperium*); and from political or military rule, liberty (*libertas*)" (Malcovati, *ORF* 32).

For many in the Roman republican tradition, securing and enhancing one's standing through patriotic action on behalf of one's country, whether politically or (even more fundamentally) militarily, was not an optional extra for individuals to be able to pursue if they wish. Rather, such participation was expected as a norm, and deviations were viewed with suspicion. Sallust and Cicero, for instance, labored hard to justify their literary efforts before their fellow elite, who would be inclined to see writing as a retreat from more respectable public activity (Baraz 2012). But some elite Romans went further and suggested that such participation was true virtue, proper for a man, and to be equated with *libertas*. Already in the poet Ennius (early second century), we read: "It is proper for a man (*vir*) to live a life with true virtue (*virtus*) and bravely to stand blameless before his foes. The man who carries himself pure and stout – that is true liberty (*libertas*). All other conduct is servile, hidden in obscure darkness" (*Ennius*, Tragedies 308–11; Warmington, Loeb). Similarly, in the preface to *Catiline's Conspiracy*, Sallust argues that nature specifies that man's natural end is the performance of deeds that bring glory (Walker 2006). Though there are different paths available to achieve this end, all require discipline and competitive, vigorous activity – what Sallust identifies as virtue. Such virtuous, active striving for glory is essential for both free men and free commonwealths.

Sallust's writings in particular reveal an intimate relationship between the pursuit of glory, honor, and status, on one hand, and freedom, on the other. Freedom and the pursuit of glory go together (*Cat.* 7.3). The desire for glory provides agency essential to contend for freedom. A citizenry sapped of the energy to contend publicly for glory is one that is prepared for slavery and mastery (see *Hist.* 1.55). To be free is to possess honor and status; to fall into mastery is to forfeit them.

Sallust, whose writings frequently showcase the struggle of the people to reclaim their liberties from a dominant oligarchical faction (see further chapter 3), portrays populist leaders urging the people to act to reclaim their liberty by linking the loss of freedom to the loss of honor (*decus*).

As in Macer's speech discussed earlier in the chapter, in *The Jugurthine War* (*Bellum Iugurthinum*), Sallust has another tribune of the plebs, Gaius Memmius (in III BCE), argue that to fail to "strive with the greatest resources on behalf of liberty" and to accept mastery is a disgrace (31.16–17). Even though the plebs never achieved full involvement in civic affairs and political rule, freedom required of them what Joy Connolly (2015: 26, 58) calls "resistibility" – the active capacity to struggle to maintain their basic civic rights and status. And, Sallust suggests, resistibility is not possible without the agency provided by honor.

Liberty's association with Roman political culture and the honor code further reveals how the concept carried different connotations for Romans living under the Republic. At the risk of oversimplification, we can arrange these conceptions on a spectrum determined by status (Roller 2001: 228; Connolly 2007: 35; Kapust and Turner 2013). At one end of the spectrum, liberty means primarily legal rights, such as *provocatio* or the institution of the tribune that helped the plebs maintain their standing by protecting them from the disgraceful indiscriminate physical punishments associated with slaves (M. T. Clarke 2014). For elite Romans at the other end of the spectrum, standing is maintained and enhanced primarily through participation in politics (Raaflaub 1984: 549; 2004: 265). In addition to the small subset of negative liberties protected by rights, many elite Romans associated liberty with participation in politics or other action on behalf of the *res publica*.

From the Free Commonwealth to Individual Freedom under Monarchy

The main authors we have been utilizing in this chapter – Cicero, Sallust, and Livy – all raise the question about the conditions for a free commonwealth. The term "free commonwealth" can refer to a polity governed under its own laws, which means that it is free from external conquest. But the main concern of these texts was protecting the commonwealth against falling into the mastery of some internal ruler or faction. How might this be avoided?

Sometimes scholars focusing on non-domination as the overarching theory of liberty, especially as it is treated in Cicero's *De republica* and Livy, suggest that law, rights, and government in the interest of the people constitute the essential preconditions of a free commonwealth (Wirszubski 1950: 129; Pettit 1997: 35–41; Kapust 2004). Such a formulation is in fact deeply Ciceronian. It strongly echoes Cicero's argument in *De republica*, in that the free commonwealth is one in which magistrates will rule in the interest of the people as a whole, and the arbitrary will of magistrates (and private citizens) will be limited and constrained by rights and law. Similarly *De officiis* 1.124 seems to reduce the essence of republican government simply to magistrates ruling on behalf of the citizen body, providing conditions for private citizens to enjoy their private liberties and rights (Manent 2013: 139).

However, while Ciceronian so far as it goes, this formulation captures only part of Cicero's republicanism, that part concerned with ownership and control. For a free commonwealth, the juridical protections, especially prominent for the plebs, are to be supplemented with the worthy standing or *dignitas* of the aristocracy, an esteem that requires the freedom to participate in politics. Likewise, the "vertical" relationship between magistrate and private citizen in *De officiis* must be supplemented by a crucial assumption about the "horizontal" question of rule on Cicero's part – that rule is dispersed among many magistracies, which will continue to be accessible to a considerable group of the elite, including "new men" like Cicero himself. Written just after Caesar's assassination that reopened public space for Cicero, *De officiis* assumes a wide arena for vigorous activity on behalf of the republic. Cicero's treatments of virtues like justice and courage are carefully calibrated to prepare active, ambitious young men for public service (Griffin and E. M. Atkins 1991: xxiv–xxv).[12]

Let's bring into sharper focus the inadequacy of seeing a free republic as prevailing so long as rights and laws constrain the will of the ruler. Consider the example of Augustus, under whose rule Rome would have been seen as unfree by a committed republican like Cicero even though such conditions existed. Augustus consolidated into his own hands the *imperium* previously distributed among the magistracies. As a result, he greatly reduced the public space available for the type of political and military glory that contributed to the *dignitas* of members of the Roman ruling class. However, as Ronald Syme notes (1939: 516), "the Principate, though absolute, was not arbitrary. It derived from consent and delegation; it was founded upon the laws." So long as the focus remains on ownership and control, on laws and rights that defend private citizens from arbitrary rule, then we can agree with Augustus' own claim to have "emancipated the commonwealth into liberty" (*Res Gestae* 1.1; Wirszubski 1950: 122).

But if we focus on whether the Principate promoted a broad public space for vigorous participation on behalf of the *res publica*, the picture is

---

[12] "Vertical" and "horizontal": Markell 2008: 25.

different. Indeed, on Tacitus' assessment, the extensive legislation that was designed to restore peace among the aristocracy led to chains (*Ann.* 3.28). In eliminating all discord, the very laws that addressed domination by the arbitrary will of would-be masters displaced citizens from political involvement and sapped them of their spirit to struggle for status. Enervated by legislation and with the space for public action reduced, citizens found themselves more as private individuals in the *res publica*, which had become in a sense the household of the *princeps* (Boesche 1987; Fontana 1993). (In fact, as we shall see in chapter 6, as Pontifex Maximus, Augustus nationalized part of his house on the Palatine Hill and transferred there the national cult of Vesta.) Thus, citizens had no choice but to live their lives effectively in the paternal power of the *princeps*. And if the *res publica* was reduced to the *res privata,* the private realm of household and private property, it was only a matter of time before emperors began to treat citizens as property. Though in some ways more subtle – Edward Gibbon called Augustus a "subtle tyrant" – the diminution of agency and political participation leads no less to the loss of freedom than lawless mastery.[13]

As a consequence of the loss of political freedom, the most penetrating discussions of liberty following the Augustan Principate turned from questions of the free commonwealth to personal freedom in an unfree state. One could, of course, try to live a private life as far from the gaze of the emperor as possible, enjoying freedom from interference to the extent the emperor would allow. Or the elite could try to find space for public action on the frontier. This was the strategy of Tacitus' father-in-law Agricola, who left Rome and the tyrannical rule of Domitian (ruled 81–96 CE) to pacify Britain, a land where there was still space for ambitious and energetic men to enhance their status by performing glorious deeds on behalf of the commonwealth. Indeed, freedom is one of the major themes of Tacitus' biography of Agricola (*Agricola*), which will be treated in greater detail later in the book.

If Tacitus in the *Agricola* explored the conditions for participation under tyrannical emperors, others tried to recover freedom by emphasizing ownership. This was the option offered by Stoics such as Epictetus, the former slave who obtained his freedom after Nero's death in 68 CE and subsequently taught philosophy in Rome and elsewhere. In the *Discourses*, a record of Epictetus' teachings presented by his pupil Arrian, Epictetus argued that if you want to be truly free and do as you wish (4.1.1), then you must ensure that you are invulnerable from being coerced to act against

---

[13] "Subtle tyrant": Cartledge 2016: 270. See further J. W. Atkins forthcoming d. Cf. Markell 2008: 25.

your will, the essence of slavery (4.1.128). The solution is to avoid identifying as your own anything that is not completely "in your own power, either to have or not to have, or to have possessions of a particular quality, or under particular circumstances" (4.1.129). Consequently, we are not to identify ourselves and our well-being with our property, social status, or even our own bodies, as all of these may be taken from us. The only thing that is completely "up to us" is the correct exercise of our faculty of choice (1.1). Since the world is governed by a rational providence that ensures that everything works out for the best, the road to freedom is to happily choose what fate ordains (4.1.131).

We might well ask with Epictetus' interlocutor: "How does this relate to freedom" (4.1.144)? Epictetus' answer is that his radical sense of self-ownership frees us from the crippling passions that beset us when we fear other people or adverse circumstances. Epictetus' freedom is a positive freedom of self-realization (in Berlin's sense) that removes internal constraints such as fear, which may keep us from achieving what we want. This view of freedom continues to have powerful resonance for people in oppressive conditions. For instance, Admiral James Bond Stockdale credits Epictetus' philosophy for helping him survive a Vietnamese prisoner-of-war camp during the Vietnam War (Stockdale 1993).[14]

Ancient and Modern Liberty Reconsidered

In this chapter, I have argued that Roman concepts of freedom are much more nuanced with respect to Athenian and modern views than Constant's dichotomy allows. When compared to their Athenian counterparts, Roman citizens enjoyed less freedom in their private lives – though unlike at Athens some small subset of their individual liberties was protected by rights. Similarly, democratic Athens, unlike Rome, emphasized (at least in theory) the equal opportunity of citizens for political participation.

When Rome is compared to modern liberal democracies, Constant's analysis yields mixed results. There is an important difference between Rome and modern liberal democracies in that these regimes place different values on public and private liberty. From the Roman perspective, these modern regimes overemphasize the individual as the subject of liberties at the expense of the household and the private at the expense of the public. Participation on behalf of the *res publica* is (at least by Roman elites) prized at the expense of private freedom, and republicans like Cicero

---

[14] For Epictetus' philosophy, see Long 2002. (In it chapter 8 relates most closely to the above discussion.)

argued for the subordination of the interests of the individual to that of the city (*Off.* 3.40). At the same time, Romans conceived of liberty in both negative and positive terms. They championed the importance of equality before the law. And most importantly, the Romans preceded modern liberal democracies in emphasizing equal rights under the law for citizens. Of course, these rights were not natural or human rights but rather rights derived from custom and law. They were relatively few in number and primarily defensive in nature. Freedom conceived in terms of participation and involvement in public affairs was tied to the desire for status and guided by an honor code that would look restrictive and dangerous in the modern world.

In conceptualizing liberty, Roman republicans join the neo-republicans in emphasizing problems of ownership and control. Inasmuch as the rule of law and rights address these problems by restraining and regularizing a ruler's otherwise arbitrary will, they establish important preconditions for liberty. To return to an earlier example, I sometimes illustrate the point in class by telling my students that the clear grading policies and reading schedule outlined in the syllabus at the start of the semester enables them to do their best by freeing them from the crippling anxiety that they would surely face if I could arbitrarily change my policies at a whim. To this extent, Cicero is right to claim, "we all are slaves to the law so that we may be free" (*Clu.* 146).

However, ultimately for Roman republicans, solving the problem of ownership and control by a master's arbitrary will proved insufficient for securing freedom. One must also emphasize participation, which depends on a desire for status and honor, deep-seated Roman notions that are typically seen as at odds with modern liberalism (but see Krause 2002). In Roman republican ideology, (elite) political participation and popular ownership were equally important conditions for a free republic.

However, as Cicero's analysis of democracy in particular suggests, ownership and political participation are not necessarily mutually reinforcing ideas. By orienting their analysis of liberty around the problem of domination, neo-republicans risk having their concern with control and ownership eclipse, and even thwart, arguments for participation.[15] Thus, Roman political thought provides a timely lesson for the modern world: when assessing institutions and laws, we must ask both whether they deal with

---

[15] See especially the critique of Pettit along these lines by Markell 2008, an important article whose distinction between "domination" and "usurpation" stimulated my thinking about the relationship between ownership and participation in Roman republican thought.

equally important for free republic

the problem of control by another's <u>arbitrary will</u> and whether they promote or stifle <u>political participation</u>. It is not clear that, absent some
motivation for <u>political</u> participation, theories of freedom that focus on
non-domination are significantly more emancipatory than Berlin's liberalism. After all, one of the lessons of Rome is that the notion of equality
before the law, suffrage, and individual rights are quite at home in a hierarchical, slaveholding regime that is ruled paternalistically, whether by a
permanent ruling class or by an autocrat.

CHAPTER 3

Citizenship and Civic Virtue

The Concept of Citizenship

Few political ideas are more fundamental than citizenship. A citizen is "a member of a political community, entitled to whatever prerogatives and encumbered with whatever responsibilities are attached to membership" (Walzer 1989: 211). This definition seems innocuous enough, but, as any observer of the current political landscape in western democracies knows, many issues related to citizenship are highly contentious. In fact, as I write this chapter in 2016, concerns about citizenship are at the forefront of politics in both the United States and Europe. Opposition to immigration was a driving force behind "Brexit," the referendum in which the British people voted to leave the European Union. In America, concerns about the economic, legal, and social costs of illegal immigration helped propel businessman Donald Trump's successful presidential campaign. Debate over immigration and citizenship has dominated the political news and brought out to the polls large numbers of voters. For some, the movement to restrict immigration and limit access to citizenship is essential for preserving law and order and fulfilling the political community's obligations to provide social and economic benefits to its current members; for others, such limitations represent an illiberal and inhumane policy, driven by insecurity and xenophobia.

The immigration debates bring to the surface a deep-seated tension within our liberal-democratic conception of citizenship. Writing two decades ago of Europe's longstanding challenge of accommodating refugees, Jürgen Habermas noted that the "process exacerbates the conflict between the universalistic principles of constitutional democracies on the one hand and the particularistic claims of communities to preserve the integrity of their *habitual* ways of life on the other" (1995: 256; emphasis in the original). How this conflict is embedded in the contemporary liberal-democratic notion of citizenship becomes clear when we consider citizenship's various dimensions. According to contemporary political theorists, the concept of citizenship is composed of three fundamental dimensions (Leydet 2014). The first involves citizens' ability to participate in politics; it highlights their capacity as political agents to share in political rule, processes, decisions, and duties. The second dimension concerns its legal aspect, that is, the rights and protections afforded to citizens by the law. Finally, citizenship provides one with a social status and identity as a member of a political community. To be a citizen in this sense is to identify with a particular way of life that shapes one's political community.

These three aspects of citizenship, however, are not all represented in our modern notion of citizenship to the same degree. The modern western, democratic concept of citizenship tends to be a predominantly liberal notion that makes the legal dimension the core of the idea – citizenship is at base a set of legal claims and rights that protect citizens' pursuit of their diverse interests in their private lives. In its legal dimension, liberal citizenship is expandable to an almost infinite group of persons irrespective of social, ethnic, gender, or even territorial differences (Pocock 1995: 45; cf. Walzer 1989: 215–16). Thus viewed from this predominant liberal perspective, citizenship tends towards universalization as more and more people are invited into its sphere of protection.

At the same time, while eclipsed by citizenship's legal aspect, the political and status or identity dimensions of citizenship are not completely absent from contemporary thinking about citizenship in liberal democracies. These dimensions are particular, and thus not easily universalized. Citizenship understood as providing members of a political community with an identity, for instance, is not easily separated from questions of national identity (Habermas 1995) and historically has been bound with a patriotic allegiance to a particular political culture or way of life (Viroli 1995).

We can now see why the conflict over immigration reveals a deeper tension within the various dimensions of the modern notion of citizenship. Such debates showcase a tension between the predominant universalizable legal aspect of citizenship and the more particularistic aspects of politics, status, and identity, which do not admit of universalization without perceived dilution or further transformation.

The tensions between these aspects of citizenship can at times be so pronounced that historians of political philosophy have identified two different conceptions of citizenship depending on which of the three dimensions of citizenship predominates. The first is the liberal conception of citizenship, which, as we have seen, focuses on citizenship's legal dimensions. The second is the republican conception of citizenship, which focuses on the first and third dimensions of citizenship, that is, those related to the citizen's standing and identity with respect to politics and social and political culture. The republican idea of citizenship emphasizes the standing, prestige, and duties of citizenship; it elevates the public over the private and the active engagement in political life over the passive enjoyment of rights under the protection of law.

Scholars trace the republican idea of citizenship back to the *poleis* of ancient Greece and to the Roman Republic, where it received its clearest theoretical treatments in the writings of Aristotle and Cicero. The liberal tradition of citizenship, according to these accounts, finds its origins in the Roman Empire, where the notion of citizenship meant being a legal being with rights and possessions regulated by law (Walzer 1989; Pocock 1995). If these accounts are correct, the tensions we noticed between the universalizable (liberal) dimensions of citizenship and the particularistic (republican) dimensions may well be traced to a historical process at Rome, the transition from Republic to Empire.

But to what extent did the Roman Republic and Empire offer two different conceptions of citizenship? This is one key question pursued in this chapter, which considers how the Romans conceived of citizenship and the related idea of civic virtue in the Republic, and how and to what extent these concepts changed over time as citizenship was extended in the Empire and civic virtue adjusted to fit monarchy. We will also consider how conceptions of citizenship and civic virtue were transformed by Christian political thought. As we will see, citizenship and civic virtue are tied to regime type, and especially to aspects of Rome's social and political culture. Hence, this chapter looks at the transformation of the Republic into Empire from the vantage point of political culture.

Roman Citizenship

In 155 CE Aelius Aristides, an Ionian Greek who possessed Roman citizenship, delivered a speech in praise of Rome at the court of Emperor Antoninus Pius. The speech drew special attention to the expansion of Roman citizenship:

> But there is that which very decidedly deserves as much attention and admiration now as all the rest together. I mean your magnificent citizenship with its grand conception, because there is nothing like it in the records of all mankind. Dividing into two groups all those in your empire – and with this word I have indicated the entire civilized world – you have everywhere

appointed to your citizenship, or even to kinship with you, the better part of the world's talent, courage, and leadership, while the rest you recognized as a league under your hegemony.

Neither sea nor intervening continent are bars to citizenship, nor are Asia and Europe divided in their treatment here. In your empire all paths are open to all. No one worthy of rule or trust remains an alien, but a civil community of the world has been established as a free Republic under one, the best, ruler and teacher of order; and all come together as into a common civic center, in order to receive each man his due.

What another city is to its own boundaries and territory, this city is to the boundaries and territory of the entire civilized world. (*Roman Oration* 59–61; trans. Oliver)

Aristides was an accomplished orator; indeed, he was one of the leading lights of a revival of Greek rhetoric in the second and third centuries CE, a movement commonly referred to as the Second Sophistic. With some rhetorical embellishment, Aristides describes how in his day Roman citizenship was extended throughout the "entire civilized world." Roman citizenship is no longer limited by, or tied to, territorial boundaries. People anywhere in the world, regardless of geography or ethnicity, may find a pathway to Roman citizenship. This extension of citizenship, according to Aristides, effectively divided the world into two groups, citizen and subject, and enabled Rome to coopt much of the world's greatest talent in the service of imperial rule.

This Roman practice of liberally extending citizenship was formally codified half a century later in a 212 CE edict by the emperor Caracalla, typically known as the Antonine Constitution, which at a stroke made all free persons throughout the Roman world – over 30 million people – Roman citizens (Ulpian, *Edict* book 22 = *Dig.* 1.5.17). The edict has been both praised as the fulfillment of the natural law cosmopolitanism of the Severan jurist Ulpian and cynically dismissed as a ploy by Caracalla to increase tax revenues for his own benefit. Whatever Caracalla's motives, neither the astounding scope of his grant of citizenship nor the high-flown words of Aristides should distract from the fact that generally speaking the extension of Roman citizenship was inextricably linked to the (at times, brutal) expansion of Roman Empire, that is, with the imposition of Roman order on and control over the world – an idea to which we will return in chapter 7.[1]

---

[1] 30 million persons made citizens by the Antonine Constitution: Beard 2015: 527. Beard draws on Lavan 2016. For Caracalla's edict as embodying Ulpian's enlightened cosmopolitanism, see Honoré 2002; 2010; as a ploy by Caracalla to enhance revenue, see Cassius Dio 78.9. Dio's account is questioned by Ando 2012: 59–60.

Caracalla's edict presupposes that citizenship is almost entirely legal and juridical. Claims to citizenship were detached from ethnicity, culture, language, civic service and duty, and political participation (Sherwin-White 1973: 287); this made it universalizable, so that all peoples anywhere in the world could become Roman citizens. Upon the disparate particularities of history, custom, religion, language, traditions, and local political and legal systems, Rome, through the extension of citizenship, superimposed a unifying legal order that provided identity without cancelling out these various differences. According to Claudia Moatti (2015: 308–13, 334–35), this predominantly legal conception of citizenship was already established in the final century of the Republic. Thus, Cicero could deeply and movingly affirm the identity-shaping ties of his "fatherland by nature," his local municipality of Arpinum, while swearing his utmost allegiance to his "fatherland by citizenship" and "by law," Rome (*Leg.* 2.5).

A convenient example of how the largely juridical view of citizenship could be separated from one's other identities is furnished by St. Paul's references to his Roman citizenship as described in the New Testament book of Acts. When addressing the crowd upon his arrest in Jerusalem, Paul identifies himself by reference to his city of origin (Tarsus), his ethnicity (a Jew), and by his new religion (a Christian convert; Acts 22:1–21). To mention his Roman citizenship before a crowd in Jerusalem might have been a red flag to a bull, and Paul discloses his identity in terms of religion and ethnicity, not citizenship. When he does disclose his Roman citizenship before Roman officials, he does so to secure its juridical protections from arbitrary beatings, particularly in the form of *provocatio* – the old Republican legal right of appeal to the people (now, to the emperor), which secured the status of Roman citizens by protecting them from the sort of arbitrary beatings exercised against slaves. This juridical benefit constituted the primary value of citizenship for provincials like Paul (see Acts 16:37; 22:23–29; 25:10–12).

Some writers living during the high Empire remark that, at least in some circumstances, the value of citizenship was diluted by its extension (Tac. *Ann.* 3.40; Plin. *Pan.* 37.2–5). But how much did the conception of citizenship change from the time of the Republic? Before this question can be answered, we first must discuss the content of Roman citizenship and its extension to others under the Republic.

Unlike under the Empire, in the Republic Roman citizenship comprised all three dimensions highlighted by modern theorists – legal, political, and status/identity.

The legal consisted of the citizens' rights described in the last chapter, such as *conubium*, *provocatio*, and *suffragium* – the rights to marry, to appeal to the people, and to vote – in addition to numerous rights under private law. In addition to these rights, Roman citizenship also carried with it numerous public and political rights, duties, and privileges. Consider a few examples. One needed to be a citizen to serve in the legions (though not in the auxiliary units). The Romans (at least with respect to the legions) fielded a citizen army throughout the Republic, and a male Roman citizen was liable for military service from the time he was seventeen, when he enrolled in the military, to the age of sixty, when he was retired. Roman men did not serve continuously during the period for which they were liable, and they became exempt from future service if they served on a substantial number of campaigns. Within the military only Roman citizens served as officers.

Another area in which citizenship mattered was paying taxes. Tribute, a direct property tax on Roman citizens to support the military, was regarded as a necessary evil (Cic. *Off.* 2.74). Rome attempted as much as possible to have provinces and subject peoples bear its financial burdens, and indeed from 167 through 43 BCE there was no tribute on the property of Roman citizens at Rome and in Italy (Nicolet 1980: 149–50).

Citizenship also mattered for political participation. A man had to be a citizen (with one exception; see below) to vote in the various popular assemblies, and being a citizen was a precondition for holding political office.

Finally, under the Republic, citizenship formed one's identity and a sense of status – to become a citizen was "to be made a Roman" (Sherwin-White 1973: 40–43; G. Woolf 1998). Roman citizenship, at least theoretically, shaped one's identity inasmuch as the Roman *res publica* encompassed and supported all that Romans loved and identified as their own. Roman citizens were members of a common republic, and as such were shaped, educated, and bound together by shared customs, religion, affections, institutions, and laws (Cic. *Off.* 1.52–57). Citizenship also provided status, elevating those who possessed it above slaves.

It is important to note that the above account, and especially the political dimension of citizenship, applied in every respect only to the adult male citizen. In both public and private law, various classes of citizens, though still full citizens, were subject to legal and political disabilities. Freedmen (former slaves), adult children under the authority of their father, independent women, practitioners of disgraceful professions (e.g., auctioneers, gladiators, actors, prostitutes), and those with physical and cognitive handicaps suffered various sorts of disabilities before the law, in comparison with the adult male head of the family (Gardner 1993).

We should also keep in mind the gap between republicanism as a theory or ideology and actual political practice under the Republic. It is true that in the high Empire Roman citizenship ceased "to be a guarantee of participation in political life" (Nicolet 1980: 20). However, as we have seen in other places in this book, in practice opportunities were limited for citizens to participate even under the Republic. While citizens had the right to participate in decision-making, neither their level of participation nor the process by which they could participate did justice to republican descriptions of an active deliberative and electoral body in which "the humblest of citizens was a member of a collective sovereignty" (Nicolet 1980: 20) – let alone to the strictures of contemporary republican and democratic theorists (see chapter 1 and chapter 5). For the most part, the many poor citizens found that their liberty largely consisted of a protective set of legal rights and the right to vote (see chapter 2). While the right of suffrage surely was more than ornamental, voting participation was very low, many votes were either "yes" or "no," and substantial financial and social obstacles rendered magistracies and senatorial positions out of reach for the vast majority of citizens (see Mouritsen 2001). An aristocracy of leading families dominated these institutions (see introduction and chapter 1). Consequently, when we turn from the type of theoretical analysis of republicanism favored by political theorists to consider political practice, we find the contrast between the "political" republican citizenship under the Republic and the "legal" or "juridical" conception under the Empire to be less stark than theorists such as Pocock and Walzer suggest. Even under the Republic, for most citizens "the core and heart of citizenship" consisted of protective private rights under law and their accompanying social status rather than participation in politics (Gardner 1993: 2; Sherwin-White 1973: 267; cf. Nicolet 1980: 21).

To stress the prior qualifications to the republican notion of citizenship in light of legal reality and political practice is not to deny, however, that the concept underwent substantial change between the Republic and Principate. The nature of this change will become more evident as we turn to consider Rome's policy of extending citizenship to non-citizens.

Rome's policy of extending citizenship liberally, though most famously exemplified in the 212 CE Antonine Constitution, was deeply rooted within Roman ideology, and distinguished it from other ancient regimes. Nicolet rightly notes (1980: 23) that from the earliest days of the Republic, Rome was "more hospitable to aliens than any other city of the ancient world."

Consider for example Athens. In the "golden age" of Athenian democracy under Pericles in the fifth century, citizenship required two Athenian parents. This requirement was consistent with democratic ideology, which held that the Athenians were autochthonous, a people descended not from colonists but from ancestors sprung directly from the land of Attica. Later, in the fourth century BCE, the Athenians implemented a process of naturalization. However, in the roughly forty-seven years between the introduction of naturalization and the end of Athenian democracy in 322, the evidence suggests that at the very most a couple of hundred people would have received citizenship through this process. (Most of these were foreign statesmen who had no interest in relocating to Athens in order to exercise their citizenship.)[2]

By contrast, the Roman foundation myths of Aeneas and Romulus portray an openness to extending citizenship to foreigners. In their distant past, Romans were not born from the Italian soil but were immigrants, foreign wanderers led from Troy to Italy by Aeneas; their first king, Romulus, built Rome by broadly extending citizenship. Reflecting these myths, the Roman republican conception of citizenship possessed a universalizing orientation. Cicero both highlighted and exploited this orientation in a significant defense speech delivered in 56 BCE, shortly after Pompey, Crassus, and Caesar had met at Luca to reaffirm their alliance. Defending the legality of Pompey's grant of citizenship to the previously non-Roman Balbus who had since become one of Caesar's most influential political advisors, Cicero could argue that in late Republican Rome, "from every state there is a road open to [citizenship in] ours ... There is no people in any quarter of the world ... so constituted that we are forbidden to adopt any one of its citizens, or to present him with the citizenship of Rome" (Cic. *Pro Balbo* 29–30; trans. Gardner, Loeb). Differences over the exclusivity of citizenship are one of the most salient factors in explaining the difference between Republican Rome and classical Athens (Konstan 2015: 13).[3]

Rome did not allow dual citizenship, though Cicero points out that many in the late Republic did not understand this (*Balb.* 29–30). They could perhaps be forgiven, since Rome included in its treaties with its allies the option to follow Roman law or local law in regulating private and local matters (*Balb.* 22). What must not be compromised is the supremacy

---

[2] Athenian citizenship after Pericles' reforms: Cartledge 2016: 88–90. Autochthony: Loraux 2000. Naturalization process at Athens: Hansen 1999: 94–95.
[3] Roman foundation myths and open extension of citizenship: Momigliano 1987: 267–74 (he also compares Rome and Athens); Beard 2015: 67, 527–28.

of Rome's empire, and most Roman treaties of the late Republic featured a so-called supremacy clause, requiring its allies to uphold the supremacy of the Roman Republic (Plb. 21.32.2; Cic. *Balb.* 35; Livy 38.11.2). Still, this clause was construed narrowly to concern primarily matters of foreign policy in order to preserve local autonomy over customs, laws, religion, and institutions (Nicolet 1980: 46).

Flexibility characterized Rome's policy of extending citizenship from the earliest days of the Republic. Rome used a number of methods for incorporating outsiders into its empire. From the early Republic to about 200 BCE, Rome conferred *civitas sine suffragio* (citizenship without the vote) on neighboring peoples. A people with *civitas sine suffragio* enjoyed the same judicial protections as other citizens but could not vote, marry Roman citizens, or occupy magistracies (Livy 9.43.23). Likewise, members of municipalities, cities of non-Roman origin, were Roman citizens with full rights and obligations, except for voting and holding Roman magistracies. Municipalities maintained their own laws and institutions.

A final means for the expansion of citizenship were colonies. There were two types. *Roman* colonies consisted of transplanted Roman citizens, often army veterans, and served as outposts to provide stability at the edges of Rome's empire. Roman colonies adopted Roman laws and institutions; they sometimes were portrayed as small reflections of the Roman people (Aulus Gellius, *Noctes Atticae* 16.13.1–9). *Latin* colonies, on the other hand, were composed of non-Romans. (But Latin ex-magistrates could automatically become Roman citizens.) Like municipalities, the Latin colonies enjoyed much autonomy with respect to living under their own laws and government. Until 89 BCE when citizenship was extended to the Latins, Latin colonists possessed a sort of halfway status between citizens and subjects. They had the rights of *commercium* (to conduct trade) and *conubium* (to marry). They could migrate to Rome to acquire citizens' rights. In the later Republic, Latins had the right to vote in the popular assembly.[4]

Despite the Republic and Empire sharing a similarly liberal and flexible policy of extending citizenship, there was a conceptual difference, which perhaps can most effectively be conveyed by noting the heated resistance that Rome's liberal policy sometimes encountered from its own citizens during the Republic. Consider a couple of examples. In 122 BCE, the populist tribune Gaius Gracchus proposed conferring citizenship on Latins so that they could enjoy the protection of *provocatio*. One might have

---

[4] My account of these classifications of citizenship generally relies on Nicolet 1980 and Sherwin-White 1973.

expected the extension of this legal protection to have enjoyed strong support – even the conservative Cato the Elder had previously railed against arbitrary beatings inflicted upon Rome's allies – but the motion failed. The reason was that the people, in particular the urban plebs, feared the political and social implications of extending citizenship. As the consul C. Fannius argued in a *contio*: "If you grant citizenship to the Latins, do you think that you will have the same position in public meetings as you occupy now, or that you will take part in the games or in festivities? Don't you think that they will take over everything?" (Malcovati, *ORF* 144).

Eventually – though it required a revolt by Rome's allies – a pathway to citizenship was opened to any free inhabitant of Italy and to free cities in 89 BCE, during the so-called Social War between Rome and her allies (91–88 BCE). While this legislation was popular among the non-citizen Italians inasmuch as it granted access to Roman political office to the elites and judicial protection to all, it met resistance from both elite and non-elite Roman citizens. The former did not welcome the additional competition for political office from the newcomers, whereas the latter feared having their votes in the assemblies diluted by additional voters. Even though Cicero's hometown of Arpinum had possessed citizenship since 188 BCE, Cicero, as we saw in the book's introduction, still faced scorn and resistance from the old aristocracy who resented his outsider status, dismissing him as a "newcomer to Rome."[5]

Both of the previous examples suggest that resistance to the expansion of citizenship occurred because of the political and identity/status dimensions of citizenship. In the late Republic, these more particularistic aspects of citizenship had not yet been completely severed from its juridical core. Hence, the resistance to the expansion of citizenship under the Republic suggests a more particularistic conception of citizenship was in play, even if its core legal and universalistic aspects were already well in place long before the Principate. By the same token, the triumph of the universalistic strain of citizenship led to the concept's dilution and increasing irrelevance. Once it was extended to all, citizenship no longer conferred status on its possessors. This had legal implications. For example, citizenship on its own no longer guaranteed all citizens protection from the types of degrading punishments that used to be inflicted lawfully only on slaves and other non-citizens. Such protections were legally guaranteed only for "the more honorable" citizens (*honestiores*), a group that included senators, veterans, and members of the municipal aristocracy – in short, the elite,

---

[5] The preceding two paragraphs are indebted to Nicolet 1980: 39–43.

wealthy, and powerful (Garnsey 1970; Beard 2015: 528–29). Roman citizenship was no longer something worth fighting and dying for, as Roman allies had done in the late Republic.

Republican Civic Virtues

In his *Politics*, Aristotle argued that what constitutes a good citizen is determined by his regime. Different regimes with their different ways of organizing society will foster different virtues or character traits in citizens. For example, liberal regimes, placing a premium on individual liberty, value the virtues of autonomy, reasonableness, and tolerance (Macedo 1990). According to contemporary republicans, regimes should value above all a patriotic allegiance to one's political community and to the common good it promotes for one's fellow citizens (Viroli 2002). A "republican liberalism" that seeks to combine commitment to individual autonomy and community might focus on the respect for autonomy and individual rights, tolerance, fair play, the cultivation of civic memory, and political participation (Dagger 1997: 196–98).

Lists of key civic virtues compiled by scholars of the late Roman Republic tend to be longer than those provided by contemporary republican theorists. This should not be surprising given the somewhat utopian nature of Republican ideology: Rome was (ideally) a nation of men ruled by virtues and affections rather than by laws. The latter were necessary when and because the former failed (Kaster 2005: 3). Thus, a greater sphere of social life and interaction was regulated by virtue in Rome than in modern liberal democracies.[6]

What virtues should citizens possess under the Roman Republic? Leading thinkers in the republican tradition such as Cato, Cicero, and Sallust addressed this question at length. These writers were especially concerned with service to and leadership of the *res publica*. In other words, they dealt with the qualities that would characterize the relatively few who would have access to office and/or military command. It was primarily through service to the *res publica*, after all, that one attained glory and status, and republican virtues constituted the qualities that enabled Romans to compete well. There was an inextricable link between republican virtues and the Roman honor code, consisting above all of the tripartite values of *gloria*, *honor*, and *dignitas* (Hellegouarc'h 1972: 362–424). The honor code was the standard by which different activities, professions, and lifestyles

---

[6] Lists of Roman Republican virtues: Earl 1967; Hellegouarc'h 1972; Schofield 2009.

would be measured. We have already noted that various dishonorable professions handicapped citizens. But beyond that, Republican writers emphasized that some ways of life were more conducive than others to the virtues that led to successful competition for the goods of the honor code. For example, Cato the Elder believed that a life on the farm was well suited for developing the military virtues essential for Republican citizen-soldiers. On the other hand, Cato, like others in the Roman aristocracy, placed a much lower value on commerce (see *De agricultura* 1.1 and Cic. *Off.* 1.150).

It is worth lingering for a moment on the primacy of agriculture over commerce in Roman republican ideology. Though agrarianism was an important ideal in the reception of Roman republicanism (especially by the founders of the American Republic), it receives little or no space in recent accounts (Kapust 2011b: 91–92; Connolly 2015: 100–101; absent from Hammer 2014). Consider Livy's influential account of Lucius Quinctius Cincinnatus. As Livy tells the story (3.26–29), during a war with a neighboring village in the early days of the Republic (458 BCE), the enemy army trapped and besieged one of the consuls and the Roman army. In desperation, the senate nominated as dictator Cincinnatus, a former consul who had left politics for farming. Traveling to Cincinnatus' farm near the Tiber to persuade him to accept the dictatorship, the senators found him working in his fields. Upon learning of Rome's need, he responded immediately. Wiping off the sweat and dirt, he donned his toga and assumed the dictator's awesome *imperium*. He raised an army and successfully relieved the besieged consular army. With his mission accomplished, he resigned the dictatorship as soon as possible, proving wrong his plebeian critics who feared that the excessive *imperium* of the dictatorship would make the man imperious. Livy leaves no doubt about the moral of the story, which he underscores by repeating the second and third Latin words of the preface to his entire history in relating it (Ogilvie 1970: 441):

> This is worthwhile to hear for those who reject all human qualities in comparison with riches and think that there is place for neither great honor nor virtue unless where resources flow in abundance. The only hope for the rule of the Roman people, Lucius Quinctius Cincinnatus, on the other side of the Tiber opposite the place where the dockyards are now, cultivated a four-acre farm, which is called the Quinctian Meadows. (3.26.7–8)

Cincinnatus was one of the American Founders' greatest classical heroes. He was considered a worthy example by John Adams, Samuel Adams, Patrick Henry, and above all, by George Washington, who actively cultivated the comparisons with Cincinnatus offered by contemporary sculptors, painters, and poets (Richard 2008: 124–27). To give but one example, on July 4, 1788, following the ratification of the US Constitution by the required nine states, celebrants in Wilmington, Delaware offered the following toast: "Farmer Washington – may he, like a second Cincinnatus, be called from the plow to rule a great people."[7] After assuming the presidency, Washington's correspondence "was littered with references to Cincinnatus and the ideal of the citizen-soldier-farmer" (Bederman 2008: 36). What Washington and his contemporaries found admirable in Livy's Cincinnatus was his patriotic devotion, a strength of character that enabled him to surrender power without being corrupted by an ambition – enhanced by his immense power – that would have destroyed Rome's fledgling republican government.

Returning to Livy's text, there are three significant apparently interrelated ideas: Cincinnatus' subordination of the desire for riches to virtue and honor; his restraint that kept him from becoming imperious or overmastering despite wielding great power; his devotion to his four-acre farm across the Tiber – the location of which Livy describes in detail. What is the connection? As we will see in the next chapter, Latin and Greek writers reflecting on Rome frequently identified greed and the excessive desire for power as sharing a common feature: a limitlessness that does not respect civic and natural boundaries and attachments. By devoting himself assiduously to the cultivation of a particular and well-defined place, Livy's Cincinnatus developed qualities of character resistant to the temptation to transgress the limits of republican government in a limitless pursuit of power, even when an emergency had given him ample opportunity. Livy's allusion to Roman topography serves as a visual marker of this ideal. The idea that the devotion to and cultivation of place can sustain communities by fortifying individuals against the tendency to transgress limits in the pursuit of power or wealth has resonance far beyond Rome. It is an important theme, for instance, in the agrarian essays of American novelist Wendell Berry.[8]

Livy's picture of Cincinnatus provides a partial view of the Roman honor code and the civic virtues that accompany it. To get a fuller picture of key civic virtues and the way in which they promoted the "good life" according to the standards of the Roman aristocratic code, consider

[7] Quoted in Maier 2010: 436. For further examples of artists portraying Washington as Cincinnatus, see Richard 2008: 125–27.
[8] Greed: Compare Balot 2001: ch. 1. Features of Rome's topography as "visual markers": Hammer 2014: 231. For a collection of Berry's agrarian essays emphasizing the theme of "place," see Wirzba 2002.

the oldest surviving fragment of a Roman funeral oration. In his eulogy delivered in 221 BCE, Quintus Metellus praises his father, Lucius Metellus, a two-time consul and hero of the first Punic War, for achieving "the ten greatest and best objectives in the pursuit of which wise men spend their lives" (Pliny, *Natural History* 7.139). These include:

(1) to be a first-rate warrior
(2) to be the best orator
(3) to be the bravest general
(4) to be in charge of the most important initiatives
(5) to hold the highest office
(6) to possess the greatest wisdom
(7) to be considered the most influential senator
(8) to obtain great wealth by honorable means
(9) to leave many children
(10) to be the most renowned man in the state.

These objectives roughly follow the order in which a senator would be expected to pass his life. He would begin as a soldier, then occupy a range of magistracies and positions of military command, before finally ending his life as a senior senator whose prestige influenced his community during his life and his legacy after his death (Flower 1996: 139–40).

Three features deserve comment. First, these objectives emphasize the predominance of the public sphere over the private realm of the household. Even the acquisition of wealth had a public dimension inasmuch as it had to be acquired "honorably" and would give an elite Roman the resources to bestow liberally favors that greased the bearings of Roman social and political life. Second, the two virtues mentioned in this passage, wisdom and courage, are esteemed precisely because they allow Romans to achieve excellence in serving the republic through politics (wisdom in deliberating) and war (courage in battle). Finally, the standing described in this passage, along with the virtues by which it is achieved, has a hereditary component. The senior Metellus was the first to establish the family name, so part of his son's task was to solidify his family's claim to a place within Rome's political aristocracy by indicating that his father measured up to the most stringent standards of Rome's aristocratic code.

The traditional aristocratic honor code emphasizing active, competitive public service as the source for standing and glory likewise shapes the accounts of virtue provided by the Roman historian Sallust and Cicero. Sallust's *Catiline's Conspiracy* and Cicero's *De officiis*, both published in the late 40s BCE, describe virtues that elite citizen-leaders would be expected to possess. Cicero's work structures what is honorable around the four cardinal virtues from Greek political thought – wisdom, justice, courage, and temperance – though each is thoroughly reworked in light of Roman values and experience. The first is wisdom (*sapientia, prudentia*), which consists of theoretical and practical knowledge (1.18–19). The second is the social virtue of justice (1.20–60). Cicero divides it into both justice in the strict sense – not to harm other human beings unprovoked and to promote the common good (1.20–41) – and liberality or generosity (*liberalitas, beneficentia*), the virtue of freely bestowing acts of kindness on one's fellow citizens and, in some circumstances, on non-citizens (1.42–59). Both justice and liberality promote social cohesion within a competitive political culture by preventing harm and promoting interdependence. No less important in this regard is *fides*, faithfulness or trustworthiness, a virtue that promotes justice (e.g., in promise-keeping or honoring contracts) and ensures that public officials govern in a way that promotes the common good (1.23, 31).

The third virtue is courage (*fortitudo*) or greatness of spirit (*magnitudo animi*) (1.61–92). As we saw in Metellus' oration, courage was traditionally the virtue that enabled citizen-warriors to achieve great glory. This well-trod path to glory makes the courageous person susceptible to the love of glory, a passion especially dangerous to liberty since those with military commands were also magistrates with political power (1.68). According to Cicero, the truly great-spirited and courageous man is secure in his own preeminence, which is anchored in correct judgments of the comparatively great value of virtue and the small and fleeting value of externals such as the approval of others or wealth or power. This makes it an especially attractive virtue for leaders, who can consequently maintain their convictions and resist corruption and flattery. Holding to one's convictions and resisting corruption were also characteristics of the virtue of *constantia*, which, along with *magnitudo animi* (greatness of spirit), was particularly associated with the Republican champion Marcus Cato, who committed suicide rather than yield to the dictatorship of Caesar (Sal. *Cat.* 54).

The "fourth virtue" actually consists of a group of related virtues that all involve in some way moderating, limiting, and calibrating one's behavior so as not to cause undue offense to other citizens (1.93–151). The most comprehensive term for this virtue is *decorum*, which involves choosing actions that will appear to others to be appropriate given the context in which they are performed. Also relevant are virtues of moderation or self-control (*temperantia, modestia*). *Verecundia* (restraint or respect) is a particularly important virtue for achieving the respect for others that the group as a whole promotes (cf. 1.99). Kaster (2005: 13) defines the term as "a kind of strategic fear that causes one to gauge one's behavior in any given social interaction and judge correctly one's standing relative to the other person, the better to monitor and restrain oneself and thus avoid giving offense." This doesn't mean that one should become a shrinking violet; rather, one should moderate one's claims when their pursuit would completely deface a fellow citizen, just as one should maintain for oneself and expect from others appropriate respect for one's own character. Another related virtue that allowed Romans to moderate social relations – though not treated in *De officiis* – is *pudor*, shame that one incurs when one sees oneself as discredited and one's *dignitas* devalued (see Kaster 2005: ch. 2).

Several other virtues deserve to be mentioned. *Pietas*, devotion to the gods, family, and country, was an indispensable virtue under the Republic. Roman republicans also held as a virtue patriotism – the love of and devotion to country as the object of citizens' greatest allegiance.[9] Finally, there is a class of virtues related to mercy – clemency (*clementia*), gentleness (*mansuetudo*), kindness (*humanitas*), and the verbs of sparing (*parcere*) and forgiving (*ignoscere*). This class of virtues was especially associated with Julius Caesar (Sal. *Cat.* 54) and gained increased political currency during the civil wars at the end of the Republic. Scholars differ about whether this increased political (as opposed to juridical) orientation of clemency initially faced resistance by elites worried that receiving mercy reduced their political status (cf. Konstan 2005 and Dowling 2006). In either case, mercy would later be embraced by elites as an important imperial virtue.

This brief review of Republican civic virtues reveals a close connection with Rome's political culture. Ideally, possessing these characteristics or excellences would allow elite Romans to excel, thereby attaining the status and honor that comprised their conception of the good life. At the same time, the possessor of these virtues – again, ideally – would also promote the social good, as the virtues were particularly calibrated to help citizens get along in a competitive, status-driven society. Thus, in the realistic utopia of social virtue ethics described by Cicero in his *De officiis*, the surest (and indeed only) pathway to personal glory and other advantages is through exhibiting virtuous and just behavior (2.43; 3.11). Given the social extension of these virtues, by benefitting yourself you would also be benefitting political society (3.26). This neat coincidence of self-interest and

---

[9] See Lucilius 1207–1208 (Warmington, Loeb); Cic. *Off.* 1.57; Cic. *Fam.* 12.14.7; Plutarch, *Fabius Maximus* 24.2.

altruism, virtue and reward, for citizens under the *Republic* was an ideal that even Cicero admitted was not always realized (1.44, 46, 64).

Civic Virtue Under the Principate

If civic virtues are related to regime type, how did they change once the Republic was transformed into a monarchy? We will focus on the civic virtues of two groups – (1) emperors and (2) the (other elite) citizens.

Scholars have generally examined the virtues of the emperor from two vantage points. The first concerns how the emperor communicates his virtues to his subjects. Such communication took multiple forms. For instance, Augustus' *Res Gestae* (34) refers to the golden shield given to Augustus by the senate in 27 BCE indicating his courage (*virtus*), mercy (*clementia*), justice (*iustitia*), and devotion to gods and men (*pietas*; see further Galinsky 1996: 80–90). Especially useful for understanding emperors' communication of their virtues is numismatics, since each coin minted at Rome officially represented the emperor and his regime to citizens of all classes throughout the empire (Wallace-Hadrill 1981; Noreña 2001; 2011). In his study of imperial coinage between 69 and 235 CE, Carlos Noreña found eleven virtues personified on coins (Noreña 2001; 2011: ch. 2). The six most communicated virtues include the following (beginning with the most frequent): *aequitas* or fairness; *pietas* or devotion; *virtus* or manly courage; *liberalitas* or generosity; *providentia* or foresight; and *pudicitia* or sexual chastity. Appearing less frequently were the juridical virtues (*iustitia* and *clementia*), additional virtues related to generosity *(indulgentia* and *munificentia)*, and finally *patientia* or endurance. One can see why an emperor would want to communicate these particular virtues. Fairness, generosity, self-control, devotion (to his subjects and gods), courage (especially in military actions on behalf of Rome), and the foresight necessary to ensure orderly rule and a peaceful succession – all suggest a stable and prosperous regime.

For the virtues of the emperor seen from the perspective of others, the key texts include Seneca's *De clementia*, Dio Chrysostom's *Orations* 1–4, Pliny's *Panegyricus* – all of which have been introduced in chapter 1. In considering the virtues ascribed to the emperor in these texts, it is important to keep in mind a tension in their presentation of the emperor vis-à-vis other citizens. On one hand, the emperor functions as a model of civic virtue in that he is conceived of as an ideal citizen. According to Pliny, he is a fellow-citizen (*civis*), "one of us," akin to a parent, not a god, master (*dominus*), or tyrant (*tyrannus*; *Pan.* 2.3–4). Under the Republican regime, citizens should compete for glory and status so long as no one citizen becomes so preeminent that he is not accountable to the laws (Livy 38.50.8). Pliny, Dio, and Seneca all praise lawful conduct by the emperor (Dio, *Oration* 3.5; Plin. *Pan.* 65.1–2; Sen. *Cl.* 1.1.4). Indeed, Pliny's *Panegyricus* contains frequent allusions to the rule of law, along with other republican themes such as the political involvement of the senate (Gowing 2005: 120–31; Wilkinson 2012: 20–26). However, all three writers acknowledge a central difference from the Republican reality: the emperor is "freed from the law" (*Dig.* 1.3.31). Hence, Seneca notes that the emperor should act "as if" he were going to have to give an account to the laws (*Cl.* 1.1.4); Pliny, that Trajan's voluntary submission to the laws was not expected of the *princeps* (*Pan.* 65.1); and Dio, that the emperor is "greater than the laws" (*Orat.* 3.10). In their praise of Nero and Trajan, respectively, Seneca and Pliny note that the emperor's power equals that of the immortal gods (*Pan.* 4.4; *Cl.* 1.1.2).

The emperor's independence from the law particularly comes to the fore when Dio and Seneca discuss the juridical virtues, justice (*iustitia*) and clemency (*clementia*). For Dio "a more exact sense of justice" is essential for "one who is greater than the laws" (*Orat.* 3.10). According to Seneca, justice may be defined as giving to each person their due, whereas clemency is a restraint from imposing a punishment that could deservedly be imposed under law (Sen. *Cl.* 2.3.2). Clemency is a virtue especially important for the *princeps*, given his freedom as a judge not subject to law:

> Clemency has a freedom of decision. It forms its judgments not according to the letter of the law but according to what is right and good. And it is allowed to acquit or to set the damages in a case at any level it likes. It does not do these things with the attitude that its action is less than justice requires but with the attitude that its decision is the most just course of action possible. (Sen. *Cl.* 2.7.3; trans. Braund)

Seneca, Pliny, and Dio supplement discussion of the juridical virtues with a range of other imperial virtues. In his third *Oration*, Dio treats the imperial virtues in terms of the four cardinal virtues of Greek philosophy – wisdom, justice, courage, and moderation. Pliny's *Panegyricus* picks out thirty-five separate virtues. Liberality (*liberalitas*), mentioned twelve times, receives special emphasis. No less important is the virtue *pietas*, mentioned eleven times by Pliny. *Pietas* covers devotion to the gods as well as both the devotion of the emperor to his citizens (2.6) and of the citizens to their emperor (24.5).

From the virtues of the emperor, we turn now to consider the virtues of the Roman elite. As in the Republic, elite virtues are determined by a particular political culture, the best guides to which are Seneca's *De beneficiis* (*On Favors*) and Pliny's *Letters*. These works describe in detail the social code of conduct among the elite. Whereas Seneca's work deals with the code in a more systematic, philosophical, and idealistic manner, Pliny's letters likewise show us prescribed conduct as "a handbook for the perfect Roman Senator" (Veyne 1990, quoted in Griffin 2000: 551).

The social code captured accurately by Pliny's letters and Seneca's *De beneficiis* in many respects differs little from the Republican code articulated in Cicero's *De officiis* (Griffin 2000; 2003; 2013). Consider the code's key features. It presumes an elite class of more or less equals who compete honorably for rank, status, and glory. Words such as *auctoritas* (prestige), *dignitas* (worthy standing), *amicitia* (friendship, alliance), *gloria*, and *honor* (glory) occur frequently in Pliny's *Letters*. Given these values, *beneficia* – free acts of kindness among relative equals – plays an important role in ensuring social cohesion among otherwise agonistic parties. Like players in a ball game, citizens learn to skillfully maneuver within socially determined roles – to know how, when, and to whom to give acts of kindness as well as how to receive them (Sen. *Ben.* 2.17.3). Proper conduct was highly contextual and depended on considerations of status and circumstance rather than on uniformly and inflexibly applied rules.

Other skills or virtues are also essential for citizens, as Pliny's *Letters* suggest. Virtues related to liberality (*liberalitas, munificentia*) are obviously important. Present too are virtues like *constantia, pietas, severitas, pudor, iustitia, verecundia,* and *prudentia.* We also find similar challenges and problems to the performance of virtuous activity as under the Republic. Romans need to consider their different obligations to fatherland, family, relatives, and friends (Plin. *Ep.* 9.30; cf. Cic. *Off.* 1.50–57). Like Cicero and Sallust, Pliny explores the relationship between virtue and glory – "glory ought to be the consequence of [our virtuous actions], not the motive for their performance" (Plin. *Ep.* 1.8) – a timely reminder given the centrality of glory to Roman political culture and the seductiveness of the attending love of fame (Plin. *Ep.* 5.8). The performance of virtue within a social culture recognizable from the Republic even holds true for book 10 of the *Letters*, addressed to Trajan, in which Pliny applies the Republican code of benefactions to the *princeps* (Griffin 2013: 65).

Despite general continuity in the honor code and Republican virtues among the elite, some works written under the Principate indicate modifications to Roman political culture, which in turn alters how citizens should display virtues. The most important modification concerns the revision of the extent and value of *gloria*. As Pliny's letters suggest, under the Principate *gloria* was still connected to traditional concepts in the Roman honor code – *dignitas* and *auctoritas*; but with the establishment of the Principate, and Augustus' emphasis on stability and law, instead of the great struggles of individuals to win glory, *gloria* became devalued and its link to *virtus* and to *nobilitas* was severed. This is especially evident in the Augustan poetry of Vergil and Horace, which, as Donald Earl (1967: 73) has observed, agreed in "dethroning *gloria* from its previous eminence in the concept of *virtus* and in dissociating this concept from the idea of *nobilitas*." To put the point differently, the institution of the Principate, with its restriction of the arena in which elite citizens could compete for public honors, altered in a subtle but significant way political culture, and that in turn impacted the exercise of virtue. This is particularly true when emperors, unbound by law, fail to act virtuously. Perhaps no work better illustrates this point than Tacitus' *Agricola*.

The *Agricola*, a complex and complicated work of literature (Whitmarsh 2006; Sailor 2008), is, among other things, a biography praising Tacitus' father-in-law Agricola, governor of Britannia from 77 to 83 CE, where his imperial and military conquest was, from the Roman perspective, a stunning success. Agricola was recalled by Domitian, perhaps, as Tacitus suggests, out of jealousy. Domitian was a tyrant, who proscribed senators, burned books, and eliminated free speech (*Agr.* 2). Conditions had improved by Tacitus' writing in 97–98, by which time Domitian had been assassinated and succeeded by Nerva. Nevertheless, Tacitus warns, "human nature is so weak that the cure lags behind the disease" (3.1; trans. Mattingly). Thus, the task of the work: an examination of the virtues of a man, Agricola, during "times hostile to virtues" (1.4). Yet Agricola's virtues are not valued for their own sake but because they bring him a certain glory – the real standard by which his life should be measured (44.3). The types of virtues that Agricola displayed are related to the glory that he managed to achieve under a tyrant. As Tacitus exhorts the reader,

> Let it be clear to those inclined to admire unlawful acts that even under bad emperors men can be great, and that subservience (*obsequium*) and discretion (*modestia*), if backed by ability (*industria*) and energy (*vigor*), can reach that peak of honor (*laus*) that many have stormed by precipitous paths, winning fame, without serving country (*res publica*), through an ostentatious death. (42.4; trans. Mattingly; modified)

As under the Republic, virtue here is tied to the honor code – to praise, greatness, glory, and fame acquired by service to the *res publica*. Almost all of the virtues exhibited by Agricola would be recognizable to Republican writers like Cicero and Sallust – including *modestia* and *industria* in this passage. At other places in the work, Agricola displays the cardinal virtues identified by Cicero – wisdom or prudence (4.1, 3; 6.3; 9.2; 19.1), justice (9.2, 4; 19.1), courage (18.2; 29.1), and words related to moderation or restraint (4.3; 5.1; 7.3; 8.1, 3; 9.3; 40.4) – even if, with one exception (40.2), words related to liberality are absent. Other familiar republican virtues are also present, including strictness (9.3), mercy (9.3), incorruptibility (*integritas*; 9.4), and steadfastness (*constantia*; 18.4).

Yet Republicans like Cicero would notice important differences in the way Agricola displays the virtues. The first has to do with the ranking of the virtues. Whereas for Cicero justice was the "mistress and queen of all the virtues" (*Off.* 3.28), Tacitus emphasizes the importance of moderation. Moderation (*modestia*) and subservience (*obsequium*) – these were the "virtues" that allowed Agricola to be great under a tyrant (30.3; 42.4). The second difference is the addition of the new virtue coupled with moderation – *obsequium* (compliance, subservience, obedience). The term is frequently used by Tacitus in his *Annals* to describe the relationship of subordinates to the emperor (see, e.g., 1.43; 3.55, 75; 6.37). It is the word Tacitus chooses to describe the relationship of the senate to Emperor Vespasian at the time of the execution of Helvidius Priscus (*Historiae* 4.3), a man who, as a principled republican like his adopted father Thrasea Paetus, resisted the Principate. From Thrasea's example, Helvidius "imbibed liberty" (*Hist.* 4.5). The comparison becomes even more interesting when one notices that the *Agricola* begins by holding out the burning of biographies eulogizing the lives of these dissident senators, Thrasea and Helvidius, as an example of the subservience and servitude characterizing the reign of Domitian (2.1–3). From the perspective of an elite republican like Cicero used to competing for and sharing in rule, such subservience would be a quality befitting a subject, not a citizen.[10]

Moderation and subservience, along with the prudence to know when and how to exercise them (42.3), paved the way for Agricola's greatness precisely by allowing him to avoid the envy that came from praise of his great deeds (8.2–3; 9.4–6; 40.1–4). He sought to avoid the agonistic striving for glory that characterized Roman political culture; the glory he acquired

---

[10] Freedom and servitude in Tacitus: Strunk 2017. Strunk discusses the cases of Thrasea Paetus and Helvidius Priscus in ch. 3.

was achieved on the frontier, far from the gaze of Domitian; and upon his return to Rome, he sought to live quietly and to deflect all attention. Ultimately he failed. Despite his precautions, he attracted glory (41.1).

In the end, Agricola's virtues and the manner in which he displayed them befitted his age (Kapust 2011b: 136), one in which the rough equality between the emperor and elite citizens conveyed by Pliny proved to be a mirage. Perhaps nowhere is this more apparent than the *Agricola*'s treatment of the one virtue that presumes equality – the bestowal of favors and thanks. Domitian, following protocol, allows himself to be thanked by Agricola for his "kindness" to Agricola in accepting the governor's request to forego a proconsulship – a request made only after Domitian's henchmen threatened Agricola and dragged him before the emperor (42.1–2). The "odiousness of this favor" should have, but didn't, cause Domitian to blush. Agricola's deference preserved his life – a "prudent" move when an assertion of liberty would have been futile (42.3). And so Tacitus claims that by elevating moderation and acquiring the non-Republican "virtue" of subservience (*obsequium*), Agricola achieved glory (42.4). As under the Republic, virtuous actions were connected to glory.

But what kind of glory? A passage from the *Annals* comes to mind, in which a Roman knight named Marcus Terentius addresses the emperor Tiberius in the senate during a time filled with fear caused by proscriptions and by senators accusing one another of treason. "To you the gods have granted supreme governance in all matters, and the glory of obeying you (*obsequii gloria*) is what is left to us" (6.8; trans. Yardley). Under despotism, virtue brings glory, but it is the glory of a subject rather than a citizen.

St. Augustine and the Christian Transformation of Citizenship and Civic Virtue

Thus far in this chapter, we have been tracing the link that citizenship and civic virtue share with political forms and the conception of the "good life" supported by the Roman honor code. The fact of this link provides the space for the potential reconception of citizenship and civic virtue by those holding different views of the "good life" from that promoted by the Roman honor code. One example of such a reconception of citizenship is furnished by Stoic cosmopolitanism, which we will explore in chapter 7. Here we will focus on another example, provided by Christianity. Already in the New Testament, St. Paul suggests that Christianity offers a new "citizenship" that could unite all human beings regardless of whether they are

Roman citizens. According to Paul, "foreigners" and "strangers" become "fellow citizens" by belonging to a heavenly city (Ephesians 2:19). Paul and his fellow Christians still retained their citizenship at Rome, but, he reminds his readers, they should not forget that that more fundamentally "our citizenship is in heaven" (Philippians 3:20).

The notion of two "citizenships" raises a version of an old tension familiar from Aristotle: the relationship between the good human being – the good citizen in the best regime – and the good citizen as determined by inferior regimes (*Politics* 3.4). Given that the identity of a "good citizen" and corresponding civic virtues are defined relative to a particular *politeia*, it is possible, perhaps even inevitable, that the "good citizen" of the heavenly *politeia* will not exemplify all of the qualities of a good Roman citizen, and vice versa. This observation generates questions. Can good Christians be good Roman citizens? Should Christians practice traditional Roman civic virtues? Should Christians occupy traditional Roman social roles and offices and perform traditional civic duties? The New Testament scriptures affirmed that Christians should submit to Roman governing authorities (Romans 13:1–7; 1 Peter 2:13–17). But as Christianity spread and Christians found themselves playing greater roles in public life following Constantine's "Edict of Milan," these questions became more pressing. The most extensive and influential answers came from the bishop of Hippo Regius in North Africa, St. Augustine.

Born in 354 in Thagaste, North Africa (present-day Algeria) to a Christian mother and non-Christian father, Augustine became an accomplished teacher of rhetoric, eventually obtaining a prestigious chair in Milan. In 386 in a Milanese garden, he converted to Christianity, an event powerfully described in book 8 of his classic spiritual autobiography, *Confessions*. In 391 he was ordained to the priesthood at Hippo Regius, where he would serve as a priest and later as a bishop until his death in 430. Augustine was a pastor and church leader rather than a professional political philosopher. Accordingly his thoughts on politics are scattered throughout sermons, letters, biblical commentaries, and theological treatises in addition to a brief series of philosophical dialogues he composed during the time between his conversion and ordination. The most significant of Augustine's writings for those interested in his political thought is the *City of God*, a monumental work of apologetics and philosophy of history that he composed between 413 and 426.[11]

---

[11] Augustine's biography: Brown 1967. For an English translation of *City of God*, see Dyson 1998, which I follow in this chapter.

Augustine originally conceived the *City of God* as a response to pagan accusations, made in the wake of Rome's sack by the Visigoths in 410, that Christianity was incompatible with the religious and civic duties that had originally made Rome great (*Letters* 137, 138). In his reply, Augustine develops Paul's ideas about citizenship further. He divides members of the human race into two "cities" according to the ultimate object of their loves. Those whose loves are shaped by the love of self are members of an "earthly city," whereas those united by love for God are citizens of the "heavenly city" (*C.D.* 14.13). The two cities do not correspond exactly to the institutional church or particular human polities. (Augustine is not always consistent in his language, and there is some debate on this matter.) In addition to living human beings, members of these cities include people from every moment in human history as well as angels (in the "heavenly city," "city of God") and demons (in the "earthly city," "city of the devil"). During their time on earth, members of the city of God constitute a "pilgrim city." However, ultimate human allegiances will not be fully revealed until God's final judgment at the end of history. During the present age (*saeculum*), citizens of each city live inextricably intermingled; they find some common purpose in the advantages of this life, especially peace (see esp. *C.D.* book 19). The first ten books of the *City of God* trace the history of the earthly city; the second twelve focus on the origin, progress, and destiny of the heavenly city.

Any discussion of citizenship and civic virtue bears on a major debate about the general character of Augustine's political thought. Drawing especially on book 19 of the *City of God*, a very influential line of twentieth-century scholarship has argued that Augustine decisively broke from the classical tradition of political thought. This "realist" interpretation emphasizes Augustine's description of civil society as corrupted by sin, his skepticism about the human capacity to cultivate civic virtue apart from divine aid, and his statements affirming civic peace as a value shared by both Christians and non-Christians. Civil authorities are not primarily to concern themselves with the cultivation of civic virtue in an effort to promote the happiness of the city; instead, their duty is to achieve peace and security by limiting the violence that characterizes human life. By thus circumscribing the role and potential of political life, Augustine, on this view, has anticipated the modern, liberal tradition. Indeed, on R. A. Markus's classic account, Augustine invented a notion crucial for the modern liberalism of political theorists such as John Rawls: the political realm as an autonomous, "neutral" common space in which groups with radically different religious views can form consensus precisely because this "secular" realm is protected from appeals to "ultimate" religious ends. Other scholars, however, find no room in Augustine's political theology for such a neutral, autonomous space and believe that "realist" readings neglect the value that Augustine places on civic virtue.[12] With this broader debate in the background, let's consider more closely Augustine's treatment of citizenship and civic virtue in the *City of God* and related writings.

No less than authors within the Roman republican tradition, Augustine recognizes a close relationship between citizenship, civic virtue, and glory. In fact, he distinguishes between citizens of the earthly and heavenly cities based on whether they seek glory from men or God (14.28). The relationship between glory and civic virtue is especially important in *City of God* book 5, where Augustine discusses the Roman honor code. Drawing on Sallust and Cicero, Augustine grants that to some extent the Roman honor code and civic virtues worked well. Virtue brought the Romans glory, honor, and power. Sallust was correct when he noted that the republican pursuit of glory produced Roman liberty and empire (*C.D.* 5.12; cf. Sal. *Cat.* 7.3). Romans' desire for human glory and praise, a vice because they did not reflect glory to God, bridled baser vices (*C.D.* 5.13–14). Christians can admire and be challenged by the virtuous behavior of Romans like Marcus Regulus and Cato the Younger, men whose devotion to virtue led to their deaths.

However, Augustine puts his finger on a problem noticed by Sallust and Cicero before him: the Roman honor code was unstable and prone to degenerate into the excessive love of glory and the destructive "lust for domination." Augustine provides two reasons for this instability. First, Roman republicanism got the relationship between virtue and the goods of the honor code backwards (*C.D.* 5.12). Since they regarded virtue as the means to "goods" such as glory and power, pagan Romans were tempted to bypass virtue for other, more convenient, means to these goods. Second, they lacked a competent judge who could assess what counted as true glory (*C.D.* 5.19; von Heyking 2001: 157). Roman republicans sought recognition for honorable behavior in the transient and unreliable opinions of elite Romans rather than in the trustworthy and sure approval of God. Thus, the Roman honor code led to serious injustices, such as Lucretia's

---

[12] Realists: Niebuhr 1953: ch. 9; Deane 1963; Markus 1970; 2006. Markus on Augustine's development of the notion of "the secular": Markus 1970; 2006. Note that Markus 2006 revisits and qualifies elements of the earlier book that he believes brought Augustine "perilously close" to "modern secular liberalism" (2006: 51). Augustine and Rawls: Weithman 1999; Markus 2006: 66–69. Critics of Markus: see, e.g., Williams 1987; van Oort 1991: 152–53; O'Donovan 2004. Augustine on virtue: Wetzel 1992; von Heyking 2001; Dodaro 2004a; Gregory 2008.

suicide due to misplaced shame, and the Roman aristocracy's subjection and exploitation of the poor (*C.D.* 1.19; 2.20; for Lucretia, see chapter 1).

The central Roman republican civic virtue of justice lies at the heart of Augustine's revaluation of virtue in the *City of God*. Much of the work's argument is bookended by two discussions of justice in light of Cicero's definition of *res publica* as entailing an agreement about right (*ius*; 2.21; 19.21). As we noted in chapter 1, Augustine argued that Republican Rome lacked true justice. The Romans lacked true justice because (as Cicero himself recognized) justice implies giving to each his due, and the pagan Romans refused to give God his due. Augustine utilizes the fact that "justice" (*ius*) along with "devotion" (*pietas*) was an integral part of Roman republican civil religion, which he critiques in the first seven books of *City of God* (on Roman civil religion, see chapter 6). True justice requires the knowledge and love of God, which is only made possible through Christ (Dodaro 2004a).

We can get a fuller picture of Augustine's account of civic virtue by turning to his correspondence with various Christian and pagan public officials from around the time he was planning and beginning to draft the *City of God*.[13] Especially important for our purposes is *Letter* 138 (c. 411–12) to Marcellinus, a (Christian) Roman civil servant to whom Augustine dedicated the *City of God*. Marcellinus had asked Augustine to respond to pagan allegations that Christian ethics – in particular, the injunctions to "return no one evil for evil" and to "offer the other cheek to an assailant" – are "contrary to the ethics of citizenship" (*Ep.* 136.2; cf. 138.9). Augustine answers by arguing that Christian virtues, such as mercy, benevolence, forbearance, poverty, justice, love, and piety, promote civil peace – the essential attribute of a city according to Augustine's reading of Cicero and Sallust, whom he cites as authorities on the matter. (Augustine combines Sal. *Cat.* 6.2 and Cic. *Rep.* 1.39.) Paying special attention to difficult cases like military service (see chapter 7), Augustine argues that Roman society would benefit from Christian citizens occupying a range of offices and social roles, including soldiers, provincial governors, "husbands and wives, parents and children, masters and servants, kings, judges, and finally even tax-payers and tax-collectors" (138.15). Christian virtue addresses not merely the symptoms of the violence that disrupts civil peace but the root of the problem: the excessive love of temporal goods (138.11).

---

[13] See especially Augustine, *Letters* 91, 104, 133, 138, 139, 153, and 155. An English translation of these letters is included in E. M. Atkins and Dodaro 2001, which I follow in this chapter.

Given that Augustine is writing to men involved in political life, these letters are naturally concerned with temporal goods, including those related to public office, such as honor, power, popular praise, and civil peace and security. As he points out in a letter to Macedonius, the vicar of Africa (413–14), these goods are secured by exercising the cardinal virtues of wisdom, justice, courage, and moderation (*Ep.* 155.10). However, just as the lower goods must stand in proper relation to the higher good of happiness in the worship of God, so the civic virtues as commonly understood in Roman thought must be transformed in light of the theological virtues of faith, hope, and, especially, love. Ultimately, the cardinal virtues reduce to a single act: loving what is good, God. And by God's grace, one can love one's neighbor as oneself, thereby fulfilling Christ's great commandment (155.10–16; cf. *C.D.* 19.14; Christ's words are found at Matthew 22:37–40; Mark 12:30–31; Luke 10:27). Without the stabilizing and transformative presence of God's grace, civic virtues in rulers will be corrupted by the pursuit of glory (155.4–6; cf. *C.D.* 5.20).[14]

Augustine's treatment of the civic virtues in *Letter* 155 to Macedonius depends on several general assumptions, which also inform his argument in the *City of God*. First, Augustine argues that citizens and the city share a common happiness based (in part) on virtue (155.7, 9; cf. *C.D.* 1.15). Second, the happy life is social (*C.D.* 19.5, 17). Third, civic goods and civic virtues require extra-political support, since, in Augustine's opinion, they must stand in relation to higher goods and to the theological virtues (155.8–12; *C.D.* 19.4, 14, 17, 20, 25). Fourth, those who rule should concern themselves with whether citizens make good use of temporal peace for their own happiness (155.10, 12); this happens when one "refers all peace, whether of body or of soul, or of both, to that peace which mortal man has with the immortal God, so that he may exhibit an ordered obedience, in faith, to the eternal Law" (*C.D.* 19.14, 17). Fifth, the completely happy life is unattainable in this life, which is marred by sin (155.5–6, 17; *C.D.* 19.27). However, even though complete earthly happiness is beyond reach, the just ruler will keep his "mind largely fixed on the heavenly commonwealth" (155.17; *C.D.* 5.24). Finally, Augustine emphasizes that the acquisition of genuine virtue requires God's grace (155.4–6; *C.D.* 5.20; 19.4, 25).

Given the preceding account, Augustine appears to have a greater role for the cultivation of civic virtue, the pursuit of social goods beyond temporal peace and security, and "religious" conceptions of the public good than do many of his "realist" and "liberal" interpreters. Indeed, political

---

[14] For *Letter* 155, see Dodaro 2004a: 206–12; Dodaro 2004b; Clair 2016: ch. 3.

theorists and theologians have attempted to draw on Augustine's conception of civic virtue in support of projects to bolster liberalism against familiar, longstanding criticisms, such as its overly individualistic and rationalistic conceptions of society.[15] With respect to Roman republicanism, it is fair to say that Augustine "re-formulates something like the traditional virtue-based concept of society, but in new terms which will give due recognition both to the reality of the moral order which makes social existence possible and to its fundamentally flawed character" (O'Donovan 2004: 63). Ultimately, Augustine's transformation of civic virtue in light of the theological virtues, especially the virtue of love, partially reconciles the good Christian with the good Roman citizen. Roman Christians can perform their Roman civic roles and duties, but with new and different motivations and virtues guiding their behavior. Still, for Augustine the reconciliation between the good Christian and good citizen cannot be complete. For as long as they remain in this world, Christians are members of a pilgrim city that is not yet home.[16]

Conclusion

The changes to the conception of citizenship and civic virtues from the Republic to the Empire were both subtle and profound. Citizenship under the Empire was distinguished by the emphasis and extension of its juridical core, which had been put in place under the Republic. Similarly, the duties and virtues of elite citizens remained largely the same from the Republic to the Empire. The difference in each case lies especially with revisions to the *political* aspect of being a citizen. Under the Empire, and indeed already in the last decades of the Republic, citizenship did not carry expectations of political involvement, and the honor code that calibrated the virtues of the elite capped the glory that one could attain. The Republican code had presumed the competition for political office among a class of more or less equal citizens. When that no longer obtained with the advent of the *princeps*, the basic civic virtues stayed the same, with the exception of the most political virtue, justice, which belonged to the emperor, and the "virtue" of subservience, which now belonged to citizen-subjects. St. Augustine, on the other hand, transformed republican civic virtue in light of a new conception of citizenship that accompanied a new view of the good life.

---

[15] Elshtain 1995; von Heyking 2001; Gregory 2008.
[16] Cf. Rist 1994: 255.

CHAPTER 4

Political Passions and Civic Corruption

Introduction

What images does the phrase "political corruption" evoke? Perhaps patronage, bribery, nepotism, and election fraud come to mind. Citizens of modern liberal democracies usually associate corruption with corrupt politicians who abuse their political power for personal gain. Many Americans will readily think of Watergate, when the investigation of a 1972 break-in of the Democratic National Committee headquarters in Washington, D.C. revealed a series of abuses of power by the Nixon administration that ultimately led to the President's resignation.

Corruption is harmful. It leads to the distrust of politicians and to cynicism about politics itself. As harmful as this may be, the solution to corrupt politicians is straightforward enough: vote them out of office. Not surprisingly, then, running against political corruption has a long history of propelling the candidacies of populist politicians, especially in American politics.

The notion of political corruption as the abuse of power for personal gain is not without analogues in the Roman Republic. For instance, in the first century BCE, as running for office became an increasingly competitive and expensive endeavor, electoral bribery increased, leading to the enactment of *ambitus* laws regulating the means by which candidates canvassed for votes (*ambitus*, a euphemism for bribery, comes from the Latin verb, *ambire*, "to go around [asking for support]"). And since many candidates entered office in debt from the election, cases of extortion (*repetundae*) by magistrates became a growing concern.[1]

When we consider the ideology of Roman republicanism, we find a much fuller and more robust sense of political corruption. In book 3 of

---

[1] For *ambitus* legislation and the related ideas of electoral corruption, bribery, and extortion, see Linderski 1985; Lintott 1990; Yakobson 1999: 22–43; Feig Vishnia 2012.

De legibus, Cicero argues, "the entire civic community (*civitas*) tends to be infected (*infici*) by the passions and vices of its leaders" (3.30). In such a case, the political leaders are both themselves corrupted (*corrumpuntur*) and corrupt others (*corrumpunt*; 3.32). In Cicero's opinion, because of their position and status a very few members of the aristocracy "have the capacity to either corrupt (*corrumpere*) or restore the habits of the civic community" (*mores civitatis*; 3.32). Though the phenomenon of corruption begins with the inordinate passions and vices of leaders, it extends to the whole civic community; it infects and diminishes civic practices and ultimately the community itself. The verb *corrumpere* often indicates harm or injury to the body. Corruption in this sense denotes a lack of health in the body politic.

Cicero's account of corruption assumes that political leaders are the key to causing and remedying the civic body's infection. A different explanation is suggested by his contemporary Sallust in his monographs *The Jugurthine War* and, especially, *Catiline's Conspiracy*. A new man born in Amiternum, a town 50 miles northeast of Rome, Sallust endured an up and down career in politics. He held the office of tribune in 52 BCE, but he was subsequently expunged from the senate in 50. After serving in Caesar's army from 49 to 44, he was made governor of a province. Once again he suffered a setback, when he was charged with extortion. At this point, he retired from political life and turned his attention to writing history.[2]

Sallust's account of corruption begins with passions and the Roman honor code. The Republic fell into corruption when the Romans' unlimited and unrestrained passions overcame their virtue. The Romans wanted too much – too much money and power, "the root of all evils" (Sal. *Cat.* 10.3). These vices perverted the aristocratic code. Under the Roman honor code, wealth was a constitutive part of a wider life dedicated to the pursuit of public office, glory, and standing – hence, it had value only if pursued "by honest means" (Plin. *Nat.* 7.139; Sal. *Cat.* 7.6). Now money was desired for its own sake, the result of "boundless and insatiable" greed (Sal. *Cat.* 11.3). Similarly, the desire for glory, which previously held value only if achieved by honorable competition, had degenerated into the desire to exercise power over others. The excessive desire for glory gave way to the desire for power, and that desire in turn led to the desire to dominate

---

[2] For Sallust's biography, see Syme 1964; for his political thought, see Earl 1961 (virtue and the honor code); Kapust 2011b: chs. 2–3 (conflict and rhetoric); Connolly 2015: ch. 2 (justice, economic inequality, and judgment); Hammer 2014: ch. 3 (memory).

others – the lust for domination (*lubido dominandi*), a dangerous desire that directly threatened freedom (Sal. *Cat.* 2.2; 5.6; *Hist.* 2.38).

Sallust's account moves beyond the corruption of aristocratic leaders considered by Cicero in *De legibus* 3 to consider broader political and economic dynamics. The proscriptions and constitutional reforms under the dictatorships of the general Sulla (82–79 BCE) intensified the struggles between the *optimates* and *populares*. Politically ambitious men appealed to the rights of the people or to the *auctoritas* of the senate to promote their careers, leading to a brutal power struggle without moderation or limit (38.4). They lost sight of the common good and mangled the *res publica* – the *common*wealth (cf. Sal. *Jug.* 41.9–10; 42.3–5). Add to this struggle for power widespread economic debt that left the poor subservient to the power of the few, and the stage was set for the revolution described in *Catiline's Conspiracy*.

Two episodes from *Catiline's Conspiracy* reveal characteristics of a corrupt political body. The first is Catiline's speech, as represented by Sallust, to urge on his supporters at paragraph 20. He points out the need of the dispossessed to reclaim their liberty from the sway of the few (20.7) who hold and control "all influence, power, honor, and wealth" (20.8). Catiline, emphasizing his followers' virtue (*virtus*) and faithfulness (*fides*), enumerates traditional Roman virtues, such as courage and hard work. Yet contrary to the impression in Sallust's introduction, the possession of these virtues does not lead to a share in the goods of the aristocratic political culture because of the many's subservience to the few (*obnoxii* at 20.7 has connotations of servitude). Their subservience is enhanced by an oppressive and widespread economic debt. Catiline emphasizes the unfairness and hopelessness of his followers' second-rate status despite their exercise of republican virtues. Despite displaying demagogic characteristics, Catiline's rhetoric reveals a deep connection between greed, economic standing, and citizenship. As Joy Connolly (2015: 105) observes, "Catiline claims that being a citizen of republican Rome is a matter not only of law and political freedom, but economic standing."

The second episode is the concluding debate in the senate between Caesar and Cato over whether to execute the leading conspirators without trial. Sallust emphasizes the "extraordinary virtue" of these two political giants. Each attained greatness and glory, but by different routes. Caesar was known for his benevolence, generosity, compassion, mercy, easiness, devotion, and hard work. He needed the grand stage of combat upon which to display his virtue. Cato, on the other hand, built his reputation on integrity, severity, steadfastness, moderation, and abstinence.

The paragon of republican virtue, "he preferred to be good than to seem good" (54.6). Yet as Sallust's readers would have known, for all of their virtues, these two men would soon find themselves opposed in civil conflict that would ultimately lead to the death of both (Cato by suicide; Caesar by assassination), and ultimately, to that of the Republic. Tethered to an unstable honor code that had lost its bearing on the common good, republican virtues could no longer ensure a free *res publica*.

Sallust links corruption to political division and factionalism, emotions like envy, greed, and the lust for power, and the loss of virtue. Corruption occurs because of a defect of the passions – either because they become inordinate and unlimited, or because they become perverted by seeking inappropriate objectives as defined by the Republican honor code – for example, mastery over others or money as a *per se* value. The defect of passions leads to a condition in which the civic virtues that facilitate cooperation among citizens are absent. Consequently, the civic body is corrupted, shredded, and diminished by faction. As the episodes from *Catiline's Conspiracy* show, a corrupt civic body is one in which part of the civic body is subservient, or in danger of becoming subservient, to another; its ill-health is manifested when displaying the "normal" social behaviors and virtues can no longer lead to civic wholeness.

For Sallust, then, corruption is a far deeper and more difficult matter than the misconduct of elected officials. As in the republican account of corruption described by the political theorist Peter Euben (1989: 223), corruption involves the

> systematic and systemic degeneration of those practices and commitments that provide the terms of collective self-understanding and shared purpose. In a corrupt society each part pretends to be the whole; each interest to be the common one; each faction to make its view and voice exclusive. Under such circumstances the common good is seen (and so comes to be) a ruse for fools and dreamers while the political arena is a place where factions, like gladiators, fight to the death.

We cannot understand Sallust's account of corruption without a deeper investigation of the passions than contemporary accounts of liberal democracy typically provide. Modern liberalism has long been suspicious of the passions, and with good reason. As Sallust himself shows, passions are instrumental in causing faction and corruption. Indeed, one of the virtues of the US Constitution, according to Madison in *Federalist Papers* 10 and 51, is that it provided devices to remedy the problem of faction arising from passions that destroyed ancient republics. In contrast, influential contemporary liberal theorists such as John Rawls largely sideline the emotions and place at the heart of liberalism a notion of justice as a principle of reason (but see Nussbaum 2013).

Contemporary liberal and democratic theories that neglect the emotions have been critiqued as being overly idealistic and offering an incomplete account of the human subject (Ferry and Kingston 2008: 4). To these considerations we may add another: by removing the emotions from our accounts of politics, we may indeed eradicate the harmful emotions (at least from our normative theory) but deprive ourselves of the opportunity to consider how to cultivate socially helpful emotions. Here the Romans are particularly useful.[3] In contrast to rationalist accounts of virtue, Sallust and other Roman authors within and beyond the republican tradition conceive of virtue in terms of the capacity to express emotions appropriately. In the words of Paul Woodruff (2001: 61–62), "a virtue is the capacity to have certain feelings and emotions when this capacity has been cultivated through training and experience in such a way that it inclines those who have it to doing the right thing."

This chapter follows Sallust's lead by looking at how select Roman thinkers deal with the key political emotions that threaten to corrupt and ultimately enslave the body politic – greed, envy, and the desire for power. These, of course, are not the only political passions – anger, for example, is an equally important political passion – but they are those most central to discussions of political corruption.[4] As in Sallust's account, the key issue before us concerns limits and restraints on the emotions insofar as they pertain to actions in public life. What dispositions or virtues should citizens cultivate to ensure appropriate emotional responses to other citizens or to events impacting the polity? How might these virtues mitigate the excesses to which the passions for power and wealth are prone, thereby forestalling civic corruption and promoting the common good?

In pursuing answers to these questions, we will focus on the thought of three philosophers – the Epicurean, Lucretius; the Stoic, Seneca; and the Platonist, Plutarch. These authors were not committed advocates of republicanism – though Plutarch would become a foundational source for the later republican tradition in both America and Europe (Richard 1994: ch. 3; Liebert 2016: ch. 2). Epicureanism, Stoicism, and Plutarch's

---

[3] Cf. Hammer 2014, who locates the ultimate power in Roman political thought in the Romans' exploration of the "affective foundation of political life" (3).

[4] On anger, see Harris 2001 and Nussbaum 1994: ch. 11 (political ramifications of anger in Seneca's *De ira*).

Platonism have each been described at times as reflecting an unrepublican shift from the flourishing of the polity to the flourishing of the individual human being. We must be careful not to exaggerate this point: in grappling with the emotions that republicans like Sallust linked to civic corruption, Lucretius, Seneca, and Plutarch never lose sight of the implications for political society; indeed, Plutarch wrote his *Parallel Lives* precisely to educate and influence statesmen. Moreover, there are advantages to watching thinkers address a central problem of the republican tradition from the outside. In emphasizing the positive emotions of reverence and gratitude as correctives to the socially destructive emotions, these thinkers point towards virtues that have been underexploited by the republican tradition. They also raise questions about the role of hope in politics.

Lucretius' Epicurean Treatment of Corruption: Reverence and the "Blessings Of Finitude"

De rerum natura (*On the Nature of Things*) is a remarkable work. The poem, written in dactylic hexameter, the traditional meter of epic, takes as its subject matter a topic of truly epic proportion – the universe itself. The work is also didactic and philosophical, instructing Romans about the teachings of Epicurean philosophy, which Lucretius takes to best capture the reality of our world, so that they can live happy lives of maximum pleasure and freedom from physical and (especially) mental pain. The founder of Epicureanism, Epicurus (341–270 BCE), established a school in Athens called the Garden. Among the topics covered by his voluminous writings are physics (the world consists of matter and void); theology (the gods live peaceful, blissful, and invulnerable lives elsewhere, unconcerned with human affairs); epistemology (he was an empiricist); ethics (a hedonist, he believed happiness was achieved by maximizing pleasure and minimizing pain); and political thought (he espoused a social contract theory of justice). Like Epicurus' Greek followers, Lucretius venerated him as a godlike hero (Lucr. 1.62–79; 5.1–12, 19–21; 6.7–8). About Lucretius, we know very little. A contemporary of Cicero and Sallust, he was born around 99 BCE and died around 55 BCE.[5]

A number of prominent Roman politicians identified as Epicureans, including the consul and proconsul Piso; the former praetor and supporter

---

[5] For Epicurus' philosophy, see the English translation of selected texts in Inwood and Gerson 1994. Long and Sedley 1987 provides text, translation, and commentary.

of Pompey, Torquatus, who fell in battle in Africa; one of Julius Caesar's murderers, Cassius; and, most likely, Caesar himself (Castner 1988). Though Epicurus exhorted his followers, "don't engage in politics" and "live life unnoticed," Geert Roskam (2007) has demonstrated that these prohibitions are not blanket statements but depend on a variable calculus that may allow a faithful Epicurean to engage in politics if certain conditions obtain (for instance, in emergencies where political abstention may threaten the Epicurean values of security and tranquility).

On the face of it, Lucretius can be particularly scathing of politics: he compares the politician seeking political power to the mythical condemned criminal Sisyphus, always pushing a boulder up a hill only to see his efforts frustrated (3.995–1002). At the same time, however, he encourages the work's dedicatee, Memmius, to continue his involvement in politics for the common good (1.41–43). Lucretius may not be as anti-political as the Sisyphus metaphor at first suggests. In describing the Epicurean position in Latin, Cicero uses the same word for "empty" to modify "desire" that Lucretius uses to modify "political rule" in the Sisyphus passage, which in Lucretius' text is immediately preceded by a discussion of the danger of the passions associated with romantic love (cf. Lucr. 3.994, 998 and Cic. *De finibus* 1.59). Perhaps in the Sisyphus passage Lucretius is targeting first and foremost not political rule but the *passion* for political rule, which Epicureans classified as an "empty" desire (cf. Fish 2011).

Regardless of Lucretius' own views on holding political office, *De rerum natura* is a profoundly political work, especially if we understand politics to take as its subject matter the *politeia*, which includes political culture as well as political offices and institutions. Lucretius engages with Roman political culture embodied in such values as *pietas, religio, honor, gloria, virtus, nobilitas, dignitas, auctoritas,* and *imperium* (Minyard 1985). In fact, as we will see, Lucretius is as concerned with the root causes of corruption, civil conflict, and inordinate passions as Sallust. He provides both a powerful diagnosis of civic corruption and a solution. According to Lucretius, Roman republicanism has failed to solve the problem of civic corruption because it has misdiagnosed the problem. At base both human happiness and social stability are threatened because human beings have transgressed the boundaries established by nature. The correct solution involves a proper understanding of and emotional response to nature's limits – for individuals, for society, and for our world.[6]

---

[6] Chapter-length overviews of Lucretius' political philosophy: Fowler 1989 (classic article); Schiesaro 2007; Hammer 2014: ch. 2. Nichols 1976 and Colman 2012 are monographs that follow the approach of Strauss 1968: ch. 5.

Civic conflict and the accompanying corruption are an important theme throughout *De rerum natura* – unsurprising, given that *stasis* was a constant feature of the first-century BCE Roman political landscape as well as a concern for Lucretius' forebears in the atomistic tradition, such as Democritus and (likely) Epicurus himself (McConnell 2012). Consider a few examples. In the introduction to book 1, Lucretius points out that the troubles besetting the commonwealth are interfering with his composition of the poem, and he indicates his confidence in Memmius' help. The prologue to book 2 describes the traditional Roman *cursus honorum* and its accompanying antagonistic contest for rank, honor, wealth, and political mastery. The wise man, secure and well-fortified by Epicurean doctrine, looks down on the others "straying everywhere as they wander about searching for the path of life, contending for intellectual preeminence (*ingenium*), competing for rank (*nobilitas*), striving night and day with the utmost effort to rise to the summit of wealth and to be the master of political affairs" (2.9–13). Some of the lines just quoted appear again in book 3, which describes civic conflict in particularly vivid terms: "Greed (*avarities*) and the blind desire for political office (*honorum caeca cupido*), which often compel wretched human beings to overstep the boundaries of justice (*transcendere fines iuris*), and from time to time as conspirators and agents of crimes, to strive night and day with the utmost effort to rise to the summit of wealth ..." (3.59–63). There is "civil war" and "the heaping of murder upon murder" (3.70, 71). Finally, the book 5 account of the origins of human society at 5.1105–60 contains another important discussion of corruption (see Schrijvers 1996). Kings – honored for their beauty, strength, and wisdom – ruled cities. After money was invented, people began to value instead reputation, power, and wealth. These desires, as well as envy, led to civic corruption, civil strife, revolution, and ultimately to violence and anarchy.

According to these passages, the cause of corruption is conflict due to passions, in particular envy and the desires for wealth and power. Commentators have noted parallels between Lucretius' and Sallust's descriptions of civil conflict and corruption, especially in the introduction to book 3 (Kenney 2014: 87; Fowler 1989: 138–39). As in Sallust, the desires for power and wealth are dangerous because they are limitless. In Epicurean terminology, they are non-natural and non-necessary, or empty, desires, which, having no natural limit, are infinite and unfillable, and therefore to be avoided. By warning human beings away from unfillable desires, Epicurus' teaching on nature "established a limit for desire and fear," as Lucretius notes later in the poem (6.25).

The key to happiness is to achieve secure and stable pleasures by holding to nature's limits. For human beings, as for other species, "a fixed limit of growth and of holding onto life has been established, and what are the capacities and furthermore what are the limits of these capacities is established through the compacts of nature" (*per foedera naturai*; 1.584–87). Human beings "have not learned the proper limit to possession" (*habendi finis*), and so they spend their lives pursuing empty, unlimited, non-natural, non-necessary pleasures, the pursuit of which leads to frustration and civil conflict (5.1430–35).

It is not just nature that has the capacity to set limits. There is an analogue in human society to the limits established through "nature's compacts" (*foedera naturai*) – the social contract (Schiesaro 2007; Asmis 2008b). In book 5 Lucretius sketches the origins of human society. This influential account, which would inspire Rousseau's *Second Discourse on the Origins of Inequality*, begins by describing a pre political condition in which human beings lacked customs, laws, and a conception of the common good (5.958–59). Life was hard. Human beings lived and died relying upon nature – that is, their own natural faculties and natural resources readily at hand. They gradually improved their natural condition through artifice: they built huts, made clothing, and developed fire and language. These developments softened human beings, both physically and emotionally. Civil society formed when early humans agreed that "it was fair for all to have compassion on the weak" (5.1023). Much as in Rousseau, the social bond consisted of compassion for bodily suffering. As a result, the first human beings established compacts among themselves "to neither harm nor be harmed" (5.1020). Although the social contract did not always ensure harmony, "the good and great part of human beings faithfully preserved their compacts (*foedera*); otherwise," Lucretius adds, "the human race would have been entirely destroyed then" (1024–26).

Four points are relevant for our discussion. First, the social contract in Lucretius echoes key features of Epicurus' own thought. Epicurus understood justice as a contract among parties who agree to forego their ability to harm in order not to be harmed (Epicur. *Principle Doctrines* (*PD*) 33 = Long and Sedley 22A). Second, while the social compact and the resulting political society belong to artifice – the city does not exist by nature, as Aristotle had argued in book 1 of his *Politics* – it is a human creation that responds to natural needs, much like the clothing and huts of early man. Third, society is based on a fundamental human desire – the desire for security (see also 5.1145–55). Epicurus taught that the desire for security was a fundamental human desire, and his successor, Hermarchus, made the desire for individual and social security the primary catalyst in his own account of the origins of political society (Long and Sedley 22N). Finally, Lucretius makes it clear that such compacts were not completely successful in preventing civic conflict, a problem that became worse as human beings developed more artifices in an attempt to fulfill even more capacious and potent desires.[7]

If the social compact and laws weren't enough to restrain the passions that lead to civic corruption and conflict, perhaps the non-institutional aspects of political culture might help? As we saw in Polybius' account of the Roman *politeia* in book 6 of his *Histories*, the Roman ruling class attempted to utilize religion as an important restraining mechanism to avoid civil corruption by checking inordinate desires (6.56.11; see chapter 1). Lucretius too recognizes the important role of religion in Roman society. However, for Lucretius the use of religious fear is doomed to fail, for at the very root of the passions responsible for corruption and *stasis* – greed, the desire for power, and envy – is the fear of death. Such passions are "nourished by the fear of death" (3.64). As Kenney (2014: 84) notes, Lucretius anchors his reasoning in Epicurean thought. Epicurus had identified the desire for security as the root of the passion for status (*PD* 7 = Long and Sedley 22C1). Lucretius simply takes the argument one step backwards, suggesting that people want security because they fear death, from which "they wish themselves to flee far away and to be far removed" (3.65–69, quote at 3.68–69). The fear of death destroys civic virtue and encourages civic corruption. It overturns key social virtues like shame (*pudor*), devotion (*pietas*), and patriotism, as well as the friendships and political alliances (*amicitiai*) at the heart of Roman political society (3.83–86).

Lucretius doesn't mean to suggest that people consciously recognize that the fear of death lies at the root of their socially destructive passions; indeed, most people "run from themselves" but "do not understand the cause of their sickness" (3.1068, 1070). But if we are going to deal with civic corruption, we must confront and accept death. This means, ultimately, that we must come to accept the limits established by nature. We are finite, mortal beings living within finite, mortal societies within a finite, mortal world. "All things gradually waste away and head to the tomb, worn out by the long lapse of time" (2.1173–74). Following his master, Lucretius argues that we must not only accept our mortality but come to realize that

---

[7] Social security and the social contract in Epicurean thought: Schofield 1999b: 748–56; Schofield 2000. Desire and artifice: Nichols 1976.

we would be no happier if we were immortals.[8] Life, a personified Nature reveals, is like a banquet (3.931–62). Eating, drinking, and conversing with friends is a pleasant experience, but, once we have had our fill of food and drink, to continue consumption would actually decrease our pleasure and make us unhappy. As Nietzsche would later note, the eternal recurrence of the same is a curse rather than a blessing (see Lucr. 3.935–49). Mortality has its own pleasures. We must come to recognize, to borrow the language of biologist and philosopher Leon Kass (2002), "the blessings of finitude."[9]

Overcoming such a deeply ingrained and seemingly natural passion as the fear of death is a tall order. The heart of Lucretius' response, of course, is to make readers aware of the scientific truth-claims of Epicureanism: "Therefore it is necessary that this fear and darkness of the mind be dispelled … by nature's appearance and underlying principle (*ratio*)" (3.91–93; cf. 1.146–48; 2.55–61; 6.35–41). But along with the rational understanding of the universe, Lucretius points us towards an emotion that arises from and promotes the recognition of human finitude and limitedness: reverence.

Lucretius' account of reverence begins by reclaiming piety (*pietas*) from religion (*religio*). Romans believed that the gods were influenced by cult practices. This Lucretius denies, but he argues that this denial does not make him impious. Religion, in fact, can lead to evil acts usually associated with impiety, as he illustrates by the example of King Agamemnon's sacrifice of his daughter Iphigenia to placate the gods so that he may launch his fleet (1.80–101). Lucretius concludes: "Such great acts of evil could religion (*religio*) urge" (1.101). In contrast to religion, properly understood, *pietas* consists of "the ability to contemplate all things with a tranquil mind" (5.1198–1203, quote at 1203). True piety, according to the Epicureans, involves the untroubled contemplation of (and indeed imitation of and communion with) the exalted nature of the gods (Fitzgerald 1951). Inasmuch as this nature surpasses human nature, it requires reverence, for "whatever is highest deserves rightful reverence" (Cic. *De natura deorum* 1.45). Epicurus noted that we should also conduct ourselves with the appropriate recognition of the exalted majesty or solemnity of the universe (*Letter to Herodotus* 77). Lucretius describes just such a response in himself to Epicurus' unveiling of the universe, nature, and the gods. "At these experiences at that time some divine pleasure seized me and a sense

---

[8] Epicurus on happiness and immortality: Epicur. *PD* 18–20; see also Cic. *Fin.* 2.87–88.
[9] Fear of death and limits: Segal 1990: ch. 5. The arguments of personified Nature: Nussbaum 1994: ch. 6.

of awe (*horror*), since by your power nature, lying so clearly open, has been uncovered in every aspect" (3.28–30). This true piety allows the Epicurean to participate in the traditional cult practices of his regime's civil religion without embracing its harmful theological beliefs (3.68–79). Unlike other citizens, he understands "by what law the capacity of each thing is limited" and nature's "deeply clinging boundary stone" (6.65–66).

The best word to capture the recognition of the exalted and majestic nature of the universe and gods – and Lucretius' own emotional response – is reverence. According to Woodruff (2001: 63), reverence is "a sense that there is something larger than a human being, accompanied by capacities for awe, respect, and shame." Reverence, Woodruff notes, is an important political virtue, inasmuch as the feelings of awe and respect come from the recognition of one's own limits. Tyrants bent on domination lack reverence.

Following his account of the plague that ravaged Athens during the Peloponnesian War, Thucydides observed that the Athenians' lack of reverence led to increased daring and lawlessness (2.53.1). Later in his *History*, Thucydides describes how daring from the lack of reverence (*eusebeia*) caused civil war and civic corruption at Corcyra, an Athenian ally, when greed and power led citizens to disregard the limits of justice and the interests of the city as a whole (3.82). Sallust, for whom Thucydides' historiography was an important model, likely found inspiration for his own account of corruption in this picture of civil conflict. Thucydides' narrative also inspired Lucretius. His poem concludes with an adaptation of Thucydides' account of the plague: Lucretius leaves his reader with the image of a distraught and lawless people fighting to the death as they struggle to burn dead bodies on funeral pyres. The "religion of the gods" counted for little. Epicurus, returning to the city a century later, would introduce a more socially salutary form of piety that accepted the transitory nature of human life and the world in which we live. Humans will become happy only when they embrace their own finitude.[10]

Gratitude and Society

There is a second socially salutary emotion experienced by those who recognize "the blessings of finitude" – gratitude, the capacity for thankfulness for past blessings leading to contentedness in one's present state. Gratitude

---

[10] Corcyra episode: Connor 1984: 95–105; Euben 1986: 226–27; 1990: ch. 6 (corruption); Balot 2001: 137–41 (greed). On Lucretius, see further J. W. Atkins forthcoming c. For a recent review of the different ways to interpret the plague, see Hammer 2014: 140–43.

was an important Epicurean emotion (Cic. *Fin.* 1.57, 60, 62; Diogenes Laertius, *Lives of Eminent Philosophers* 10.122). In his writing on the topic, Seneca notes that Epicurus deserves credit for emphasizing the importance of this emotion (*Ben.* 3.4). Gratitude from reflecting on past blessings enables the Epicurean sage to experience joy on his deathbed just as his prior life was marked by gratitude from the habitual mental renewal of past blessings.[11] Fools, on the other hand, lack gratitude. As a result, they live lives of agony and fear, constantly grasping after the empty desires of wealth, power, and fame (Cic. *Fin.* 1.60).

This general testimony is consistent with Lucretius' portrayal of gratitude. Gratitude is an essential condition for dying at peace (3.935–43). People who chafe at death live lives marked by ingratitude. They overlook the giftedness of nature and therefore are constantly chasing after insatiable pleasures. Overlooking the definite and secure past, their hopes are in the limitless future, which is why they get so bitter at the prospect of death removing that future (cf. Cic. *Fin.* 1.60 and Sen. *Ben.* 3.4).

Ingratitude also characterizes civic conflict and corruption. Book 6 of *De rerum natura* begins by remarking how Epicurus had observed the habitual ingratitude that characterized the lives of the Athenians in their endless pursuit to fulfill their limitless desires (6.11–23). Given the importance of gratitude for confronting death in adverse circumstances, it does not surprise that the end of the book shows Athenian society utterly and spectacularly collapsing as it is beset by the plague.

One final point about gratitude emerges from *De rerum natura* book 6: a link between ingratitude and security. Epicurus noted that the ungrateful Athenians enjoyed to the greatest possible extent a secure life (6.11). It is not hard to see how a sense of security could lead to ingratitude. Those who are secure forget the fragility of life, thereby taking their current favorable circumstances as givens rather than as precious gifts to be appreciated while present because they might be taken away (or not even have been bestowed in the first place). Interestingly, studies show that in the initial weeks following the September 11, 2001 terrorist attack on the World Trade Center in New York City the most common emotion felt by Americans was gratitude (Watkins 2007: 50).

But gratitude is not an important emotion for Epicureans alone. According to Cicero, "gratitude is not only the greatest virtue but the mother of all the others" (*Pro Plancio* 80). Seneca, incredibly, ranks ingratitude as the greatest vice – worse than murder, tyranny, theft, adultery,

---

[11] Gratitude as sage faces death: Cic. *Fin.* 1.62. Epicurus' own deathbed experience: Cic. *Fin.* 2.96.

sacrilege, and treason (*Ben.* 1.10.4). Ingratitude is the mark of a tyrant. According to Seneca, lack of gratitude accompanied Alexander the Great's unlimited desire for glory, which led him to become "a robber and plunderer of nations" (*Ben.* 1.13.3). What makes gratitude the premier social virtue among Romans of both the Republic and Principate? How precisely is this emotion related to civic corruption?

Perhaps the best place to start is with Seneca's *De beneficiis*, a work that tackles problems posed by ingratitude as part of its principal message (Inwood 1995). The chief philosophical inspiration behind *De beneficiis* is Stoicism. According to the Stoics, the cosmos is endowed with, and ordered by, reason, which human beings share. This reasoning capacity unites human beings to the gods and to one another, and virtue – the possession of which is both necessary and sufficient for happiness – consists in using our reason well, that is, according to the norms of nature. Human beings are by nature social animals born for the common good and mutual assistance (Sen. *Cl.* 1.3.2; *De ira* 1.5.2; Cooper and Procopé 1995: 187).

De beneficiis advises the reader about how to appropriately, that is, rationally, give and receive benefits in the context of Rome's "gift economy" (Griffin 2003; 2013). For our purposes, the relevant features of the Roman gift economy, which Seneca describes in detail, may perhaps be grasped most easily through a contrast with the sort of "capitalist meritocracy" characteristic of a liberal democracy like the United States of America (Brooks 2015). A capitalist meritocracy puts a high premium on individual autonomy, performance, and independence. The most important social virtue is justice. One's social duties regarding justice take the form of respecting rights and honoring contracts, so that all parties get what they deserve or are entitled to. In the Roman gift economy, by contrast, society – especially elite society – is held together by mutual freely given favors or kindnesses between individuals. Generosity was just as important a virtue as justice. When an individual receives a gift, there was a strong expectation that he would repay it in some way at some time, even if only by exhibiting a kind disposition to the benefactor. However, repayment was emphatically not offered as part of a contract, which legally stipulates conformity. Neither is the gift an investment whose primary purpose is to secure a future return. Moreover, the gift-giver is to be guided by the best interests of the recipient. Altruism and interdependence are built into this economy.

From Seneca's various discussions of gratitude in *De beneficiis*, we might generally define gratitude as an affection or cognitive state that duly recognizes a freely given gift from a personal giver to whom one becomes subsequently indebted. Gratitude is also a virtue: there are not just grateful *responses* by people in certain situations, but there are actually grateful *people*, people whose characters are disposed towards gratitude. Like other virtues, for Seneca the virtue of gratitude contributes to its possessor's happiness or flourishing. Gratitude thus is both individually and socially beneficial.

Two additional important aspects of gratitude stand out in Seneca's discussion. First, like Epicurus, Seneca emphasizes the indispensable link between gratitude and memory: "Memory makes gratitude" (*Ben.* 3.4.2). Gratitude sharply contrasts with hope: the former looks to the past; the latter, to the future. Ungrateful people do not adequately store up memories of past kindnesses, goods, and blessings. Because we tend to take our present goods for granted, not recognizing their contingent nature, we devalue them and become dissatisfied. We look towards the future in order to acquire more, which in turn makes it harder to feel grateful for the past; there is a reciprocal relationship between memory and gratitude.

Second, gratitude recognizes dependence and fosters interdependence. A grateful person acknowledges that he is dependent on others for what he has. He recognizes that there are some things that he has received by others' good graces and not merely by his own effort. As a result, he is willing to reciprocate in giving freely to others. Thus, the recognition of dependence leads to interdependence. When we recognize that we need one another and contribute to the good of others (even if they are not strictly deserving), society is strengthened. That is why, for Seneca, "nothing so dissolves and disrupts the concord of mankind as this fault. Our safety depends on the fact that we have mutual acts of kindness to help us" (4.18.1; trans. Cooper and Procopé).

Incidentally, the idea of dependence on a personal gift-giver provides Seneca with the opportunity to critique the Epicurean ideas of gratitude and reverence before the gods. Gratitude by definition requires a personal gift-giver to whom one is grateful. Yet notwithstanding Lucretius' personification of "Nature," the Epicureans do not recognize a personal gift-giver for the gifts of life. Can you really be grateful when "you have not had any favors from him [god], but have been congealed out of atoms and these motes of yours by blind chance?" (trans. Cooper and Procopé; 4.19.3). Rather, on the Stoic account, grateful human beings recognize their dependence upon the gods, leading to a socially interconnected city of gods and human beings (*Ben.* 2.29–30; for the cosmic city, see chapter 7).

Finally, Seneca links the loss of gratitude to civic corruption. The principal causes of ingratitude are the emotions that destroy society. The first is undue self-regard. We tend to overvalue our own worth, which leads us to treat the good gifts bestowed on us less as gifts than as required payments. Such a high self-estimation leads to ingratitude (we are not thankful for what we deserve) and even to indignation if we feel we have been undervalued. The other emotions are familiar from Lucretius and Sallust: greed – which Seneca links to both avarice and the desire for power – and envy (*Ben.* 2.26–28).

Plutarch on Gratitude, Hope, and the Passion For Power

Perhaps no writer focuses more intently on greed, envy, and the passion for power than Plutarch. A Greek who eventually attained Roman citizenship, Plutarch (46–120 CE) studied philosophy and rhetoric; he was also active in public life, holding political office in Chaeronea, a city in his native Greece, and a priesthood at Delphi. He was granted equestrian status by the emperor, though in his case it did not lead to a career in imperial administration at Rome; nevertheless, he had access to the Roman elite in Italy (Jones 1971). His *Parallel Lives* sought to instruct the Roman ruling class by providing examples for emulation or disapprobation from the lives of leading Greek and Roman statesmen. As Stadter notes (2014: 25), Plutarch wanted his readers to move from the specific circumstances in the lives of these individual statesmen to consider larger, timeless themes. Central among these themes is civic corruption and the related emotions of envy, greed, and above all, *philotimia* (ambition or the love of honor) and *philarchia* (the love of political office and power). In Plutarch's *Marius* and *Pyrrhus*, his presentation of corruption and the political passions intersects with our earlier treatment of gratitude and amplifies the concerns expressed by the Epicureans and Seneca with the contrasting emotion of hope.[12]

Considered biographically, the link between Marius (157–86 BCE) and Pyrrhus (318–272 BCE) is not obvious. They were born 150 years apart. The former held the Roman consulship an unprecedented seven times and extended Rome's empire; the latter was a Greek who numbered among Rome's most formidable enemies. But for Plutarch they share a common struggle. Though supremely accomplished men of immense natural talent, both were undone by a lack of contentment, coupled with greed,

---

[12] For Plutarch's treatment of statesmanship (broadly conceived) in the *Lives*, see de Blois et al. 2005. Liebert 2016 brings Plutarch's *Lives* into conversation with concerns in contemporary political theory.

ambition, and immoderate hope for the future (Duff 1999: 103). In the case of both men, this condition led to civic conflict and corruption.

Perhaps the best way into Plutarch's treatment of these issues in the *Pyrrhus* is through an encounter between Pyrrhus and an accomplished Thessalian orator named Cineas. The conversation occurred as Pyrrhus, enjoying a period of secure and peaceful rule over his native Epirus, was preparing to act on a request for help that would bring him into war with Rome. When asked by Cineas about his plans once he had conquered Italy, Pyrrhus replied that he would move on to Sicily. "Would the taking of Sicily be the end of our expedition?" Cineas wondered (14.4–5). Pyrrhus assured him that it would be the prelude to the conquest of other Mediterranean powers like Libya and Carthage in North Africa – the acquisition of which, Cineas adds, will no doubt help Pyrrhus reacquire Macedonia and solidify rule in the rest of Greece. But what, Cineas asks, will Pyrrhus do once he has managed to conquer the world? Upon hearing Pyrrhus describe how they will live a contented life of peace, pleasure, ease, and friendship, Cineas finally has Pyrrhus set up: Why not live this way now without incurring the costs of war (14.7)? At this "Pyrrhus was more troubled than he was converted; he saw plainly what great happiness he was leaving behind him, but was unable to renounce his hopes of what he eagerly desired" (14.8; trans. Perrin, Loeb).

Cineas' questioning laid bare Pyrrhus' motivations. Despite already having the resources at hand for happiness, he cannot be content until he has satisfied his desires for power, a desire that is limitless and will not be satisfied until he has conquered the world. Like the dashing Greek general Alcibiades, who in a parallel passage had his own ambitious hopes exposed by Socrates (Plato, *Alcibiades* 1 104e–105e), Pyrrhus wants power for power's sake. Thus Pyrrhus' life is characterized by several interrelated themes: disregard for boundaries and limits, inordinate desires (especially for power), lack of contentment, and hope. All of this has profound political implications. Driven by these desires, leaders pursue advantage regardless of justice (12.3), and the people, seeing such examples, imitate them and do likewise (12.7).

In the case of Marius, Plutarch provides his thesis statement at the outset. Marius was a naturally gifted leader and politician – indeed, Plutarch notes that Julius Caesar, the greatest of the Romans, looked to him as a model (6.2). But he dismissed an education in Greek language and literature; he scoffed at the idea of learning a literature "whose teachers are enslaved to others" (2.2). As a result, he put the "ugliest crown upon a most illustrious career as a general and politician when he was driven aground upon the shore of a most premature and savage old age by the blasts of passion, untimely love of rule, and insatiable greed. However, his actual deeds will at once bring this into clear view" (2.3).

Plutarch's account delivers on this promise. In Marius we see a discontented man whose desire for power knew no limit (34.4). After his fifth consulship, he was as desirous of a sixth as another man would have been of his first (28.1). And as he faced the approach of his enemy, Sulla, as a seventy-year-old man, now wealthy and having held Rome's highest office more frequently than any other man, he yet lamented the fact that he was dying with his desires for power still unsatisfied (45.7).

Plutarch concludes the work with his own assessment of Marius' condition by contrasting his discontented and ignominious death – his ambitions seem to have driven him mad – with the deaths of the philosophers Plato and Antipater of Tarsus. Much like Epicurus, these philosophers were able to meet death well by remembering past blessings with gratitude.

> Unmindful and thoughtless persons, on the contrary, let all that happens to them slip away as time goes on; therefore, since they do not hold or keep anything, they are always empty of blessings, but full of hopes, and are looking away to the future while they neglect the present. And yet the future may be prevented by Fortune, while the present cannot be taken away; nevertheless these men cast aside the present gift of Fortune as something alien to them, while they dream of the future and its uncertainties. And this is natural. (46.3–4; trans. Perrin, Loeb)

The *Marius* concludes with a now familiar account of gratitude, but it is the contrasting passion of hope that receives the more sustained treatment in the *Pyrrhus* and *Marius*. The word for "hope" appears twenty-one times between the two biographies, with thirteen of those within the *Pyrrhus*, as befitting a man who "was always entertaining one hope after another" and allowed "neither defeat nor victory to put a limit to his troubling himself and troubling others" (30.2; trans. Perrin, Loeb).

In order to grasp fully Plutarch's account of hope, we must recognize the influence of Thucydides. Thucydides contrasts hope with foresight and planning. Hope is a comfort in danger, but a cold one, for it causes individuals and states to take unnecessary and unwise risks. It is an irrational expectation of success given one's resources and likely challenges. It is the plight of the desperate that no more saved Nicias, the Athenian leader of the disastrous Sicilian expedition, than it did the Melians, who were destroyed by Athens despite their reliance on hope. Through these episodes, Thucydides seems to suggest that human beings have a natural disposition to rely on hope and to take unnecessary risks, a disposition that good leaders should recognize and counter. As Diodotus mentions in Thucydides' version of the Mytilenaean debate in book 3, "hope and desire are present in every situation ... Desire thinks out a plan and hope offers an abundant supply of good fortune. These passions cause the greatest harm, and because they are unseen they are stronger than visible dangers" (3.45.5).[13]

Plutarch's critique of hope echoes Thucydides'. Hope unites with passionate desire (see esp. *Pyrrhus* 26.1) to drive leaders always to believe they can attain the next object that their passion for power places before them. In the process, they trade the securities of the present for the uncertainties of the future. Like Thucydides, Plutarch suggests that hope is "natural" for human beings; people generally are seduced by hope into trading present goods for an uncertain future. Like contemporary philosopher Roger Scruton (2010b), Plutarch warns of "the dangers of false hope," especially when hope is embraced by naturally talented and ambitious leaders.

What is Plutarch's solution? If human beings have a natural tendency to overestimate their capacity to achieve their desires in the future, they should undergo a liberal education in order to reshape their natures. Through education and the development of our rational capacities, we may attain an appropriate foundation for dealing with life's "external goods," thereby forestalling our soul's chase after an endless stream of unattainable desires (*Marius* 46.4).[14]

Conclusion

Reverence, according to Paul Woodruff, is a "forgotten" social and political virtue. The same has been said about gratitude (Scruton 2010a; Ceaser 2011; Leithart 2014). Still, these virtues are part of the American political tradition. Abraham Lincoln's first public address to the Young Men's Lyceum in Springfield, Illinois – "The Perpetuation of our Political Institutions" – proposed in response to increasing violence and factionalism the cultivation of the "reverence for the laws." As Ceaser (2011) notes, one of the problems Lincoln tackled in this address was how to promote gratitude to those from whom we have inherited our political institutions and way of life when they are no longer living.

---

[13] On hope in Thucydides, compare Schlosser 2013, who holds that hope is "chastened" rather than "rejected."

[14] For the psychology of Plutarch's leaders, see Duff 1999: 72–98.

One common set of devices for promoting public gratitude are monuments, memorials, and national memorial days like Memorial Day in the United States or Remembrance Day in the United Kingdom and other commonwealth nations. Monuments and observances utilize the link between gratitude and memory noted by the Epicureans, Seneca, and Plutarch to instill in citizens a sense of dependence upon those who have gone before. They also undermine the sense of entitlement that comes with taking for granted one's current security. By remembering past struggles and considering the possibility that past events could have turned out differently, we become aware of the contingency of our present blessings. We remember the fragility of life.

One might object that gratitude is a vestige from the ancient world that modern liberal democracies would do well to forget. Gratitude in the ancient world was an instrument for stabilizing a hierarchical order; inasmuch as it emphasizes dependence, it perpetuates the status quo by squelching the independence necessary for change and revolution. Gratitude is a virtue for those in power; for the oppressed, hope – generally denigrated by the ancient Greeks and Romans – is the more appropriate virtue.

Before dismissing gratitude, consider at least the three following points. First, the memorialization of past blessings required for gratitude need not lead to the nostalgic desire to turn back the clock to the good old days. Gratitude reminds us that our present blessings were contingent upon past actions, and frequently the persons and events that we memorialize involve past struggles for a better world that current citizens should both appreciate and imitate. The repayment of gratitude prompted by memorials involves living out past virtues in order to make a better future. For instance, citizens might be reminded of the principles by which they can, from patriotic allegiance, question aspects of the present political order – one of the functions of the Vietnam Veterans' Memorial in the National Mall according to Charles Griswold (1986).

Second, hope need not be the sort of dangerous, groundless optimism disparaged by Plutarch and Thucydides. In fact, as the influential twentieth-century historian and social critic Christopher Lasch argued, hope, unlike optimism, expects disappointments; indeed, hope is "the disposition to see things through even when they don't [work out for the best]" (1991: 81). Unlike but not opposed to gratitude, hope requires a belief in and commitment to justice, and like gratitude hope "rests on confidence not so much in the future as in the past" (Lasch 1991: 81). Working from a different perspective, political philosopher Cornel West (1999: 12) likewise distinguishes hope from optimism, while emphasizing commitment to justice and the "best of the past" for the "prisoner of hope." Such conceptions of hope necessarily complement rather than compete with gratitude since they emanate from a common root: dependence on what has been given already and thus presently exists (e.g., the principles inherent in the natural or divine order of our world, God). Whereas gratitude is the emotion derived from backwards-facing dependence, hope pivots and faces the future expectantly in light of the past.

Third, as the republican tradition warned, independence and assertiveness may lead to civic corruption. If this tradition is correct, then liberal democracies need virtues like reverence, which fosters respect for others in light of the acknowledgment of one's own limitations, and public gratitude, which is a necessary handmaiden of "our communal aspirations towards wholeness" (Griswold 1986: 691).

CHAPTER 5

Rhetoric, Deliberation, and Judgment

Rhetoric and Its Critics

Rhetoric, according to classical accounts, is the art of persuasive speaking (Quintilian, *Institutio oratoria* 2.15.3; cf. Aristotle, *Rhetoric* 1.2). Oratory was essential for Roman political leadership. The idea that a distinguished man should be a capable public speaker was deeply woven into the fabric of Roman political culture (Plin. *Nat.* 7.139; Cic. *De oratore* 1.14–16). The successful orator in many ways exemplified traditional Roman virtues. As Cato the Elder wrote to his son, "the orator is, Marcus my son, a good man skilled in speaking" (*Ad filium* fr. 14, Jordan). This basic notion of an orator would be echoed by Cicero at the end of the Republic and by Quintilian under the Principate.

For contemporary readers "rhetoric" carries largely negative connotations. It readily attracts the modifiers "empty" and "mere." It is a type of sophistry that makes the weaker argument appear stronger. It conceals biases and falsehoods. It is a synonym for "spin" – "no rhetoric, just facts" runs the common slogan.

This popular suspicion of rhetoric is nothing new. Indeed, for all of their stress on the importance of oratory, many Romans were suspicious of speech too elaborately adorned according to principles found in Greek rhetorical handbooks (Crook 1995: 34). As Cato, known for his rough and ready style, also advised: "Stick to the subject; the words will follow" (*Fil.* fr. 15, Jordan).

Of course, rhetoric has also faced more theoretical criticisms. Consider three of the most important. First, rhetoric is constantly beset by the twin dangers of flattery and manipulation, dangers well illustrated in Plato's dialogues *Gorgias* and *Menexenus*. In the former, Socrates both unmasks the manipulative power of rhetoric over those who lack knowledge (464d–465e) and shows that even the most independent-minded and strong-willed political leader in democratic Athens is bound to the will and desire of the people, to whom he must pander in order to acquire and maintain power (513a–c); in the latter, which contains a parody of an Athenian funeral oration, Socrates shows the power of rhetoric to bewitch and manipulate its audience through ornate embellishments (234c–235c).

The second criticism comes from Thomas Hobbes, the influential seventeenth-century English philosopher and translator of Thucydides. Rhetoric, insofar as it stirs up the mind's passions, perverts the judgments of the people, thereby undermining popular government. Consequently, regimes that rely on rhetoric are fractious and turbulent, until eloquence is regulated by a single sovereign authority (Remer 1996; Skinner 1996; Garsten 2006: ch. 1).

Finally, according to more recent "deliberative democrats," legitimate democratic power requires rational deliberation among participants of equal standing in a conversation that is equally accessible to all. According to this account, rhetoric as it is usually understood and practiced is unable to meet the standards of rationality and equality necessary for deliberation and judgment about the public good.[1]

With these criticisms in view, this chapter explores the relationship between rhetoric, this critical art for Roman leaders and statesmen, and its relationship to important aspects of political decision-making such as deliberation and judgment. Roman rhetoricians illuminate the way in which institutions shape deliberative practices, the role of non-rational resources in deliberation and persuasion, and the relationship between deliberation and political order, on one hand, and political conflict, on the other. They also offer valuable discussions of the conditions for the free and frank political speech necessary for political deliberation and judgment.

Rhetoric and Republican Institutions

While traditionalists like the elder Cato may have been content to leave successful oratory to practice and experience, in the last century of the Republic Romans began to systematize their approach to rhetoric, as they were also doing with grammar, law, philosophy, theology, ethnography, architecture, and medicine (Rawson 1985; Moatti 2015). Two of these Republican rhetorical handbooks would survive (and in fact greatly influence education in rhetoric in the Middle Ages and Renaissance) – Cicero's

---

[1] Conditions for deliberative democracy: Gutmann and Thompson 2004. See also the collection of essays in Bohman and Rehg 1997. Remer 2017: ch. 6 offers a Ciceronian critique of deliberative democracy.

De inventione (composed in the late 90s or early 80s BCE) and the anonymous *Rhetorica ad Herennium* (likely composed in the 80s BCE). Following
earlier Greek handbooks (cf. Arist. *Rhet.* 1.3.1358b), these guides divided
oratory into three types: epideictic, deliberative, and judicial (Cic. *Inv.* 1.7;
Rhet. Her. 1. 2).

Though deliberative oratory is most closely tied to the theme of this
chapter, and has been the recent focus of historians interested in Roman
politics, it is important to remember that the authors of the handbooks
saw all types of oratory as relevant for politics (Cic. *Inv.* 1.6; *Rhet. Her.* 1.2).
As the author of the *Rhetorica ad Herennium* notes immediately before
his threefold division of rhetoric (1.2), "the task of the public speaker is to
discuss capably those matters which law (*lex*) and custom (*mos*) have fixed
for the uses of citizenship, and to secure as far as possible the agreement
of his hearers" (trans. Caplan, Loeb). According to this author, there is a
relationship between the art of persuasion and civic institutions and laws.
Taking our cue from the *Rhetorica ad Herennium*, let's consider in turn the
three types of rhetoric, paying special attention to their relationship with
Republican Rome's civic institutions.

Epideictic ("display") speech is that which is related to praise or censure.
While occasions for purely epideictic rhetoric were relatively infrequent –
the chief example was the funeral oration – the author of *Rhetorica ad
Herennium* suggests that epideictic is still important because it was frequently incorporated into deliberative speeches in the senate and *contio*,
or into judicial speeches in court (3.15). Covering themes such as birth,
education, wealth, civic and moral virtues, power, glory, citizenship,
friendships, and physical characteristics, these display speeches provided
an opportunity for the development of character (*êthos*, *mores*, *natura*) in
the audience, informing them what they should value and embedding discourse within a shared civic and political culture.

Judicial speeches concern rhetoric in civil and criminal trials (see Crook
1995). By the late Republic, trials involving crimes that impacted the public were normally conducted in standing criminal courts, presided over by
a magistrate, and involving up to seventy-five jurors. Civil trials involving cases of a private nature usually consisted of much smaller juries but
could on occasion involve more jurors than in criminal trials. Trials featured speeches by a prosecutor and a defendant, who was represented by
advocates who spoke on his behalf.

Criminal trials at Rome were often held in the Forum, where a ring
of bystanders (*corona*) would frequently gather and voice their approval
or disapproval of various arguments. The popular attention and increased

standing for successful advocates and prosecutors could launch their political careers.

Deliberative speeches involve a choice between two or more courses of action on which a body of persons must deliberate to determine which course of action carries greater advantage (*Rhet. Her.* 1.2; 3.2). In political deliberation, questions of advantage involved consideration of both "security" and what is honorable and right (*Rhet. Her.* 3.3; cf. Cic. *Inv.* 2.157–78, which arranges these categories somewhat differently). The former involves discussion of available resources to achieve one's goals by force or by non-military means; the latter requires consideration of whether a course of action is right and praiseworthy (*Rhet. Her.* 3.3–7). For instance, should Rome destroy Carthage or allow it to remain in power (3.2)? (A question discussed in the senate frequently in the second century BCE.) To answer this question, senators will need to consider Rome's interest (*utilitas*) and exercise prudence to determine which course of action best promotes it when relevant advantages and disadvantages are weighed.

The senate was in fact the regular place for deliberative speeches. Senators were called upon to speak according to seniority, beginning with the consuls-elect, followed by the ex-consuls, praetors, and so on down the list. This procedure meant that, following Sulla's increase in membership to 600 in 81 BCE – a quorum was 200 (Cic. *Q. Fr.* 2.1.1) and a well-attended meeting had more than double that number – most senators had little opportunity to contribute, even though all possessed the right to speak. Junior senators, whom we might think of as "backbenchers" or "footmen" (*pedarii*), primarily showed their opinion on the speakers' views by physically moving to one side of the senate house or the other when the question was called. While debates could be heated, with banter between speakers, interruptions, and sophisticated rhetoric, they were relatively restrained compared to the rhetoric in another potential arena for deliberative speech, the *contio*, or popular assembly (Cic. *de Orat.* 2.333–34, 338).[2]

As we saw in chapter 1, the *contio* is a non-voting, non-decision-making popular assembly in which a magistrate convenes and addresses the people (see Pina Polo 1996; Morstein-Marx 2004). He may do so for a number of reasons: to read out a fresh decree of the senate; to relay important news from the battlefield; to eulogize the dead who fell there; to address the people at the end of a procession following a triumph; to promise he would conduct himself lawfully upon taking up his magistracy and to affirm he in fact kept that promise upon laying it down. Last, but certainly

---

[2] The standard view of lack of participation by junior senators is usefully complicated by Ryan 1998.

not least, *contiones* were places where legislation was presented prior to being put to the vote by the people. While it was possible for the audience to hear opposing views on legislation at a *contio*, there was no expectation that this would be the case, and in some instances the gathering was closer to a "rally" attended by the speaker's supporters (and sometimes interrupted by protestors). In this sense, it is comparable to an American town hall meeting (Pina Polo 2011b: 286). Nevertheless, its role as a venue for the people to hear legislation made the *contio* a potentially important link in the process of political deliberation and judgment.

Cicero elevates the act of addressing the people assembled in a *contio* from the rostra (speaker's platform) in the Roman Forum even over speaking in courts or the senate (*Brutus* 186). After all, this act brought one face to face with the "sovereign" decision-making body of Rome, the *populus Romanus* (Cic. *Pro lege Manilia* 1–2; Morstein-Marx 2004: 53–54). The experience was without a doubt most exhilarating (Cic. *de Orat.* 2.338). It was also challenging. Crowds at the Forum could be immense, perhaps upwards of 15,000–20,000, and very loud. The audience was highly variable, though the craftsmen and shopkeepers working near the Forum likely formed its typical core. Holding the attention of a large, diverse crowd which could come and go at any time was challenging; so too was addressing a hostile crowd. The *contio* in the Forum was the meeting place between the people and senate, and it could make or break the careers of those senators who spoke.[3]

Some historians have recently portrayed the *contio* as the place where the Roman people exercised their sovereign authority by deliberating on and judging proposals placed before them, thereby forcing the elite to take into account the popular will (Millar 1995; 1998). In particular, the people were presented with an opportunity to weigh different views, which they could hear debated at a single *contio*, or else hear presented individually at separate *contiones* (Brunt 1988: 26–27).

However, Robert Morstein-Marx, the author of the standard treatment of the *contio*, argues that several factors significantly hampered the *contio* as an arena for public deliberation. First, while it was standard procedure to have both proponents and opponents of legislation speak before a vote, a number of factors (such as the power that the presiding magistrate has over who speaks, in what order, and for how long, as well as his ability to convene a partisan crowd) limited the potential for a balanced exchange of

---

[3] Size of crowd at Forum: J. T. Ramsey 2007: 124. Forum as meeting place for people and senate: Morstein-Marx 2004: 12, 55.

ideas. Moreover, when addressing the assembled people, almost all speakers portrayed themselves as "men of the people" (*populares*), at the expense of whatever ideological positions they might otherwise have held. This even included Cicero, who elsewhere aligned himself with the supporters of the senate, "the best ones" (*optimates*), and denigrated the "men of the people" (*populares*; *Sest.* 96–135). Thus, debate concerned people, not ideas, institutions, or ideologies; the main question was whom the people should trust as representing their true interests (Morstein-Marx 2004: 212, 229–34, 257).

Morstein-Marx (2004: 15–33) further compares the oratory of the Roman Forum to the standards for deliberation advocated by the philosopher Jürgen Habermas, an exercise that lends itself to a critique of rhetoric along the lines of that attributed to deliberative democrats in the previous section: the lack of equal opportunity for all to engage in and consider rational argumentation leaves one far from the "ideal speech situation" required for legitimate democratic deliberation. Of course in addition to popular assemblies, Habermas's standard for deliberation would also call into question as potential venues for deliberation the Roman senate and, for that matter, the Athenian council of 500 and assembly (*ekklesia*), for in each case size precludes all members from having the equal opportunity to speak.

One must be careful about assuming that deliberation and judgment is primarily a matter of the reciprocal exchange of speeches. For instance, Daniela Cammack (2013) has argued that in democratic Athens, deliberation was an internal rather than external process, which allowed a large number of citizens to make decisions guided by the speeches of a few leading citizens. There are many salient differences between the Athenian assembly and Roman popular assemblies. To name just one, whereas debate at the Athenian assembly resulted in a vote, the several-week gap between the presentation of legislation at a *contio* and the up-or-down vote at a *comitia* allowed a number of extraneous factors to supervene on the decision-making process (for further differences, see chapter 1). Thus, Cammack's Athenian model, which requires deliberation to conclude in a vote, cannot apply directly to Rome. Nevertheless, an internal model for deliberation raises the possibility that political deliberation and judgment could happen on a larger scale, and Gary Remer has recently argued for an "internal-reflective" style of deliberation in the Roman *contio* and senate.[4]

---

[4] Remer 2017: 195–97. Remer borrows the term "internal-reflective" from Goodin 2000.

Regardless of the issue of scale, oratory performed and heard in the Roman Forum would still seem prone to the criticisms of Plato and Hobbes, inasmuch as pandering and manipulation threatens popular judgment, thereby undermining popular government. These dangers were no doubt real; in fact, they were addressed by oratory's greatest practitioner and defender at Rome: Cicero.

Cicero on Rhetoric, Deliberation, and Judgment

Cicero thought hard about rhetoric throughout his life. He devoted the first of his theoretical writings to the topic, *De inventione* (*On Invention*) – a handbook that he would later dismiss as a crude work of his youth (*de Orat.* 1.5). His next work on the topic was his masterpiece, *De oratore* (*On the Orator*). Written in 55 BCE as the first of a trilogy of Platonic-style dialogues that also included *De republica* and *De legibus*, *De oratore* presents a fictional conversation from 91 BCE at the outset of the Social War and just a few years before the beginning of the civil wars that would end with Sulla's dictatorship; its main characters featured two of the most accomplished orators of the day, Marcus Antonius and Lucius Crassus, Cicero's teacher. A decade after composing *De oratore*, Cicero continued to deal with rhetoric in his works *Brutus* and *Orator* – the *Brutus* in particular provides an invaluable history of rhetoric and rhetoricians in Republican Rome. His final theoretical work, *De officiis*, also contains relevant material. While Cicero's treatment of rhetoric, deliberation, and judgment matured, it is nonetheless possible to see a general approach to these issues emerging from *De inventione*, *De oratore*, *Brutus*, *Orator*, and *De officiis*. In these works, he grapples with some of rhetoric's most longstanding criticisms.

Early in *De inventione* (1.6) Cicero establishes rhetoric as "part of political science" and articulates a crucial distinction between the function (*officium*) of rhetoric, to speak appropriately for persuasion, and the end (*finis*) of rhetoric, to actually persuade. The function and end of rhetoric do not always align. Just as a doctor's function to use appropriate medical techniques to treat a patient might not result in healing, so the function of a rhetorician to find the appropriate means of persuasion might not lead to his audience being persuaded. Indeed, Antonius suggests in *De oratore* that the better the orator, the more profoundly he is aware of the potential gap between delivering a good speech and actually persuading one's audience (1.120–22). Thus, one problem for persuasion is how to ensure that the orator's function and end coincide.

A second set of problems raised by Cicero involves Plato's concerns with the orator either manipulating or pandering to his audience. Indeed, Plato's *Gorgias* was one of two Platonic dialogues (the *Phaedrus* is the other) that establishes the theoretical challenges to which the *De oratore* responds (Fantham 2004: ch. 3). The potential for manipulation is inherent in the power of oratory "to get a hold on assemblies of men, win their good will, direct their inclinations wherever the speaker wishes, or divert them from whatever he wishes" (1.30; cf. 1.202; 2.32, 176; trans. Rackham and Sutton, Loeb). The dialogue puts this dangerous capacity on the table early when one of the characters, Scaevola, challenges Crassus' initial praise of rhetoric as essential for establishing and maintaining polities. On the contrary, Scaevola suggests, when orators succeed, people are "not so much convinced by the reasoning of the wise as snared by the speeches of the eloquent" (1.36; trans. Rackham and Sutton, Loeb). He subsequently cites examples where persuasive rhetoric damaged rather than helped the *res publica* (1.38), an argumentative move also made by Socrates in the *Gorgias* (515c–519e).

However, the potential for the orator to manipulate is limited by the necessity of conforming one's arguments to the tastes and opinions of one's audience, a point greatly emphasized in *De oratore*.[5] Oratory is subject to the control of opinion (1.108). This can lead to pandering. A vivid example in *De oratore* is Crassus himself, who as a young man in 106 BCE shamelessly pandered to the people in a *contio*. Pleading on behalf of the senate, he beseeches the people: "Do not let us be slaves (*servire*) to anyone except to you as a body, whose slaves we are able and ought to be" (1.225). This "sacrifice of … principle to opportunism" by the orator (Fantham 2004: 220), Antonius points out, would not have been approved by Plato (1.224–25) – a statement loaded with irony since Crassus had earlier portrayed Plato as embodying his (Crassus') ideal of the union of philosophical knowledge and rhetoric by his writing of the *Gorgias*, the dialogue in which he most viciously attacked rhetoric in the name of philosophy (1.47).

How does Cicero address these dangers of rhetoric that threaten to hamper deliberation by binding the capacity for judgment of both the speaker and audience? We should begin by noting, as many commentators have, that Cicero follows Aristotle in holding that belief is engendered by emotion (*pathos*) and character (*êthos*) in addition to rational argumentation (*logos*). Cicero would disagree with critics like Habermas who suppose

---

[5] See, e.g., *de Orat.* 1.83, 94, 108, 119, 125, 213, 223; 2.72, 159; 3.65–66, 223; cf. *Orator* 24; *Brutus* 185.

legitimate deliberation consists only of a rational weighing of arguments to
the exclusion of the emotions. Such a view, on Cicero's account, is unre-
alistically utopian, since people judge far more things by emotions than
by truth (*de Orat.* 2.178). Moreover – and somewhat ironically for criticisms of oratory by advocates of deliberative democracy – Cicero suggests
that rhetoric that engages the emotions makes speech even more demotic
and widely accessible (*vulgus*), since, unlike rational argumentation, such
speech may be open to those who do not share a common language or
manner of discourse (3.223).[6]

Cicero in fact has more faith in the common people's capacity to judge
than many of rhetoric's detractors. The orator seeks to win the goodwill of
his audience by adapting himself to their "judgment (*arbitrium*) and will,"
which in turn is governed by prudence (*prudentia*), that is, "a practical
grasp" that allows for effective judgment (*Orator* 24; see Kapust 2011a: 99).
When it comes to assessing the effectiveness of rhetoric as a whole – taking
into account rational argumentation, the ethos of the speaker, and the
capacity of the speech to move the audience – Cicero believes that the
judgment of the multitude and crowd is up to the task; indeed, it is not
inferior to the judgments of experts (*Brutus* 185). Crassus makes a similar
point in *De oratore*. Nature gives everyone, even the inexperienced crowd,
the capacity to discriminate in matters of rhetoric (*de Orat.* 3.195). There
is little difference between the expert and common man when it comes to
judging (3.197). Rhetoric must be "adapted to the ears of the crowd" (*de
Orat.* 2.159), but as in music there are some things so discordant to most
people's ears that they can never be admitted into a speech (1.113–15).

Political judgment, Cicero stresses in his *Orator*, involves both the
speaker and audience. Both must judge what arguments and style are
appropriate given the circumstances and the character (*persona*) of both
speaker and audience (70–74). The terminology here – *persona* – evokes
the idea of an actor playing a role in the theater. One of the great challenges of both oratory and life is determining how to play one's role appropriately (70), which requires prudence, judgment, and the possession of
decorum, the virtue concerned with appropriate speech and behavior.

Cicero's most extensive and considered treatment of these themes is
found in *De officiis*. Here again he reaffirms the capacity of the audience
to judge worthy and appropriate performances in the theater (1.97). But
Cicero goes further and extends the idea of characters or parts (*persona*)

to all of life (Schofield 2012). We must play our parts in a manner that is appropriate or decorous. Cicero enumerates four roles or parts (*personae*) in all. But the first and most fundamental role is the one nature has given to us as rational beings. This involves a sense of restraint and respect for others (*verecundia*) as well as self-respect, both of which promote society (1.98; Kaster 2005: 17–18, 22–23). One who plays the role of human being well, living justly, wisely, and courageously (*Off.* 1.94), "springs ready to view" (1.95) or "shines out in life" such that he "arouses others' approval" (1.98). (The word for "approval" can refer to an audience's approval of an orator.)

Here, then, is one key reason for Cicero's confidence in popular judgment. At a deep level, all of us inasmuch as we are human have the capacity to perceive when words, thoughts, and actions are discordant, that is, when they are disrespectful of other human beings and disruptive of human society. As Cicero's metaphors of music and theater suggest, this sense can be effectively aroused by auditory and visual means in addition to rational arguments. Neither strictly rational nor irrational, this aesthetic sense when engaged can shape and change predominant popular opinion. To take a more recent example, late eighteenth-century English abolitionists used seals with the images of slaves and graphic depictions of overcrowded slave ships to convey visually the dehumanization caused by the slave trade (Swaminathan 2009: 186–87). The visual imagery appealed to a common notion of human dignity that rational argumentation alone could not unlock.

Cicero's insistence that judgment has a touchstone beyond conventional opinion in a natural, innate instinct common to human beings goes back to his first treatment of deliberative oratory in *De inventione* (2.161). Here Cicero adds to nature a second means of regulating and shaping opinion about the issues on which one deliberates: customary law and time-honored principles that have received widespread popular approval over the years (2.162). In other words, Rome's customs and constitution provide another means of shaping opinion and guiding appropriate judgments on behalf of both the orator and audience. This is the reason why, as the *Rhetorica ad Herennium* suggested, epideictic oratory, which reminded the audience of fundamental Roman values, could play an important role in deliberative speeches.

De oratore likewise emphasizes the importance of the Republican constitution, customs, and institutions. Oratory is dependent on such republican institutions as the forum, *contio*, law courts, and senate (1.35, 44), the Twelve Tables and other public law (1.194) establishing Roman political culture (1.193–96), and the "spirit, customs, and way of life" (*mens, mos, disciplina*) of the fatherland that Romans love (1.196). It is not accidental that in the drama of *De oratore* the pending upheavals of the Republican constitution led to the death of the great orators who spoke in the dialogue (3.8–11; Garsten 2006: 166).

Morstein-Marx has described oratory within the *contio* as a "political drama" (Morstein-Marx: 2004: ch. 7). Given Cicero's use of theatrical imagery, the same could be said for his theoretical account of rhetoric (Connolly 2007: ch. 5). The orator and audience both play their parts, each making judgments according to (if we may extend the theatrical analogy) a common "script" that dictates appropriate arguments. This script in turn is determined by nature and by the republican constitution, institutions, and customs that maintain and uphold Roman political culture. The existence of this script provides grounds for Cicero's denial that oratory is nothing more than the sophistic manipulation of one's audience (cf. *Orat.* 65; *de Orat.* 3.55).

It is interesting to note that the two main sources of the script that enables judgment, *mores* (customs, character) and *natura* (nature, character), are Latin words that Cicero uses to render the Greek *êthos*. As for Aristotle, *êthos* for Cicero refers to both the character of the audience and orator (J. May 1988: 2–3). Character is one of the bases for mutual judgment by orator and audience. The former judges what arguments will be persuasive given the character of his audience; the latter judges whether the orator is trustworthy. The script for speaker and audience provides a communal or common character that informs what both parties find persuasive.[7]

The existence of a script offering common standards for judgment for both speaker and audience points towards Cicero's answer to the question of the alignment between good rhetoric and persuasive rhetoric, between rhetoric's function (*officium*) and its end (*finis*). The orator can have confidence that persuasive rhetoric will indeed win over his audience because it takes place within a recognizable and common context, which is established by nature, mores, laws, and the Roman constitution and institutions. This script informs and limits what is persuasive.

It also serves as an essential precondition for political judgment. It does so in two interrelated ways. First, by informing and limiting what both audience and orator finds persuasive, the script provides a mutual standard for judgment. Contents of the script such as nature and republican institutions, customs, traditions, and laws provide a flexible standard

---

[7] For the *êthos* of a community as a standard for judgment in Aristotle, see Garver 2004. Cicero cautions that the orator's speech must not stray far from the *sensus communis*, the political community's general perception of what is appropriate (*de Orat.* 1.12; see Remer 2017).

for judgment that ensures the possibility of persuasion is not destroyed by the arbitrary and absolute imposition of the will of the speaker over the audience or vice versa. That is, because of the script, the relationship between speaker and audience does not necessarily reduce to either pandering (absolute rule of audience over speaker) or manipulation (absolute rule of speaker over audience). There is mutuality in judgment, even though, especially in contexts such as the *contio*, the reciprocal judgment between orator and people does not exclude hierarchy (Remer 2005: 155). Here we find Cicero's response to the Platonic critique of rhetoric as prone to manipulation and pandering.

Second, the script facilitates political judgment by enabling decision-making to transcend the mere amalgamation of private opinions and judgments. It opens up the possibility for public, shared, and therefore truly political, judgments. Political philosopher Ronald Beiner (1983: 141) makes a deeply Ciceronian point when he argues that political judgments are possible

> because of a common tradition and shared history, public laws and obligations to which all are subject, common ideas and shared meanings. These 'public objects' or public things (*res publica*) allow for judgment of a public character, for these things concern all of us who participate in these traditions, laws, and institutions, and who therefore share in common meanings. Such judgments concern not merely what *I* want or the way of life *I* desire, but rather, entail intersubjective deliberation about a common life (how *we* should be together).

It is important to note that on Cicero's account of judgment, the relationship between rhetoric and script runs in both directions: just as the script guards judgment from the potential excesses of rhetoric, so rhetoric contributes to the script that informs judgment. Public oratory, especially epideictic, reinforces and perpetuates a shared notion of what is honorable, a notion itself embedded in the shared history, traditions, meanings, and ideas that comprise much of the script. Roman funeral speeches, for instance, portray and reinforce a common notion of the "good life" for the political community. This notion of what is honorable is essential for political deliberation and judgment.[8] Similarly, Cicero's allowance that judgment involves aesthetics means that rhetoric may use auditory and visual stimuli to make visible and persuasive nature's contributions to the script, which a political society's particular customs, institutions, and laws

---

[8] Epideictic as concerned with what is honorable, which in turn is one of the two important elements for deliberation: Cic. *Inv.* 2.12. Roman funeral oration: Plb. 6.53–55; Plin. *Nat.* 7.139.

might have occluded. (Consider again how visual imagery in pro-abolition arguments led to the revision of custom, practice, and law.) Thus, contra Hobbes, rhetoric itself might be an asset, rather than a liability, to judgment.

My account of Cicero's rhetorical theory has said little about the role of rational argumentation in deliberation and judgment. This is not to suggest that Cicero found argumentation unimportant. *De inventione* and *De oratore* both treat at length rational proof. The topic of *De inventione*, the *inventio*, is after all a speech's formal argumentative structure (cf. Cic. *Inv.* 1.9). And in *De oratore*, Crassus complains on multiple occasions that the philosophical method (associated with followers of Aristotle as well as skeptical followers of Plato) of being able to argue on both sides of a question rightfully belongs to the orator. However, deliberation on matters that call for judgment about what is advantageous and honorable has little traction apart from common standards, values, and institutions that create space within which meaningful discussion can occur. This part of Cicero's teaching will be confirmed by later Roman theorists of political rhetoric writing when the Republic was but a distant memory.

Quintilian and the Decline of Rhetoric

Following Cicero's death and the inauguration of the Principate, rhetoric declined – or so writers such as Seneca, Petronius, Quintilian, Tacitus, and "Longinus" suggested in a number of "decline narratives" in the first century CE. Kennedy (1972: 446–64) points out several possible reasons: Romans were naturally attracted to decline narratives; Cicero's brilliance overshadowed later orators; and legal and bureaucratic developments solved problems more efficiently without recourse to rhetoric. Cicero himself may even have contributed to this narrative by offering a more pessimistic view of oratory in his *Brutus*.

The reason most pertinent to our concerns in this chapter, however, has to do with changes to the Republican institutions that supported rhetoric. Augustus abolished the *contio* in 14 CE. A short time later, elections were removed from the people when Tiberius transferred electoral powers to the senate. The triumph, an occasion for epideictic, was limited to the emperor's family. Finally, from the end of Augustus' reign until the time of Diocletian (284–305 CE), a great deal of influence was wielded by the imperial council (Crook 1955), an informal but important group of advisors consisting of the *princeps*'s supporters and family members; the council was closed to the scrutiny of most senators (Connolly 2007: 255).

Rhetoric in general, and especially the deliberative rhetoric so essential to Republican politics, declined because institutions like the senate and the *contio* that supported it were weakened or banished.

Within this context, Quintilian wrote his *Institutio oratoria* (*Institutes on Oratory*), the longest, most detailed surviving didactic work from the classical world (Morgan 1998: 245). In this work, Quintilian, who served as a teacher and orator from the late 50s under Nero to his retirement in 88 CE under Domitian, sought to describe the education of the complete or ideal orator (*orator perfectus*; 1.pr.9). Borrowing Cato's words, Quintilian defines such an orator as "a good man skilled in speaking" (12.1.1, 27, 44; 12.2.1). This implies that he possesses the cardinal virtues of wisdom, courage, justice, and self-control (1.pr.12; cf. 12.2.1–7).

Quintilian defines rhetoric as "the science of speaking well" (2.15.38). As Quentin Skinner notes (1996: 100), Quintilian's formal definition of rhetoric focuses on the rhetorician's task or function (*officium*) of speaking well rather than on his goal (*finis*) of persuasion. This is not to say that Quintilian neglects persuasion. Indeed, he readily admits that most orators speak in order to persuade an audience to agree with their viewpoint (2.17.23). Nevertheless, he adamantly insists that a speaker's success is independent of whether he actually persuades. "But our orator and his art, as we have defined it, do not depend on results. The orator certainly aims at victory, but when he has spoken well, even if he does not win, he has fulfilled what is required by his art" (2.17.23). Quintilian later revises the Ciceronian formulation by identifying speaking well as the goal of rhetoric rather than, as Cicero would have it, as its function (2.17.25).

Why does Quintilian revise Cicero? We should begin by noting that Quintilian drops persuasion as the goal of rhetoric under pressure from critics who point out the frequent failure of rhetoricians to persuade. Quintilian, it would appear, is so sensitive to such criticisms because he is less confident than Cicero in the ability of good rhetoric to actually persuade. Quintilian recognizes that in practice there will be a significant gap between "speaking well" and "speaking persuasively." Thus, to hold out persuasion as the major criterion of success and failure would be to agree to a standard that rhetoric could not reliably meet.

In other ways, however, Quintilian tracks Cicero closely. For instance, the complete orator, like Cicero's ideal orator in *De oratore*, will combine philosophy and political life (12.2.4–8). He will be able to argue on each side of a question in order to discover the truth (12.1.35–36, 2.23–25; cf. *de Orat.* 3.80, 107). He will recognize that what is honorable will vary by circumstances (12.1.36–37; cf. Cic. *Off.* 1.31, 59) and that sometimes circumstances will force the orator to depart from what one would usually consider to be honorable (12.1.36–45; Cic. *Off.* 1.31–32; 2.60).

Comparison between Quintilian and Cicero is especially instructive when it comes to deliberative rhetoric, discussed along with the other genres of rhetoric in *Institutes* book 3. Like Cicero, Quintilian distinguishes between the honorable and advantageous in deliberation. He emphasizes that when it comes to deliberation one must speak according to common conceptions and consider the consensus about what is advantageous (3.8.39). Successful rhetoric depends on the "character of the audience" and "commonly accepted opinion" (3.7.23). Throughout this section (3.8.35–54), Quintilian emphasizes the importance of adapting rhetoric for persuasion in a way that suits the mind of one's audience. Like Cicero, he argues that the effective orator must engage in role-playing, adapting his speech and mannerisms according to the diverse character types in his audience. According to Quintilian, such impersonation is the most difficult thing about oratory (3.8.49). Last but not least, like Cicero before him, Quintilian argues for the importance of the non-rational aspects of persuasion, such as the emotions and trust.

Despite widespread agreement with Cicero, Quintilian's discussion departs from his predecessor's in terms of emphasis at a couple of significant points. The first concerns *paradiastolê*, the rhetorical redescription of actions using different terms than one's opponent to persuade one's audience to see actions in a different moral light. The goal is usually to excuse or lessen one's own vices or to reveal as a neighboring vice what one's opponent claims as a virtuous action. The trick is to recognize that the difference between virtue and vice often depends on details that admit of different interpretations. For example, one might describe a course of action one's opponent calls "courageous" as "reckless." This device is present in Cicero but receives clearer expression in the *Rhetorica ad Herennium*, where it is identified as a technique in deliberative rhetoric (3.3.6), and in Sallust (Skinner 1996: ch. 4). In fact, Quintilian cites Sallust's account of the Catilinarian conspiracy, in which he claims that Sallust redescribes Catiline's reason for evil actions as due not to wickedness but to "indignation", that is, due to an appropriate response to a slight to one's honor (*Inst.* 3.8.45). Later in the monograph, Sallust's Cato decries the redescription of vices as neighboring virtues as evidence of a systemic breakdown of Republican values: "we have lost the true vocabulary for things" (*Cat.* 52.11). Sallust's suggestion that *paradiastolê* characterizes speech in a factious and corrupt polity in turn echoes Thucydides' famous account of *stasis* in Corcyra during the Peloponnesian War, where the phenomenon of rhetorical redescription is depicted if not named (Th. 3.82). For Sallust no less than for Thucydides, "political corruption and linguistic corruption imply one another" (Euben 1990: 189).

The second difference in emphasis between Quintilian and Cicero has to do with the importance of the *contio*. Quintilian points out that Cicero was interested mainly in deliberative rhetoric because of its importance for politics; furthermore, he recognizes that at the heart of political rhetoric for his great Republican predecessor was the *contio*. Echoing what we have already seen in our discussion of Cicero, Quintilian suggests that such rhetoric is based on the resources of the city and the character (*mores*) or nature (*natura*) of its citizens (3.8.14). Quintilian endeavors to enlarge the field of deliberative rhetoric far beyond popular assemblies and other political institutions (3.8.14) to include exercises in the schools and rhetoric within historical writing (see, e.g., 3.8.67). However, Quintilian's expansion of opportunities for deliberative rhetoric in book 3 decenters the *contio*, limiting the "opportunity for great oratory" (Kennedy 1972: 511).

Commentators have noted the effect. Connolly (2007: 255) points out that Quintilian "does not expect his students to participate in the ruling practices of Cicero's age." Quintilian as a result "transposes" Ciceronian public rhetoric "into a domestic key" (Connolly 2007: 256). Describing the cumulative effect of Quintilian's account of genres of rhetoric in book 3 and of the ideal rhetorician in book 12, Kennedy (1972: 509) writes:

> Rather heavy emphasis is put on the orator's personal morality and technical competence, rather less on his political and intellectual leadership. His role in the law courts seems more evident than in the council chamber or before the people. Such practical matters as delivery play considerable part in his success … In other words, the picture is much what one might have expected from a teacher of rhetoric who inherited a rich tradition and lived under an autocratic government.

Returning to the matter of the gap between persuasive rhetoric and good rhetoric, Quintilian himself never provides an answer. However, from Cicero's perspective his lack of confidence in the capacity of good rhetoric to persuade would be well founded. With the loss of opportunities for oratory before the assembled citizen body and senate, the orator can no longer count on the broader civic character to provide shared standards for discourse. The danger of losing a shared moral vocabulary identified by Sallust's Cato has if anything intensified from the Republican perspective, for the very institutions and occasions that reinforced commonality have declined. As Quintilian notes in his discussion of *paradiastolê*, "what is called liberty in some is called license in others" (3.8.48). With the degeneration of common character (*natura, mores*), the orator finds himself having to accommodate the manifold versatile characters of private individuals (*personae*), a most difficult task (3.8.49). The attendant danger in such a situation is that the orator will lose space for independent judgment, and deliberation will turn to flattery. This problem is explored with penetrating insight by Tacitus.

Tacitus on Rhetoric Under the Principate

Tacitus was born in either northern Italy or modern Provence, France, around 56 CE, near the beginning of Nero's reign. He was a teenager when Nero committed suicide in 68, which was followed by a year of constant civil war as four emperors successively claimed power. Though a "new man," Tacitus progressed steadily through the *cursus honorum*, eventually holding the consulship. He was away from Rome from 89 to 93, when the emperor Domitian, jealous to maintain his power against suspected challengers, unleashed a reign of terror. Leading senators were killed, and the investigations of self-appointed "informers" (*delatores*) who denounced and prosecuted critics of the *princeps* led to a condition of extreme slavery in which it was no longer possible to speak freely (*Agr.* 2). After Domitian's assassination in 96 CE, the rule of his successors, Nerva and Trajan, inaugurated a time of relative peace (*Agr.* 3).

Over the next twenty years, Tacitus appeared to have been intermittently involved in public life. He was consul in 97. Along with Pliny, he served as the prosecution in the highly publicized extortion trial of Marius Priscus (governor of Africa) in 100. In c. 112/113 he was proconsul of Asia, a plum position that capped a successful senatorial career. During these decades, he also wrote. He published his *Agricola* (see chapter 3) in 97–98, followed soon after by the *Germania*, an ethnographical work dealing with the peoples who lived beyond the Rhine and Danube Rivers in the western part of the Roman Empire. Later in life he turned to history, publishing the *Histories* and the *Annals*, which between them covered Roman history from 14 to 96 CE. The *Annals* cemented Tacitus' legacy as a writer and historian of the first class, and is itself an important contribution to political thought (Hammer 2014: ch. 7). For Tacitus' treatment of rhetoric, however, we turn not to his historical writings but to his contribution to the genre of dialogue, *Dialogus de oratoribus* (*Dialogue on Orators*).

Published in the early years of the second century, the *Dialogus* self-consciously, in its style as well as matter, recalls Tacitus' great predecessors in the dialogical genre, Plato and Cicero. The Ciceronian works invoked most frequently include *De republica* and *De oratore* (Köstermann 1930). Like these Ciceronian dialogues, the dialogue is set just before the death of the main character, Maternus, whose death presumably is caused by his political opposition to the Principate (Saxonhouse 1975: 59, 65–66). As in the Ciceronian works, the dramatic date of the conversation is set in the past and narrated by the author (cf. Tac. *Dial.* 1.1–4 with Cic. *de Orat.* 1.24–27 and Cic. *Rep.* 1.13). Of the Platonic dialogues, the *Dialogus* most extensively echoes Plato's *Gorgias*, unsurprisingly given the *Gorgias*'s theme and its influence on Cicero's *De oratore*.[9] As we noted earlier, one of the main issues raised by the *Gorgias* was the problem of pandering to those who had power. In the case of democratic Athens, according to Socrates the democratic orator was subservient to the people. The *Dialogus* too raises the problem of oratory's subservience to those in power.

Maternus is a senator and orator who plans to turn from oratory and public life to a quiet life of composing tragedies. He is joined by two law-yers, Aper and Secundus, and by Messalla, a young aristocrat. The dialogue consists of three pairs of set speeches arguing on opposite sides of three questions: (1) Maternus and Aper debate the respective merits of com-posing drama and giving speeches (4–13); (2) Messalla and Aper debate whether ancient or modern oratory is superior (14–23); (3) Messalla and Maternus debate the reasons for rhetoric's decline (24–41). Although not apparent at first, all three debates turn out to be related.

The *Dialogus* is an artfully crafted work that must be read and inter-preted with care (Saxonhouse 1975; Bartsch 1994; Kapust 2011b; van den Berg 2014). For example, in the first exchange between Aper and Maternus, it becomes clear that, despite the latter's initial claims, his decision to write tragedy does not constitute a retreat from public life, not when he has recently composed a controversial tragedy about the Republican hero Cato the Younger (2.1). Cato, a Stoic and staunch republican, committed sui-cide rather than endure the rule of Julius Caesar. As Bartsch (1994: 109) notes, Tacitus' readers would readily recognize that the *Cato* was being read in public at the same time as a self-styled contemporary Cato, Helvidius Priscus, was being punished by "the emperor whom Maternus himself has offended and through the *delatores* whose power he deplores." Such activ-ity would eventually cost Maternus his life. Drama rather than oratory is seen as the politically dangerous medium of speech.

---

[9] *Dialogus*'s engagement with Plato's *Gorgias*: Kapust 2011b: 130, 132; Saxonhouse 1975: 57–58.

This and subsequent debates suggest that oratory is less politically dangerous than tragedy because it is less politically effective. The political power of oratory is limited due to oratory's dependence on political institutions. With the abolition of the popular assemblies and reduced scope of the senate, the orator under the Principate finds himself with a limited role and limited audience. The *princeps* was the ultimate arbiter of political speech, and, beginning with Tiberius (ruled 14–37), those who spoke words deemed hostile to the emperor could be prosecuted under the *lex maiestatis* – a type of law (or rather a series of laws) that under the Republic had prohibited acts of treason against the "supremacy" (*maiestas*) of the Roman people (Williamson 2016). The first-century CE expansion of the *lex maiestatis* to include speech and acts held to be hostile to the emperor led to the rise of *delatores*. In return for monetary awards from the imperial treasury and/or for the promise of public honors, these "informers" would accuse Roman citizens of politically seditious or offensive speech. Under the *Lex Iulia maiestatis*, a statute sponsored either by Julius Caesar or Augustus, even slaves and legally handicapped citizens (e.g., women) could make allegations (Williamson 2016: 339). The presence of the informers impacted every area of life, both public and private, leading to a "political psychology of despotism" that leveled and isolated by breaking down social status and breaking apart community; it resulted in "the loss of the will to speak" (Hammer 2014: 345–53, quotes at 345 and 351).

Given our discussion of liberty and status in earlier chapters, it is easy to see how this "psychology of despotism" worked. Tacitus' discussions of liberty across his corpus seem to yield a position similar to that with which we concluded our discussion of republican liberty in chapter 2: liberty is lost both when one is subservient to another's arbitrary will and when the avenues of participation in politics are foreclosed (Strunk 2017: 23–37). The Republican status-saturated Roman honor code remained largely intact under the Principate (see chapter 3) even as the traditional Republican venues for achieving political glory were either abolished or dominated by the *princeps*. The institution of the Principate stifled political speech through this combination of the supremacy of the *princeps*'s arbitrary will and the continuation of the Roman desire for status. That speech was subject to the *princeps*'s arbitrary will meant that one could never be completely sure that political speech would not offend. And the cost of offensive speech was high: the loss of status or life. At the same time, the desire for monetary gain or enhanced public status ensured that there would be some members of society who "embarked" on informing as "a form of life" (Tac. *Ann.* 1.74, with Hammer 2014: 346). As a result of this system, fear caused the Roman elite to self-censure their political speech, even in private. Better to flatter than to risk offense.[10]

The institution of the Principate and corresponding political psychology shapes the discussion of the *Dialogus*. In his argument on behalf of oratory, Aper cites imperial orators Eprius Marcellus and Vibius Crispus as examples of men who have achieved power and fame through oratory. Eprius Marcellus had a reputation as a flatterer (*adulator*) and informer (*delator*; Strunk 2017: 127). And in Tacitus' later account in his *Histories*, we find that for Marcellus and Crispus "oratory as a means toward power and fame had meant nothing more than subjection to the current political system" (Saxonhouse 1975: 60; cf. Strunk 2017: 87; see *Hist.* 4.42–44). The system of flattery and fear that they inhabited and perpetuated ensured oratory's lack of political potency and the security of the prevailing political order. Later in the *Dialogus*, Maternus traces this condition back to the institution of the Principate itself. Under Augustus there was "continuous leisure (*otium*) for the people and perpetual tranquility for the senate; the very great order imposed by the *princeps* had pacified eloquence itself, as it also had everything else" (38.2; cf. *Ann.* 3.28). Lost along with eloquence was republican liberty (*libertas*; 27.3).

Maternus' emphasis of peace and order points to another crucial reason why the diminished importance of Republican institutions under the Principate resulted in the loss of republican oratory and liberty: the loss of such institutions eliminated the conflict these institutions presupposed and supported. Conflict is to the great political oratory of the Republican *contio* as air is to fire. Just as air fuels fire, so conflict and motion fuels and fans republican rhetoric (36.1). Readers familiar with the *Federalist Papers* will recall that Madison uses the same metaphor when comparing liberty and faction in *Federalist* 10.

Despite his concerns with faction, Madison suggests that the abolition of liberty is too great a price to pay for the elimination of faction. At least on the face of it, Maternus comes to a different assessment. The diminished influence enjoyed by orators under the Principate corresponds to the existing *res publica* that is "well-ordered, peaceful, and prosperous" (36.2). By contrast the grand old Republican oratory is "a foster-child of license (*alumna licentiae*)," which "does not arise in well-ordered civic communities" (*in bene constitutis civitatibus*; 40.2). With these quotations, Maternus is subverting Cicero, who had identified the "prosperous" political society with the Roman Republican constitution (Cic. *Rep.* 4.3; 5.8; Mayer

[10] Status and the honor code in Tacitus: see chapter 3. Fear: Hammer 2014: 345–53; Strunk 2017: 36.

2001: 211). Likewise, in his *Brutus* (45) Cicero argues that Republican oratory is the "companion of peace and friend of leisure, a foster-child (*alumna*), so to speak, of an already well-ordered civic community" (*bene constitutae civitatis*). A peaceful civic community is a necessary (though perhaps not sufficient) condition for oratory.[11]

In so appropriating Cicero's language, Maternus is denying that the Republican constitution was as "well-ordered" and as productive of liberty (*libertas*) as republicans had supposed. Instead, he suggests that Republican institutions such as the *contio* served as the loci for "factions among the aristocracy and the constant power struggles of the senate against the plebs. Even if all of these in turn tore the *res publica* to shreds, nevertheless they sustained the oratory of those times" (36.3–4). For Maternus looking back on the Republic, civil unrest appears to accompany and produce great oratory; the greatness of a Cicero requires the threat of a Catiline (37.6). Surely such unrest is too steep a price to pay for republican liberty?

What is more, Maternus suggests that republican thought has foolishly mistaken license (*licentia*) for liberty (*libertas*; 40.2). The term *licentia*, used at 36.2 and 40.2, goes back to Cicero's translation of Socrates' condemnation in Plato's *Republic* of a democratic freedom that assumes a radical equality (Cic. *Rep.* 1.66–68; Pl. *R.* 8.562d; see Mayer 2001: 199–200). In the hands of Maternus, the vocabulary used by Cicero to dismiss democracy is now applied to the Republican constitution. At the end of the day, Rome's constitution is grouped with the democratic constitutions of Rhodes and Athens. In these regimes, oratory flourished but "all power was in the hands of the people" (40.3). The problem with these democracies and Republican Rome alike is that assemblies require the ignorant multitude to make decisions about political matters (41.4). This is a recipe for tumult. Instead, decisions should be made by "the single wisest man" (41.4). This will likely eliminate rhetoric, as was the case at Macedon and Persia (40.3), but this is a small price to pay for peace and order. Arguing from the history of the late Republic, Maternus has anticipated Hobbes's later criticism of rhetoric: politics will remain tumultuous until rhetoric is in the hands of a single sovereign.

Maternus' closing speech in which he argues for monarchy and against republicanism seems to clash with his willingness to take risks in venerating the Republican hero Cato. Commentators have offered several solutions: perhaps Maternus' praise of the emperor is ironic; perhaps we are to read his devotion to Cato as innocent and imprudent; or perhaps he

---

[11] The *Dialogus* and the *Brutus*: Mayer 2001: 211; Gowing 2005: 117–20.

is intentionally employing "doublespeak," language designed to offer different meanings to his different republican and pro-imperial audiences.[12]

It is important to note that Maternus' critique of republican rhetoric links oratory to the type of conflict associated with the breakdown of the Republican constitution, whereas Cicero, in the very passage from the *Brutus* cited by Maternus, links effective rhetoric to a functioning republican constitution. Cicero grants that rhetoric can't function if a constitution isn't already established, if a commonwealth is constantly engaged in war, or if it is "constrained and shackled by the mastery of kings" (*Brut.* 45). Likewise, while Cicero's *De republica* identifies the mixed constitution as a prosperous and stable regime in the passages alluded to by Maternus, book 2 of Cicero's work makes clear that the Republican constitution provides an ordered system that allows for conflict while limiting its effects. Thus, Maternus does not accurately capture the Republican relationship between conflict and oratory. Republican oratory is not the result of conflict *simpliciter* but conflict channeled through a republican constitution and institutions.

Whatever Maternus' reasons for criticizing the Republic and praising the imperial system, he does not essentially disagree with the theoretical point at the heart of republican thought, namely, that rhetoric and liberty rely on a republican constitution. Maternus himself notes that ancient liberty and genuinely powerful rhetoric are both absent under the Principate (27.3; 38.2). Republican rhetoric is no longer an option because of the Principate; with the Republican constitution gone, attempts to reform the system from within lead only to subservience, as in the case of Eprius Marcellus and Vibius Crispus (8.1). Thus, one who wants to have real political power to exercise change without being reduced to flattery must go outside the traditional venues for oratory, now crabbed and subservient to the emperor.

Maternus' solution is theater. Here, unlike in the senate, there is no opportunity for debate or deliberation; however, like the Republican *contio*, the theatre does provide a popular audience before whom the dramatist can make a case without submitting to the arbitrary will of the *princeps*, an audience of one. In the end, the imperial poet, writing plays to be performed before a crowd in the theater, is "the closest approximation to the republican orator" (Bartsch 1994: 118). Drama, on which Cicero had drawn to convey the task of the Republican orator, has replaced oratory as the central means of delivering free and critical political speech.

---

[12] Ironic: Saxonhouse 1975. Imprudent: Kapust 2011b: 130. Doublespeak: Bartsch 1994: 115.

Conclusion

On a first reading, the major texts on rhetoric by Cicero, Quintilian, and Tacitus might well come across to modern readers as inaccessible, dry, and irrelevant for contemporary politics. Nothing could be further from the truth, as my experience teaching these texts has shown me. Indeed, fewer works of either Greek or Roman political thought provoke a more vigorous response from my students. Equipped with terminology from Quintilian, we can, for instance, identify and analyze the widespread use of rhetorical redescription that characterizes the current factious state of American politics no less than the Roman Republic of Sallust's day.

Or consider Tacitus' discussion of flattery and the suppression of political speech. Some educators and observers have suggested that the increasingly common practice on American university campuses of reporting incidents of bias (including biased speech) to "bias response teams" in pursuit of the laudable goal of reducing bias and discrimination might have the unintended side effect of creating an environment in which faculty and students avoid frank conversations about difficult issues out of fear of causing offense – a fear that is enhanced by uncertainty about what speech is liable to be perceived as offensive. Similarly, outside of the university, there is increased worry that social media may enable an environment of mutual surveillance that contributes to conformity out of a fear of being "publicly shamed."[13] My students find Tacitus' account of the psychology behind frank speech and its loss valuable to reflect on as they work out their own thoughts on these difficult issues.

This is not to say that they should recognize their own situation in Tacitus' work. There are significant differences between America and Rome to be considered. For instance, America has political and legal institutions protecting free speech unknown to imperial Rome. Similarly, shame and honor were much stronger motivating forces for the Romans than for contemporary Americans. But the differences themselves contribute to the value of these ancient texts for modern readers. By reading Tacitus we enter into a cultural, political, and legal framework very different from our own. But in the context of this foreign framework, we encounter familiar or at least recognizable concerns. (For more on this approach to the contemporary use of Roman political thought, see the book's conclusion.)[14]

---

[13] "Rhetorical redescription" (and classical rhetoric more broadly) in the 2016 United States presidential election: J. W. Atkins 2016. Bias task forces: Snyder and Khalid 2016. Public shaming: Ronson 2015.
[14] For self-censorship as a phenomenon both ancient and modern, see Watts 2014.

In addition to speaking to such timely issues, Roman texts on rhetoric squarely articulated and confronted perennial criticisms of rhetoric: rhetoric falls short of the rational standards required for decision-making, deliberation, and judgment; it inescapably leads to flattery, manipulation, and deep political division. Cicero, Quintilian, and Tacitus, contemplating first the assault on (Cicero) and then the loss of (Quintilian and Tacitus) republican institutions, show the important relationship between rhetoric, judgment, political culture, and political institutions. Rhetoric depends for its political efficacy on public institutions and political culture. However, it also contributes to the common ethos necessary for shared, and hence truly political, judgments. Thus, to rhetoric's critics, the Roman tradition offers the following counter-claim: despite the dangers that attend rhetoric, to abandon oratory is to abandon all hope for *political* deliberation and judgment.

CHAPTER 6

Civil Religion

Republican Civil Religion: Ancient and Modern

The term "civil religion" was introduced into modern political thought by Jean-Jacques Rousseau in the concluding chapter of his *On the Social Contract* (1762). Because "no state has ever been founded without religion serving as its base" (4.8; trans. Cress), Rousseau considers the political efficacy of a number of historic and current religions. The "religion of man," Christianity as represented by Jesus in the New Testament Gospels, although in Rousseau's estimation true, was too heavenly minded to do much civic good. Far more politically useful (but less true) was the "religion of the citizen" – ancient paganism. However, returning to paganism in post-Reformation Europe was not feasible. After considering these and other historical religions, Rousseau sketches his own civil religion. Its principles are general and minimal; they must be embraced and followed by all good citizens on pain of banishment or death. They include the following: (1) The existence of a powerful, intelligent, beneficent, provident divinity; (2) the afterlife; (3) the happiness of the just and the punishment of the wicked; (4) the sanctity of the social contract and law; and (5) the intolerance of intolerance. In addition to these five, Rousseau is adamant that the same rulers should oversee both religious and state affairs.

Rousseau may have coined the term "civil religion," but the basic concept of a religion that supports political society was an important idea in Rome. The Republican polymath Marcus Terentius Varro (116–27 BCE) used the term "civil theology" (*civilis theologia*) to describe "everything that a political community ... claims to be necessary for the gods to receive proper worship, expressed at Rome by the notion of maintaining the *pax deorum*, the good-will of the gods" (Rüpke 2007: 130). In return for this worship, the gods (the Romans were polytheists) protected and upheld the

136

political community. The Romans had a particular name, *sacra publica*, for those rites that a community undertakes to fulfill its duty to the gods who sustain its social order. Religion was a fundamental part of Roman political culture, as Polybius recognized when he treated it as the foundation of the Roman *politeia* in book 6 of his *History* (6.56.6–7; see chapter 1). Modern notions of religion, which frequently associate belief in God, gods, or the divine with the private expression of the individual conscience, open up cleavages between religion and politics unknown to the Romans, who integrated religious practices seamlessly into the political institutions and practices that defined their constitution (see below).

Cicero provides the fullest theoretical treatment of Roman civil religion in works such as *De natura deorum*, *De divinatione*, and, especially important for our purposes, *De legibus*. Designed as a companion piece for his *De republica* and modeled on Plato's *Laws*, Cicero's *De legibus* is best known for its account of natural law in book 1. However, book 2 provides an extensive religious law code designed to fit the Roman mixed constitution described in *De republica*. Cicero draws these laws from a number of sources, including the Roman religious tradition, the Twelve Tables, Greek lawgivers such as Solon, Plato's *Laws*, and his own experience (Dyck 2004: 290).

Like Rousseau, Cicero supposes that religious laws are most fundamental to establishing a commonwealth (*Leg.* 2.69). Other similarities between the two accounts exist as well. Like Rousseau, Cicero argues for the existence of powerful, intelligent, provident gods (2.15); he also affirms an afterlife and the happiness of the just and punishment of the wicked (2.15, 19, 24). As Rousseau maintains the sacredness of the social contract and his laws, so Cicero invokes the presence of the gods to ensure the sacredness of the community of citizens (*sancta societas civium*; 2.16). The public priest should condemn as impious violations of the law code (2.22; cf. 2.37). Finally, Cicero, like other Romans, would have agreed with Rousseau's later claim that the same individuals should administer the affairs of religion and state – a point Cicero most forcefully made in an earlier speech before the pontifical college in 57 BCE (*Dom.* 1).

Despite these similarities, the differences between Rousseau and Cicero are substantial. Cicero follows Plato in providing an in-depth commentary on his religious laws, whereas Rousseau sets himself apart from his predecessors by offering his principles with no substantial commentary. Second, there is far more specificity to Cicero's law code – unlike Rousseau, Cicero names specific priesthoods, rites, and customs.

The difference in structure and detail points to deeper philosophical differences. Cicero believes that there should be an intimate relationship between civil religion and the Roman constitution: the constitution should guide the religious laws, and the religious laws should support the constitution (2.23, 30). For Rousseau, on the other hand, severing religion from a polity's constitution was important: "Since, therefore, each religion was uniquely tied to the laws of the state which prescribed it, there was no other way of converting a people except by enslaving it, nor any other missionaries than conquerors" (4.8; trans. Cress). From Rousseau's point of view, the danger in the ancient republican constitutional embodiment of religious principles was that it invited imperial conquest and slavery.

The thinness of Rousseau's civil religion can in part be explained as an attempt to promote tolerance – a key driving force behind Rousseau's civil religion. This tolerance is limited to those who are prepared to tolerate others, not only in the context of civil society but also in the theological realm – "it is impossible to live in peace with those one believes to be damned" (4.8; trans. Cress). Another limit to toleration concerns those who agree to, and then break, the laws of political society. Indeed, one might conceive of the chief function of Rousseau's civil religion as providing a mechanism to sanctify the laws of the state: for the most part, citizens may believe whatever they want in private, so long as their deeds don't contravene the laws of the state. Rousseau's concern with action over belief shares an affinity with Roman civil religion, which emphasizes cult practice and ritual. Still, on the face of it, there appears to be a difference here between Cicero and Rousseau: Cicero's law code codifies religious intolerance, proscribing certain religious rites (2.21).

These differences between Rousseau and Cicero set the agenda for this chapter, which examines Roman civil religion. What is the relationship between civil religion and the constitution at Rome under the Republic and under the Principate? What is religious toleration? Did the Roman regimes practice it? What role, if any, did political form play in promoting toleration? What arguments, if any, did Romans and inhabitants of the Roman world develop on behalf of toleration? Was Rousseau justified in worrying about ancient republican civil religion's potential for driving imperialism? Underlying many of these questions is a concern with the relationship between universal principles and particular religious practices, a challenge acknowledged by both Cicero and Rousseau, as well as by influential treatments of civil religion in our own day.

Civil Religion, Republican Institutions, and the Mixed Constitution

As modern scholars correctly note, "the religion of later republican Rome reflected closely the ideas and institutions characteristic of the whole republican order" (Beard, North, and Price 1998, 1: 54). Under the Republic, the interconnection between politics and religion encompassed magistracies, institutions, and political culture. Though priesthoods were technically not magistracies, Roman priests, like magistrates, wore the purple-bordered *toga praetexta*, and senior magistrates at Rome and generals in the field regularly performed religious sacrifices. Indeed, most priests were also magistrates or ex-magistrates. Meetings of the senate, popular assemblies, and elections were preceded by the taking of auspices, in which presiding magistrates in consultation with priests (augurs) sought to determine the will of the gods through such means as studying the flight and behavior of birds, interpreting thunder and lightning, or seeing if sacred chickens would eat special food. The taking of auspices designated a space as sacred, as a *templum*. The Roman senate always met in a *templum*. Similarly, the taking of auspices made elections religious as well as political events (Beard, North, and Price 1998, 1: 21–23; Rüpke 2007). The English terms "political" and "religious," "sacred" and "secular," tend to imply a sharp contrast unknown to the Romans.

Beard, North, and Price have argued that the close connection between politics and religion led to the development of a particularly *"republican type of religion"* characterized by the diffusion and decentralization of religious authority among the various priesthoods (1998, 1: 61; emphasis original). In addition to the augurs, there were three other colleges of priests, the *pontifices, fetiales,* and *duoviri.* The *pontifices* advised on law, especially matters of family law (e.g., wills, adoption, inheritance), kept annual records of important public events, and were in charge of the calendar, including dates for festivals and for the meetings of the assemblies, senate, and courts. The *fetiales* advised the senate on aspects of foreign policy and, according to Livy, originally served as ambassadors, messengers, and possessed the right to declare war (Livy 1.32.6–14; cf. Cic. *Leg.* 2.21; see further chapter 7). The *duoviri* were in charge of the Sibylline Books, which contained oracles in Greek verse consulted during times of crisis.

Livy's history of the Republic presents the priesthoods as subject to the same political pressures as political institutions and offices. For example, as we saw in chapter 2, Livy's narration of the struggle of the orders between the plebs and patricians included plebeian efforts to open up magistracies formerly reserved for patricians. Livy's telling of the story similarly presents the priesthoods as being gradually opened to the plebeians, a process that concluded in 300 BCE with the passage of the *Lex Ogulnia*, a law that added four plebeians to the pontifical college and five to the augural college, bringing their total numbers to eight and nine, respectively (Livy 10.9.1–2).

In Cicero's estimation, the republican nature of civil religion extended beyond the decentralization of the powers of the various priesthoods to include the very character of the Roman constitution. Thus when he proposed his religious laws, he advised that they should be those that maintain and support the Roman constitution (*Leg.* 2.23). In particular, Cicero ensured that his laws corresponded to the mixed constitution described in *De republica*.

De republica advocates an "equitable" constitutional balance between a popular element based on liberty and equality, and an aristocratic element emphasizing the authority (*auctoritas*) and judgment (*consilium*) of the senate (2.57; cf. 1.69). This is reflected in the religious code of the *De legibus*. For instance, luxury should be removed from worship since "if we want poverty and riches to be equitable (*aequalis*) among human beings, why should we prohibit poverty from access to the gods by adding an expense to the rites?" (2.25). As *De republica* 2.27 makes clear, this "popular" element was one of the religious reforms to the Roman constitution ascribed to Numa, the second king of Rome known as the founder of Rome's religious system. Cicero presents the Roman constitution as gradually acquiring some popular-aristocratic features characteristic of the Republican mixed constitution already under the early monarchy. Similarly, Cicero's commentary on religious laws emphasizes that part of the value in these laws lies in the aristocracy's capacity through them to guide the people and check the popular excesses that characterize pure democracies. In Cicero's opinion, the Roman mixed constitution provides guidance for the people – *consilium* and *auctoritas* – and Cicero's religious legislation seeks to contribute to this constitutional feature. As Cicero notes again, "it upholds the commonwealth [to ensure] that the people (*populus*) are always needing the judgment (*consilium*) and authority (*auctoritas*) of the nobility" (2.30).

Specific religious institutions and priesthoods are also designed to ensure that the mixed constitution functions well. Consider augury, which Cicero knew well, as he himself was a member of the augural college. The practice of taking auspices is useful to the commonwealth (*Leg.* 2.32). Augurs may serve the commonwealth by using their powers to delay business in the senate and to dissolve popular assemblies at especially important times. Moreover, the taking of auspices is useful inasmuch as it adds an element of sacrosanctity to various political and military initiatives. Because of their political utility, Cicero publicly defends augury and divination, even if privately he may have had doubts about the validity of divination (cf. *Div.* 2.28, 32, 70, 75). As Varro once reportedly said in regard to the philosophical critique of popular religious practice, some teachings "our ears are able to bear more easily within the walls of the lecture hall than outside in the forum" (August. *C.D.* 6.5).[1]

On Cicero's aristocratic view, the powers of augurs are perhaps most important when it comes to popular assemblies, the "democratic" component of the mixed constitution. The augurs' capacity to dissolve popular assemblies helps to guard against what Cicero sees as a potential hazard of popular rule: the proneness of popular assemblies stirred by passion to act in haste and make rash decisions. From as early as Thucydides, this has been a criticism of democracies such as Athens. Elsewhere in Cicero's writings, he criticized the Athenian democracy for "the immoderate freedom and license of her assemblies," which led to many hasty and poor decisions (*Flac.* 16). Augurs may use their powers to delay votes in the assembly in order to give the people's passions an opportunity to cool. A judicious use of this power allows the augurs to serve the *res publica* in times of great crisis by thwarting unjust or unwise legislation (3.27, 43).

Roman Civil Religion and the Principate

Just as Augustus claimed to have restored the Republic, so he represented himself as having restored a civil religion neglected during the turbulence of civil war. The Roman biographer Suetonius reviews Augustus' renewal of religious cult practices (*Augustus* 29–31) along with his other conduct "in power and magistracies" (*Aug.* 61). Augustus was known for his *pietas* or devotion to the gods, a virtue that also has important social and political significance. Given the interconnection between the polity and religion under the Republic, it is unsurprising to see religious reforms accompanying Augustan political reforms (see further Galinksy 1996: ch. 6).

Augustus' carefully calibrated religious reforms had two components (Scheid 2005). First, Augustus restored Republican religious institutions, traditions, and buildings in a way that displayed his piety and respect for

---

[1] Cicero on divination: Beard 1986; Schofield 1986. Augury: Linderski 1986 (augural law); Linderski 1995 (Cicero's views).

Republican traditions. Second, he established an imperial cult at Rome as well as in Italy. This second component of Augustus' religious reform subtly undercut the apparent republicanism of the first. In 12 CE, Augustus was elected *pontifex maximus*, took control of the Sibylline Books, and moved the pontifical residency from its traditional location in the Forum to his house on the Palatine hill. He transformed his private residence into a palace shared with Vesta and Apollo. The former was the goddess of hearth and home whose fires Rome's founder, Aeneas, had transported from Troy (Vergil, *Aeneid* 2.296, 567); the latter was the god of music, prophecy, and the sun. As Ovid writes, "Vesta has been received by her relative's home – so the senators have rightly decreed. Phoebus Apollo occupies one part; another part has been given to Vesta; the remaining third part, Augustus himself occupies ... A single house holds three eternal gods" (*Fasti* 4.949–54). Since Augustus never claimed to be worshiped as a god, Ovid is engaging in either flattery or biting irony, depending on one's understanding of Ovid's general stance towards the Principate (Fantham 1995; 1998). In either case, the outcome of the event Ovid describes remains the same: Augustus has literally made the *res publica* his private *domus* – a phenomenon we observed from different vantage points in chapters 1 and 2. From Augustus' time on, the emperor alone became *pontifex maximus*, the head of Roman civil religion (Beard, North, Price 1998, 1: 188–92).

The quotation from Ovid counts Augustus as a god along with Vesta and Apollo. The emperor's divinization was another component of the development of the imperial cult. Once again, Augustus moved cautiously, portraying himself as a pious respecter of Republican tradition. In 19 BCE upon returning to Rome from a campaign, Augustus refused most of the honors offered by the senate but did accept a festival to Fortuna Redux – the goddess of safe return. But there was a twist: the senate named the holiday *Augustalia*, as if the god to be honored were actually Augustus (*Res Gestae* 11, with Scheid 2005: 190). In 2 BCE, the same year the senate bestowed on Augustus the title of "father of the fatherland," the Temple of Mars Ultor (Mars the Avenger) was dedicated, an act that reinforced Augustus' lineage that ran through Julius Caesar back to the goddess Venus (Cartledge 2016: 269). By linking the *princeps* to the legendary founders of Rome, Aeneas and Romulus, the architecture and imagery of the temple, like that of all other Augustan temples, was carefully calibrated to communicate Augustus' greatness (Zanker 1988: 110–18). Even though Augustus, like his adoptive father Julius Caesar, became divinized only after his death, he laid the groundwork for the emperor to be regarded as the vice-regent of the gods while alive and a god after death.

While at Rome the developing imperial cult led to the consolidation of the powers of the priesthoods into the hands of Augustus, when one looks outward to the provinces, one finds a very decentralized religious order (G. Woolf 2012: 121). As in the "polis religion" that characterized the Greek world, religion in the Roman Empire was rooted in the local civic customs and institutions of the various cities under Roman rule.[2] As Roman rule spread, Roman religion may have been "exported" (see below), but Rome imposed no overarching organizational religious structure. Civil religion remained organized around local customs and civic structures. The Augustan age maintained the late Republican practice of allowing Rome's allies to maintain local customs, laws, institutions, and religious practices – provided only that they upheld the supremacy of Rome (Nicolet 1980: 46).

This picture remained broadly accurate until 249, when Emperor Trajan Decius issued an edict that all of the inhabitants of the Roman Empire must support the welfare of Rome by sacrificing to the Roman pagan gods and eating the sacrificial meat. Local magistrates had the responsibility of enforcing this edict. We do not know Decius' motives behind issuing the edict, and, though a number of different sources convey its gist, the edict's exact words have not survived. But its effects were undeniable. It led to the centrally organized and widespread persecution of Christians, who refused to worship pagan gods, in place of the previous local, scattered, and ad hoc persecutions. Unsurprisingly, scholarly discussion of this edict usually occurs in the context of religious persecution (see below). However, this global persecution reflected a general shift in policy represented by the edict. There was now a universalized religious practice to which individuals were expected to conform. As James Rives (1999: 152) points out, "by insisting that every inhabitant of the Roman Empire had a specific and immediate religious obligation to the imperial government," Decius established a single, "thin," "religion of the Roman Empire." In this we can find a parallel to the expansion of citizenship in the late Republic and Principate, which we examined in chapter 3. Just as the universalization of citizenship imposed a superordinate structure upon a mishmash of local citizenship practices, so too imperial Roman civil religion added order to the diverse local cult practices.[3]

To sum up the argument of the last two sections, Roman history reveals a relationship between civil religion and regime type. The Republic saw the

---

[2] Polis religion: Sourvinou-Inwood 1990; cf. the critique by Kindt 2012.
[3] Edict of Decius: Rives 1999; G. Clarke 2005: 625–35.

decentralization of the powers of the priesthood, whereas the imperial cult that began with Augustus featured the consolidation of religious authority in the hands of the *princeps*. The third century CE saw attempts to unify Roman rule with a universal but thin notion of civil religion as well as citizenship. Finally, looking at the matter from a theoretical perspective, Cicero argued for a close relationship between the Republican mixed constitution and the civic institution of religion.

Civil Religion and Roman Toleration

Rome has a reputation for being especially tolerant of foreign religions (MacMullen 1981: 2). From the outset, the Romans had a habit of appropriating other gods and religious practices. As we saw above, Aeneas brought Vesta along with his household gods from Troy to Italy. Many of the gods in the Roman pantheon had Greek equivalents, e.g., Jupiter, Juno, and Minerva corresponded respectively to Zeus, Hera, and Athena. Rome also assimilated a number of foreign cults such as Cybele, "The Great Mother," from Asia Minor, Isis and Osiris from Egypt, and Sybil, priestess of Apollo, from the Greek colony of Cumae. But does this openness to foreign deities signify "tolerance"?

Not necessarily. Rome's "openness" to foreign gods must be placed in the context of its imperial expansion. The Romans believed foreign cities to be protected by their gods. If the Romans could appropriate or assimilate foreign gods for themselves, they thought they could gain an advantage over their enemies. The Romans had a name for the process – *evocatio* – "a summoning away." For example, Livy (5.21.1–7) records how the Roman dictator Camillus in 396 BCE attempted "to summon away" Juno, the patron goddess of the Etruscan city of Veii. After the Roman victory, "Queen Juno," as the Romans called her, received a temple on the Aventine hill in Rome. Whatever we may be speaking of when we speak of toleration, we certainly do not have in mind the cultural appropriation of another's gods as a means of conquest! As Peter Garnsey writes (1984: 8), "Roman-style polytheism was disposed to expand and absorb or at least neutralize other gods, not to tolerate them."

To leave our discussion of toleration there, however, would be to miss out on an important opportunity to think about the concept offered by the Roman world. Let's begin by defining toleration. Care is needed. Discussions of toleration often link the idea to modern liberal notions such as the recognition of human moral autonomy, human rights, and the inherent value of diversity. As a result of these associations, some scholars view toleration as a "distinctly modern" concept with no relevance to the ancient world. However, as Rainer Forst (2013) has argued in his important, historically rich study of toleration, such a position mistakes a particular *conception* of toleration for the more general *concept* itself. Most generally, toleration aims at the peaceful coexistence of individuals and groups within a political community when the beliefs and practices of one or more individuals and groups are believed by others to be false, bad, or harmful. It requires the exercise of restraint or forbearance on the part of those with the power to persecute those whose views or practices they find repugnant. A regime may be characterized as tolerant if its rulers refuse, for any number of reasons, to take action against people in its midst with whom they disagree.[4]

One pathway into the concept of toleration at Rome begins with the mistaken connection between toleration and the number of gods worshiped. Rousseau's contemporary, the Scottish philosopher David Hume, famously argued in chapter 9 of his *Natural History of Religion* that polytheistic religions were tolerant of minority and foreign religious practices, and that monotheistic religions were inherently intolerant. It is only mildly ironic in this context to note that Rousseau's tolerant civil religion is monotheistic, whereas Cicero's polytheistic civil religion proscribes certain religious rites (*Leg.* 2.21). In his commentary on the relevant provision of the law code, Cicero endorses the "strictness of our ancestors in these matters," which was on full display when the Roman senate regulated the religious practice of the Bacchanals in 186 BCE (2.37). It is worth lingering for a moment on this historic example of intolerance by polytheistic Rome, as it will point us towards a principle to account for religious toleration and its limits with much greater explanatory power than the number of gods of a given regime's civil religion.

The Bacchanalia were festivals related to the cult of Bacchus (known as Dionysus to the Greeks), the god of wine. The cult was of foreign origin, coming to Rome from Greek "colonies" in southern Italy, and contained elements of the Greek mystery religions. Livy condemned their nocturnal meetings as violent, drunken orgies (39.8). But it is unlikely that the senate suppressed this group simply because of immorality. In his reconstruction of the cult, John North argues that it consisted of groups of cells widely spread throughout Italy. These cells were composed of a broad-based

---

[4] Modern toleration linked to autonomy, human rights, and diversity as valuable: Streeter 2006: 231; cf. Mendus 1988. Toleration as "distinctively modern": Beard, North, and Price 1998, 1: 212. My general definition of the concept of toleration is indebted to Garnsey 1984 and Forst 2013: ch. 1.

membership (e.g., slave/free, Roman/non-Roman, male/female) bound by oaths, who pooled a common fund administered by the group, and each of which had its own organizational structure. Membership in the cult was voluntary. Taken together these aspects of the cult of Bacchus seem to have placed it outside "the normal basis of State control and supervision of religion" as well as "the normal regulations and structure of the life of the city" (North 2003: 212). As such, Livy presents the cult of Bacchus as constituting a "second nation" (*alter populus*; 39.13.14). It makes its participants unfit to fulfill basic civic duties like serving in the military (39.15.13). In a word, participation in this alternative regime challenged *pietas* or devotion to the republic (Riedl 2010: 53–54). Apparently Roman senators could not tolerate the cult of Bacchus because they saw it as a threat to the Roman order.

Consequently, the senate passed a decree strictly regulating the worship of Bacchus. The decree did not eliminate the cult, but struck at the heart of the features that made it an alternative regime. Its common fund was eliminated, and its organizational structure dismantled. Broad-based participation cutting across classes was undermined when the number of worshipers at any one time was strictly limited; participants first had to apply to the senate. Violation of this decree was punishable with death (Warrior 2006b: 85–88).

The Roman senate's treatment of the Bacchanalia illustrates a fundamental principle accounting for the limits of a regime's capacity to tolerate difference: a religion cannot be tolerated when it threatens the foundational principle(s) of the constitution and the way of life that defines it.[5] As Matthias Riedl observes (2010: 54), "religious toleration is, in the first place, not a question of polytheism or monotheism. Toleration is possible as long as the constitutive self-understanding of a society is not endangered, as long as the logic of the political order, from which the dominant part of the society derives the meaning of its existence, is not questioned." Interestingly, this principle explaining the limits of toleration may have been at play in antiquity's most famous case of polytheistic intolerance, the conviction and execution of Socrates for (among other charges) acts of impiety. From the perspective of the Athenian jury, Socrates' impiety – not duly acknowledging the gods of the city and introducing "other new divinities" – made him a threat to the democratic community (Cartledge 2009: 76–90).

If toleration is related to the political order, then one might gain insight into political and religious toleration by studying how and to what extent

---

[5] This is similar to what Forst (2013: 27–28) calls the "permissive conception" of toleration.

toleration is achieved by various political forms. This is Michael Walzer's project in *On Toleration*. Tolerance is a chief liberal-democratic virtue, but liberal democracies according to Walzer do not necessarily promote toleration most effectively. Instead, Walzer (1997: 15) surprisingly suggests, "imperial rule is historically the most successful way of incorporating difference and facilitating (requiring is more accurate) peaceful coexistence." An imperial regime counts as a "regime of toleration" in so far as imperial officials tolerate the religious practices of various communities under their rule, even if members of these separate communities promote a way of life that is closed to members of other religious traditions under the same imperial rule. The imperial officials are concerned with communities rather than individuals. So long as imperial rule is peacefully upheld, the imperial magistrates don't usually interfere with the internal lives of these communities. The secret to the imperial regime's tolerance is ironically that which makes this form of rule most distasteful from a liberal-democratic perspective: its autocratic, distant, disinterested nature leads to an even-handedness in its treatment of subject communities (Walzer 1997: 14–15).

Forst (2013: 19) has suggested that Walzer's imperial "regimes of toleration" does not really capture the idea of toleration since it by definition requires the disapproval of rather than indifference to "tolerated" views or practices. Despite this objection, Walzer's model still has the potential to describe toleration. First, one could conceivably construe the disinterestedness of an imperial regime as implying not that imperial officials hold no negative value judgments about the beliefs of various communities but that the force of these negative judgments has been blunted and relativized by the officials' larger loyalty to the peace and order of the empire. Second, in such an imperial regime, one might see toleration as describing not only the "vertical" relationship between magistrates and subjects but also the "horizontal" relationship among communities. The threat of repercussion by imperial magistrates for any disorderly conduct might incentivize communities to endure the presence of other communities with which they passionately disagree. With these possibilities in mind, let's look closer at whether Walzer's description of imperial regimes of toleration accurately describes imperial Rome. We will take as our test cases the Roman regime's treatment of Jews and Christians, arguably the best-known instances of Roman imperial "tolerance" and "intolerance" of deviant religious groups.[6]

First, Jews. Roman writers frequently, though not invariably, described Judaism as a "superstition" (*superstitio*), a term with negative connotations

---

[6] I borrow the use of "vertical" and "horizontal" in this context from Forst 2013: 6.

(see below). Judaism or Jews are mentioned at least in passing by a number of non-Jewish writers of the late Republic and early Empire. These authors write in a wide range of genres, such as epic poetry (Lucretius, Vergil, Lucan), elegy (Tibullus, Ovid), satire (Horace, Persius, Petronius, Juvenal), history (Curtius Rufus, Livy, Tacitus), oratory (Cicero), didactic (Columella, Quintilian), philosophy (Seneca, Epictetus), grammar (Erotianus), and antiquarian and encyclopedic writings (Varro and Pliny the Elder). Roman writers most frequently commented upon Jewish practices of Sabbath-keeping, dietary restrictions (especially abstaining from pork), circumcision, their worship of a God without images, and their unwillingness to pray to the gods of Roman society. These references to Judaism run the gamut from sympathetic, to amused, to hostile. For example, according to St. Augustine, the first-century BCE polymath Varro implied that the Jewish custom of worshiping their God without an image more closely reflected the devout reverence of the "ancient Romans" than Roman polytheism as practiced in his day (C.D. 4.31). Varro's slightly younger contemporary Cicero, on the other hand, during his successful defense of Lucius Valerius Flaccus against charges of corruption, portrays Judaism as "a barbaric superstition" that was deeply incompatible with Roman values and ancestral institutions (Flac. 67–69). The hostility with which Romans viewed Judaism increased in the late first and second centuries CE, following the Jewish rebellions of 66–70, 115–17, and 132–35.[7]

Despite the tendency of some elite Romans to mock and scorn Jewish religious practices and customs, imperial Rome generally exhibited tolerance. Until the Great Revolt of 66–70, Rome had granted partial autonomy to the Jewish nation, which was governed by a complicated arrangement involving the Temple priests, the Roman procurator (the overseer of a province appointed by the emperor), the Herodian family, and the governor of Syria (Schwartz 2014: 86–87). Roman authorities would often make special accommodations for Jews by allowing them to live in accordance with their own customs and laws. Edicts promoted toleration by exempting Jews from Roman prohibitions on religious associations ("vertical toleration") or protecting Jews living outside of Judea from persecution by majority groups in their communities ("horizontal toleration").[8] The

[7] For overviews of attitudes of Roman writers towards Judaism and Jews, see Schäfer 1997 and Goodman 2008: ch. 10 (list of Roman authors at 366). Increase in Roman hostility towards Judaism following the Jewish revolts: Goodman 2008: 505.
[8] Hostility towards Jews by Greeks and Egyptians was particularly severe in Alexandria, Egypt in 38 CE, prompting two delegations to Rome. See Philo, Legatio ad Gaium; Josephus, Antiquities of the Jews 18.257–60; Schäfer 1997: ch. 8.

Jewish writer Josephus (37–c. 100 CE), a Jerusalem priest who served as a general for the Jewish forces from the outset of the Great Revolt until he was captured by the Romans in 67, collected a number of documents showing Roman favor to Jews in books 14 and 16 of his *Jewish Antiquities*.

As the favorable decrees collected by Josephus make clear, Roman toleration extended to Jewish communities often originated in response to petitions by Jewish leaders. Until the second century CE, Jews were able make good use of the networks of friendships, favors, and obligations that constituted the Roman system of patronage. Patrons could ask the emperor for favors on behalf of communities. Roman authorities sometimes justified these exceptions by pointing out special services or favors that the Jewish people performed for Rome.

A good example of patronage at work is furnished by Agrippa I, appointed King of Judea by the emperor Claudius in 41 CE. The previous year, Agrippa leveraged his friendship with the emperor Gaius to dissuade him from placing a statue of his likeness in the Temple of Jerusalem to be worshiped. In a letter to Gaius, as reported by a contemporary observer, the Jewish exegete and philosopher Philo of Alexander, Agrippa appealed to a number of factors: his friendship with Gaius, the respect shown to the Temple by Gaius' grandparents and Augustus, and the ancient lineage of the Jewish tradition of worshiping without images.[9] This last point in particular would have appealed to the Roman value of ancestral religious tradition. In fact, one reason why the Romans tolerated Judaism was their belief that, unlike gentile Roman Christians who had abandoned the cults of their ancestors, Jews had always sacrificed only to their own God. The Jews thus did not risk angering the traditional gods of Rome by abandoning them (Goodman 2008: 374).

The Romans were far from uniformly favorable towards and tolerant of Judaism. Jews were expelled from Rome by Tiberius in 19 CE and by Claudius around 49 CE. Following the Jewish defeat in 70 CE, Vespasian levied a special Jewish tax for the rebuilding of the Temple to Jupiter. This annual tax would continue indefinitely, perhaps even to the time of Constantine, as the price for the Jews to continue to practice their ancestral customs (Schwartz 2014: 89). These instances of Roman intolerance of Judaism occurred in the contexts of political or civic upheaval, which necessitated the emperor to act to restore order or "to manipulate his

---

[9] Philo, *Legatio ad Gaium* 278–79, 290–92. This paragraph is indebted to the discussion of patronage by Goodman 2008: 76–85.

image in order to ensure support for his regime" (Goodman 2008: 369–70, 428–33, quote at 442–43).

Now consider Christianity. Jesus and the earliest Christians were Jews, but Christianity gradually separated itself from Judaism. According to Luke's account of the rise of the early church in the Acts of the Apostles, Roman authorities regarded disputes between Christians and Jews with impartial indifference, so long as the resulting civic disturbances were not too great. To single out just one instance, Luke describes how Gallio, proconsul of Achaea and Seneca's older brother, refused the requests by Jewish leaders to judge St. Paul for what Gallio considered to be disputes about Jewish law and religious tradition (Acts 18:12–17). Luke concludes his account of the incident by noting, "none of these matters was a concern for Gallio" (18:17). This seems to be a great example of evenhanded "toleration" of different religions due to imperial indifference.

But the situation looks different when one considers the first persecutions of Christians by Roman authorities in 64, when Nero selected Christians as scapegoats for the fires in Rome (Tac. *Ann.* 15.44). From this time until around 250, persecutions of Christians were sporadic and local.

Why were Christians persecuted? Our evidence from pagan Roman writers is scanty. Tacitus, appropriating a common anti-Jewish motif, notes that Christians were charged for their "hatred of the human race" (*Ann.* 15.44). For Tacitus, Christians were "inferior Jews," a pernicious "superstition" that has left Judea and, through proselytization, has infected Rome (Schäfer 1997: 191).

More instructive is correspondence between Pliny the Younger, serving as governor of Pontus-Bithynia, and the emperor Trajan (c. 112 CE). Pliny outlines his own procedure in dealing with Christians. Non-citizens denounced for their Christianity were executed upon confession, whereas citizens were sent to Rome for trial. Given the vast numbers affected due to the growth of Christianity, Pliny decided to halt the proceedings against Christians and seek advice from Trajan. Perhaps the spread of Christianity – an infectious "superstition" (*superstitio*) – would slow if Christians were offered the opportunity to change their minds (Plin. *Ep. Tra.* 10.96)? Trajan commends Pliny's procedure, and acknowledges that when dealing with religious dissidents there is no general rule that can be indiscriminately applied. Christians "should not be hunted down, but if they are accused and convicted, they must be punished" (10.97).[10]

---

[10] For discussion of Pliny's letter and Trajan's reply, see Sherwin-White 1966. See also Wilken 2003: ch. 1.

It is worth pausing to consider further Pliny's correspondence with Trajan. First, notice that Pliny refers to Christianity as a "superstition." The Latin *superstitio*, often contrasted with *religio*, "correct practice," was, by the time of the first century BCE, a term of disapproval. The boundaries defining what counted as *religio* and *superstitio* were fluid and context-dependent. Practices designated as *superstitio* were those that remained outside the traditional Roman civil religion: these included religions such as Judaism and Christianity, but also private rituals such as soothsaying, nocturnal meetings, and astrology. Classification as a *superstitio* did not in itself constitute grounds for punishment under law. Thus, it is noteworthy that Pliny mentions the damage that Christianity had for a time caused to the local cult practices. Given the relationship between pagan cult practices and civic life, Pliny is likely suggesting that Christianity threatened the local civic order.[11]

Threats against or disturbances of the established civic order were for the Romans a serious matter. One thinks, for instance, of Luke's account in Acts 19 of the civil disturbance in Ephesus as a result of Christianity's threat to the traditional Artemis cult. Luke's narration in the chapter "does not press for 'toleration' of a politically innocuous group but, instead, displays the deep and often troubling cultural destabilization inherent to the early Christian mission" (C. K. Rowe 2009: 49). Given imperial expectations that governors would keep their provinces "settled and orderly" by removing "bad people" from their midst (*Dig.* 1.18.13.pr.; 1.18.3), de Ste. Croix (1963: 16) suggests that provincial authorities may be likely to side against unpopular minority groups like Christians in the interest of maintaining peace. If this is correct, the type of persecution described by Pliny represents an example of an imperial power's commitment to peace and order leading to intolerant persecution rather than to the fair and impartial administration of justice.

Even more significantly, as in the case of the Bacchanalia, Christianity had its own internal order, institutes, and governance separate from that of the pagan civil religion. This order supports a way of life that "maintain[s] that the overall pattern of life that constitutes pagan culture is deeply problematic" (C. K. Rowe 2009: 171). Christians too were "another nation" and thereby a threat to the way of life undergirding Rome's political order. Unsurprisingly, Christianity eventually became one of the targets of a series

---

[11] *Religio* as "correct practice": Streeter 2006: 232. *Religio* vs. *superstitio*: Beard, North, and Price 1998, I: 215–27; Streeter 2006: 232–33; Kahlos 2007: ch. 4. Evolution of *superstitio* into a term of disapproval: Grodzinski 1974.

of laws passed from the first century BCE to the third century CE banning private associations and clubs (Beard, North, Price 1998, 1: 230).

Persecutions continued to be sporadic ad hoc matters under the authority of local magistrates until Decius' 249 edict, discussed in the last section, launched a temporary, widespread persecution resulting in the death of Christians in both the eastern and western portions of the Roman Empire (G. Clarke 2005: 632–35). Under Decius' successor, Trebonianus Gallus (ruled 251–53), this persecution subsided. Christianity was broadly tolerated and troubles were confined to occasional local disturbances. The exceptions were few but significant. In 258 the emperor Valerian (ruled 253–60) began what one historian has described as "a deeply divisive and bloody conflict throughout the empire" when he sent a rescript to the senate directing that officers in the Christian Church should be put to death, and socially prominent Christians should lose their status and property (G. Clarke 2005: 645). And in 303 Diocletian initiated a series of edicts that launched the persecution of Christians across the empire. Persecution (except for a brief revival around 320 in the east under Licinius) gave way to a policy of toleration that was promoted by Constantine from 313. The persecutions under Decius, Valerian, and Diocletian were possible because imperial edicts had moved beyond concern with communities and placed direct religious obligations on individual subjects of the empire.

Our examination of Rome's treatment of Jews and Christians presents a far more complex picture of Rome as an imperial regime of toleration than that suggested by Walzer's model. In the case of Jews, in important instances both the vertical toleration by Roman authorities and the horizontal toleration by other religious and ethnic groups were achieved by the partial granting of favors through the system of patronage rather than through a distant, detached, impartial authority. Moreover, as both the cases of Christians and Jews attest, the imperial desire for peace and order may lead to the intolerant punishment of minority groups rather than to tolerant, dispassionate, even-handed treatment. However, one key feature of Walzer's model is generally affirmed: the imperial regime of toleration's focus on communities rather than individuals. In the Roman Empire, global persecutions did not occur until the imperial cult had to do with individuals rather than with groups.

Arguments for Toleration

Toleration grounded on alliances and the need of the regime's rulers to maintain peace, order, and stability has drawbacks, as we have seen.

Dependent upon the stability of the local and imperial political orders, toleration could be revoked without warning. Moreover, toleration was extended unevenly among different groups, as it relied upon the extent to which groups were seen as a threat to the predominant civic order. For both Christianity and Judaism, competition between their own religious institutions and the Roman civil religion caused conflict with Rome.[12] Thus, those liable to face persecution might look to articulate new reasons for toleration. Let's consider a few of the most important.

The word *tolerantia* ("endurance") first occurs in Cicero's *Paradoxa Stoicorum*, where he describes the "endurance of fortune" as a virtue of the Stoic sage (27), and later in the writings of Seneca. This use of *tolerantia* translates the Greek verb *hupomenô* (to endure, to abide patiently). As John Lombardini (2015) has shown, later Greek Stoics such as Epictetus and Marcus Aurelius employed the verb *anechô* and its cognates to describe the obligation that human beings have to "put up with" or tolerate those with whom we disagree. According to these Stoics, "tolerant" human beings correctly recognize that the incorrect beliefs of others cannot impair their own happiness, and that, at any rate, they lack the capacity to correct others' beliefs.

"Endurance" (*hupomonê, tolerantia*) and the acknowledgment of the limits of our responsibility to judge others' beliefs would likewise play an important role in early Christian discussions about toleration. For instance, in his work *De bono patientiae* (*On the Good of Patience*), the third-century Carthaginian bishop Cyprian set *tolerantia* among the Christian virtues of humility, mercy, patience, and love. Jesus showed these and other virtues "in patiently enduring the Jews" (*in Iudaeis tolerandis*); by his humility and humiliation, he set an example for Christians to follow (6). Similarly, St. Paul joined the virtue of endurance (*tolerantia*) to love (15). (Cyprian cites 1 Corinthians 13:7: "Love endures all things.") Therefore, Christians should love one another "in mutual forbearance" (*mutua tolerantia*), and "by the strength of forbearance" (*firmitate tolerantiae*) they must obey Christ's command to love their enemies (15). A little later in the treatise, Cyprian argues that Christians should endure the persecutions they suffer at the hands of Jews, pagans, or heretics without retaliation because judgment is ultimately God's prerogative.

---

[12] For the conflict between Roman and Jewish institutions, see Schwartz 2014: 69 and the lengthy comparison in Goodman 2008. For Christian institutions as an alternative regime, see the discussion above.

Like the Stoics, Cyprian inextricably links tolerance to endurance and
to the acknowledgment of the limitations of one's responsibility to judge
and correct others, but he is working from within a significantly different theological and eschatological framework. Whereas the Stoics saw the
endurance of others' mistaken views as a function of the sage's own invul-
nerability to the opinions of others, Cyprian connected it to the suffering and humiliation of Christ. For the Stoics, to act intolerantly towards
another is to impair your own happiness by trying to achieve something
that is not "up to you"; for Cyprian, it is to usurp God's position as judge.

Cyprian's account of *tolerantia* has to do with horizontal toleration: why
Christians should forebear in the face of persecution without retaliating
against other communities with which they disagree. But what about the
vertical toleration of Christianity by Roman authorities? (Cyprian himself fell victim in 258 to the persecution launched by Valerian.) This question arose in the apologetic literature of Cyprian's fellow North African
Christians, Tertullian, Lactantius, and Augustine.

Tertullian, an accomplished and creative apologist and theologian
writing from Carthage in the late second and early third centuries, first
coined the term "freedom of religion." In his *Apologeticum* (*The Apology*;
c. 197–98), a work addressed to Roman magistrates, Tertullian defends
Christianity against the charge of impiety (*irreligio*) directed at them
because of their failure to participate in the Roman civil religion. At one
point in this highly polemical work, Tertullian turns the tables on pagan
accusers. It is they, not Christians, who are guilty of impiety. Tertullian
creatively argues that one reason for the impiety of pagan Romans is their
persecution of Christians: "See to it, whether this too may be part of the
charge of impiety: to take away the freedom of religion (*libertas religionis*),
to forbid a choice of divine being (*optio divinitatis*), so that I am not permitted to worship whom I wish, but I am compelled to worship whom
I would not. No one, not even a human being, wishes to be worshiped by
an unwilling person" (*Apol.* 24.6). "Piety" or "correct religious practice"
(*religio*) requires willing worshipers, so it is "impiety" or "incorrect religious practice" (*irreligio*) to compel worship. Situated within its broader
argumentative context, Tertullian's talk of "freedom of religion" is part of
a deliberate attempt to controvert the Roman notion of *religio* (Streeter
2006: 232–35).[13]

In a letter written c. 212 to the African proconsul Scapula, Tertullian
once again argues for the toleration of Christianity:

[13] Dates for Tertullian's life and works follow T.D. Barnes 1985.

> You suppose that others too are gods, whom we know are demons. However, it belongs to human law [or "it is a human right"] and one's natural power (*humani iuris et naturalis potestatis*) for each person to worship whatever he wishes. The religious practice (*religio*) of one person neither injures nor helps another. It is not the place of religion (*religio*) to compel religion (*religio*), which ought to be undertaken willingly (*sponte*), not by force. (*Ad Scapulam* 2.2)

This influential passage was cited to support early modern views about religious toleration. For example, in the only full-length book he ever wrote, *Notes on the State of Virginia* (1785), Thomas Jefferson argued that natural rights guarantee individual religious freedom:

> Our rulers can have authority over such natural rights only as we have submitted to them. The rights of conscience we never submitted, we could not submit. We are answerable for them to our God. The legitimate powers of government extend to such acts only as are injurious to others. But it does me no injury for my neighbor to say there are twenty gods, or no god. It neither picks my pocket nor breaks my leg.[14]

In his private copy of the *Notes*, Jefferson supplemented this passage by writing out by hand the Latin text of *Ad Scapulam* 2.2, a passage underlined in his private edition of Tertullian's text (Wilken 2014; 2016; Shah 2016b).

It is tempting to read Tertullian through a Jeffersonian lens. And in fact, many commentators see this text as establishing – for the first time in the history of political thought, and some fifteen or sixteen hundred years before John Locke, William Penn, and Thomas Jefferson – the freedom of individuals to worship as a universal human or natural right.[15] These scholars usually render *humanum ius* in the passage as "a human right."[16] Robert Louis Wilken bolsters this translation by suggesting that the term works "in tandem" with "natural power" to form a single idea: a "'right' that precedes and is independent of any action by the ruling authorities" (Wilken 2016: 64).

Wilken's rendering is plausible (option A). As we saw in chapter 2, in Roman law "right" (*ius*) paired with power (*potestas*) indicated an individual right, a claim based on a particular power possessed by an individual.

---

[14] Query VII, "Religion." Text quoted from Shah 2016b: 57.
[15] Natural or human right in Tertullian: Rist 1982: 159; Bélanger 1985: 289; Pagels 2012: 131–32; Randall 2013: 5; Shah 2016b; Wilken 2016: 64–65. First occurrence in the history of political thought: Shah 2016b: 57. For the later development of natural rights and religious liberty, see Tierney 1996.
[16] Forst 2013: 43; Randall 2013: 5; Shah 2016a: 8; Shah 2016b: 52; Wilken 2016: 64; Bélanger 1985: 289 (in French). Compare the paraphrase by Rist 1982: 159.

Ius humanum is a common enough term in both Roman historical and philosophical writings, though in these contexts it virtually always means "human law" rather than "a human right." As for "natural power," the term occurs at only one other place within Tertullian's own corpus: a passage in *De anima* (21) that describes the human capacity for choice (*potestas arbitrii*) as a "free" (*libera*) and "natural" (*naturalis*) power. If this is what Tertullian means by a "natural power" in *Ad Scapulam* 2, then Tertullian clearly has in mind the "subjective" natural capacity of the individual will to choose freely. In this case, it is natural, though not necessary, also to construe *ius* in the "subjective" sense as "a right" possessed by the individual rather than as an external "law" outside of and binding on the individual. Drawing on Tertullian's anthropology, we might further suppose that this "right" or natural power of choice is endowed to human beings by virtue of their being created in the image of God (Genesis 1:26–27; Wilken 2016: 65). In short, the pieces are there for the idea of an individual "human" or "natural right" (subject to the qualifications discussed below). Given Tertullian's propensity to use legal, philosophical, and theological concepts in creative and innovative ways, and given that he has already shown a willingness to coin new phrases and play with terminology when defending religious toleration, he might very well have put them together.[17]

However, a second rendering is possible (option B). One could construe *humanum ius* in its common sense as "human law," which would then, relatively easily to Roman ears, establish a contrast between two types of law: "man-made law" and "natural law" (Garnsey 1984: 14–15; Streeter 2006: 234). "Human law" in Latin literature is often paired with "divine law," and elsewhere Tertullian identifies "natural law" as God's "divine law" that is revealed to all (*Adversus Iudaeos* 2; cf. *De corona militis* 5–6). So one could also plausibly argue that Tertullian is making a point about an individual's freedom to worship in relation to the external legal and divine order: "It is ordained by both man-made and natural law that each person may worship whatever he wishes" (trans. Garnsey 1984: 14). In this case, individuals would possess a "right" to freedom of worship as the implied correlative of the duty of human beings to obey the God-ordained natural law that true worship cannot be coerced. This would still count as a highly innovative argument for religious toleration, but, much as Cicero's

---

[17] *Ius humanum*: in Seneca's thought, see Inwood and Miller 2007: 161–62; it is a common term in Livy (see, e.g., 5.37.4) and Tacitus (see, e.g., *Ann.* 1.40 and next footnote). Tertullian's creative use of law: Young 2000: 646. Tertullian's creative use of philosophy and theology: Osborn 1997.

articulation of natural duties discussed in chapter 2, on this interpretation the notion of natural rights is not articulated directly but must be
inferred.[18]

With either option A or B, however, substantial differences remain
between Tertullian's thought and Jefferson's – a point that can be obscured
by using terms as loaded with modern connotations as "human rights."
For Jefferson, natural rights imply indefeasibility: such rights cannot be
taken away, and any government interference or restriction of these rights
without the consent of the governed is illegitimate. Moreover, for Jefferson
natural rights also entail the correlative natural duty for others to recognize
those rights (Zuckert 1996: 73–78).

If we construe Tertullian as innovatively arguing for a "human right"
in terms of a "natural human power," then he is leaving it to Scapula and
his other elite Roman readers to fill in the corresponding natural duty,
and it is doubtful that he would have expected them to do so. He certainly wouldn't have conveyed a correlative "natural duty" by alluding
to a "natural power" as understood in Roman law, for the jurists saw no
incompatibility between conceiving of freedom as "one's natural power of
doing what one pleases" and this natural power being limited "either by
coercion (*vis*) or by law (*ius*)" (*Dig.* 1.5.4). Option B does specify a natural
(or divine) duty applicable to all human beings, though at the expense of
explicitly articulating the idea of "natural rights."

Nor should we assume that Tertullian shared Jefferson's preoccupation
with legitimacy. Commentators on *Ad Scapulam* 2 sometimes anachronis-
tically introduce abstract terms like "state" and "government" into their
analysis of Tertullian's text, thus opening up space for the question of
legitimacy: if individuals have the natural rights of the freedom of worship independent of "the state," then they could demand that legitimate
"state" action be justified in terms of these rights (for legitimacy, see also
chapter 1).[19] However, Tertullian never develops such an argument. In
the subsequent text of *Ad Scapulam*, he condemns the unjust treatment
of Carthaginian Christians by previous African governors, but he never
questions the legitimacy of their rule and strongly affirms Christians' support of imperial government (see also *Apol.* 30). Elsewhere he dismisses

---

[18] *Ius humanum* and *ius divinum*: Tac. *Ann.* 2.14; 3.70; 4.38; 6.26; *Hist.* 2.91 (to give only a selec-
tion from Tacitus, a historian with whom Tertullian was familiar). By "human law" Bowen and
Garnsey (2003: 46 n. 186) suggest that perhaps Tertullian, who was familiar with the correspondence between Trajan and Pliny discussed earlier in this chapter, means to evoke Trajan's instructions
that Christians should not be actively hunted down.
[19] Compare Wilken 2016: 64.

"all secular powers and dignities" as "hostile to God," but this condemnation follows from his general "anti-world rhetoric" in texts designed "for
internal Christian consumption" rather than from a concern with legitimacy (Young 2000: 649; see *De idolatria* 18–19).

The closest Tertullian comes to questioning the "legitimacy" of acts of
religious persecution occurs in his earlier *Apologeticum*, where, despite the
fact that Christianity had not yet been proscribed by senatorial or imperial decree (T.D. Barnes 1968), he condemns persecutors as promulgating
"unjust laws." Law by its nature commands the "good" and promotes "fairness" and "justice." It is measured by "truth," and its justice should be open
to the scrutiny of those whom it commands (4.13). Otherwise, it is "mere
force" (*vis*) and "unjust mastery" (*iniquam dominationem*; 4.4). Tertullian's
argument, though rhetorically clever, exploits traditional Ciceronian and
republican themes.[20] Thus, Tertullian seems to stand closer to the "republican" and natural law tradition of Cicero than to the "modern" natural
rights tradition of Jefferson. If he is concerned with "legitimacy," this concern is a matter of the justice of "law," not of "the legitimate powers of
government" given fundamental human rights.

One final difference between Tertullian and Jefferson: Jefferson focuses
on an individual's private and inward convictions – "the rights of conscience." Tertullian's argument, while forcefully articulating the individual
dimension of religious liberty, does not strip the notion of "religion" of its
important "communal and public dimensions" (Shah 2016b: 54). In fact,
Tertullian's preeminent concern is to secure the freedom for Christians to
practice their religion within the context of a particular community, the
(orthodox) church, and to achieve this goal, he employs in his apologetic
writing a variety of rhetorically sophisticated arguments. His defense of
individual liberty is a byproduct (albeit an important one) of this larger
goal, not an abstract principle to be independently asserted (Streeter
2006: 236). This is perhaps one reason why we don't find Tertullian
acknowledging individual freedom to worship as a legitimate defense for
"heretics" within the church (Stroumsa 1998).

Tertullian's argument for toleration on the basis of the "freedom of
religion" is elaborated upon by his fellow North African, Lactantius (c.
250–c. 325). A world-class teacher of rhetoric, Lactantius was provoked
by the Great Persecution of Diocletian launched in 303 CE into writing a

---

[20] Cf. Cic. *Leg.* 1.19: "fairness"; *Leg.* 2.11: "justice and truth"; *Leg.* 1.44; 2.13: "the good." On the republican account of law, force and mastery (*vis* and *dominatio*) is what law (*lex* and *ius*) prevents (see
chapter 2).

defense of Christianity, *The Divine Institutes*. Lactantius agrees with the presupposition of pagan persecutors that religion has important public benefits and should be defended. But he argues that persecuting those who dissent from the Roman civil religion is the wrong way to go about it. The value of religious acts of worship depends on the will of the worshiper; sacrifices made by those who are not spiritually engaged are of no value (5.19.23). Whereas Tertullian had enigmatically anchored this notion in "human law" and man's "natural power," Lactantius more extensively argues for the notion that religion should be voluntary based on God's prescription, especially as revealed in the life and acts of Christ. Since God does not value unwilling worship, it is no use forcing worship through compulsion. Religious disputes should be settled by arguments and persuasion, not coercion. Moreover, potential persecutors of Christians should forebear for the very practical reason that persecution tends to increase the very worship they wish to suppress (Bowen and Garnsey 2003: 46–48).

Neither a relativist nor a pluralist, Lactantius believed that there is one true God for all people, the Christian God, and that those who don't worship him are in error, and even liable for eternal divine judgment (see, e.g., 5.18.16). One might suppose that such beliefs would lead to intolerance. But Lactantius argues this is not so. Christians are not to get angry if God is not worshiped or to seek revenge if they themselves are persecuted. Interestingly, he argues for this from his belief in God's "supreme power" to avenge both affronts to his own honor and injustices committed against his people (5.20.9–10). Unlike Rousseau, Lactantius believed that one could live in civic peace with those whom one thinks are damned, and, perhaps somewhat paradoxically, he grounds his argument for nonviolence in his belief in divine punishment.

The arguments for toleration in Cyprian, Tertullian, and Lactantius had a mixed legacy in Christian thought. For example, their more influential North African successor, St. Augustine, writing after Christianity had become the prevailing Roman religion, reproduced and further developed arguments for toleration from its relationship to virtues such as love, patience, and humility, the role of God as ultimate judge, and religion as a necessarily free act on behalf of the worshiper (Forst 2013: 48–51). However, while Augustine initially followed Lactantius' commitment to persuasion rather than coercion, he eventually had a change of heart when confronting the Donatists, a North African sect who believed they alone were the true church with valid sacraments (cf. *On True Religion* 16.31 and *Letter 93 to Vicentius* 17).

Still, as Jefferson's citation of Tertullian suggests, the legacy of Tertullian, Lactantius, and St. Augustine on toleration would stretch well beyond the ancient world. By arguing for religious liberty as "an attribute of individuals, not the exclusive possession of an *ethnos* [a people] or *polis*," the African apologists broke with the views of democratic Athens and Republican Rome (Garnsey 1984: 16). By further grounding freedom from coercion in the idea that religious worship is an act of the will, the African apologists provided one plank in the groundwork for the principled religious toleration familiar from founders of the modern liberal tradition such as John Locke. As Locke argues in his *Letter concerning Toleration*, arguably the most important modern text on toleration, "saving Religion consists in the inward perswasion [sic] of the Mind, without which nothing can be acceptable to God. And such is the nature of the Understanding, that it cannot be compell'd [sic] to the belief of anything by outward force" (Tully, ed., p. 27).[21]

Empire and the Exportation of Religion

Rousseau worried that civil religions inextricably linked with constitutions would incentivize imperialism, since conversion would be yoked to conquest. For his part, Rousseau severed the link between religion and constitution. In the place of national religions championed by his predecessors in the republican tradition, such as Machiavelli, Rousseau crafted a civil religion, derived from principles of right, which is both minimalistic in its details and universalistic in its scope. Rousseau's solution is not completely satisfactory (Beiner 2011). It is hard to see how such a minimalistic, universalistic religion will satisfactorily bind citizens more deeply to their particular civic community, as any civil religion must.

How far does Rousseau's worry about religious imperialism pertain to Rome? As we discussed earlier in the chapter, Roman civil religion was closely linked to the history and institutions of the city itself. Even as the empire grew, religious practices outside of Rome remained decentralized. Yet it is also undeniable that as Rome's empire spread, so too did its gods. Most famously, religion and empire are linked in Vergil's *Aeneid*. "Pious" Aeneas is divinely led to found the Roman people, to whom Jupiter promises "empire without limit" (1.279). Later Aeneas visits the underworld, where he sees a procession of Rome's future leaders and is told: "You, Roman, remember to rule with power (*imperium*) over other peoples

---

[21] Locke on toleration: Goldie 2010; Forst 2013: 210–37.

(these will be your arts), and to impose the ways of peace, to spare the conquered and subdue the proud" (6.851–53).

Given the interplay between Rome's imperialist ideology, history, institutions, and religion, we might wonder whether the link between the constitution and civil religion led to the imperialistic exportation of religion. In one set of circumstances, it did. Roman colonies, settlements of Roman citizens outside of Rome, represent the direct exportation of Roman religion. Often colonies were not completely new settlements but were preexisting communities to which Roman citizens were added. As evidence from surviving charters demonstrates, Rome provided the model for these colonies' constitutions, including provisions for Roman civil religion. For instance, in the legislation drafted in 44 BCE for the Spanish colony of Urso, we find described duties for three of the four major priestly colleges at Rome. With Rome as the model, dress, responsibilities, and privileges are spelled out for the priests of Urso. This imitation of Rome was not unique: the charter contains language that suggests there was a general set of regulations for priesthoods for Roman colonies (*Lex Coloniae Genetivae Iuliae* ch. 66, ll. 35–37).[22]

But generally speaking the spread of Roman religion was indirect and unsystematic. Though conquered territories might incorporate some Roman rituals, they would also maintain many of their own practices. While the Roman gods accompanied imperial expansion, a commitment to exporting Roman religion was not among the most important causes of imperial conquest (G. Woolf 2012: 122).

Imperial expansion did prompt questions regarding the relationship between Roman religion and the idea of a single cosmos, and more specifically between Roman gods and foreign gods. Even if, as Woolf suggests (2012: 121), pagan Romans never worked out an agreed-upon authoritative answer, intellectuals such as Varro and Cicero nevertheless creatively attempted to analyze traditional civil religion in light of reason and the universalization of Roman rule (Moatti 2015). Once again, Cicero's *De legibus* represents the most sustained surviving example of this project.

De legibus book 2 provides a theoretical treatment of Roman civil religion in light of natural law, "the highest reason, implanted in nature, which commands what should be done and forbids the opposite" (*Leg.* 1.18). This law exists independently of popular legislation. Universal in scope and eternal in duration (2.8, 10), natural law regulates a cosmic city of gods and human beings (1.23, 33, 60–61). This conception of law follows

---

[22] See text, translation, and commentary in Crawford 1996, 1: 393–454.

closely that of earlier Greek Stoicism, though Cicero does not attribute it to the Stoics explicitly. Given the existence of this natural law and cosmic city, *De legibus* invites questions on a number of important relationships.[23]

The first concerns nature and convention: how do the laws of Cicero's law code, passed by Cicero and his dialogue partners playing the part of a Roman assembly, meet the requirements of natural law (which, Cicero suggests, they must do if they are to be valid)? The second, the universal and particular: how are Rome's religious laws to apply to cities beyond Rome if they do not depart much from ancestral and current Roman religious customs (cf. 2.23 and 2.35)? Third, the relationship among the various particulars in light of the universal: how does Roman civil religion relate to the different religious practices of other peoples in light of the cosmic city? Depending on Cicero's answers to these questions, he could be seen as providing a philosophical justification for the type of religious imperialistic conquest feared by Rousseau. For if natural law prescribes what is good universally, and if the religious laws designed to fit Rome's constitution – the best of all constitutions – constitute natural law, then doesn't natural law justify the universalization of Roman religious laws as good for all people?

It does not. Here is a summary of what I take to be Cicero's position:[24]

(1) Natural law establishes right and wrong conduct; it is action-guiding for human beings and enjoins them to perform virtuous actions (*Leg.* 1.18–19, 42–43, 58; 2.8–12).

(2) As virtue is necessary for human happiness, natural law promotes human happiness (*Leg.* 2.11; see Annas 2013).

(3) An important social virtue prescribed by natural law for human beings is *pietas*, devotion or respect for the gods and for one another (*Leg.* 1.43, 60; 2.15).

(4) Implicit in all human legislation is the intention to promote "the security of states, the health of citizens, and a peaceful and happy life for human beings" (*Leg.* 2.11). Thus, human legislation follows natural law in promoting human happiness.

(5) Cicero's law code reflects natural law in prescribing *pietas* (*Leg.* 2.19, 22), which is a quality that "all good men have" (*Leg.* 2.28).

---

[23] For Cicero's creative appropriation of the Stoic (and Platonic) natural law traditions in *Leg.* 1, see J. W. Atkins 2013: ch. 5 (with bibliography on the question of sources).

[24] For a fuller explanation and defense, see J. W. Atkins 2013; 2017. For alternative views, see Girardet 1983; Asmis 2008a; Annas 2013; Sauer 2015; Straumann 2016.

(6) Following Plato's *Laws*, Cicero holds that natural law will be instantiated differently in different political communities, depending on contingency, necessity, non-rational aspects of human nature, and form of constitution. For instance, the Greeks and Romans differ from the Persians in promoting piety (*Leg.* 2.26).

(7) The constitutions to which natural law should be adapted themselves admit of contingency, necessity, and the non-rational aspects of human nature.

(8) The mixed constitution is the best practicable or humanly attainable constitution, which is the form of constitution that best serves free peoples (*Leg.* 3.4).

(9) The Roman constitution is the *best example* of the mixed constitution, that is, the best example of the best practicable constitution (cf. *Rep.* 1.70; 2.21–22, 52).

(10) The Roman constitution grew organically over the centuries as a number of leaders responded to various contingencies. Its design could not be precisely replicated even if the world's best and brightest legislators were assembled in one place at one time (*Rep.* 2.2).

(11) As (9) and (10) suggest, the mixed constitution can be (and should be) widely exported, but Rome's particular version cannot be exported, and certainly not in every detail.

The above account addresses *De legibus*'s concerns with the relationships between nature and convention, particularity and universality, and the various religious customs of particular regimes. It accounts for passages that acknowledge the affinity of Cicero's laws to Roman religious customs as well as those that describe the naturalness of this legislation (cf. *Leg.* 2.23 and 2.61–62). It also explains in what sense it is true that "we are giving laws not for the Roman nation but for all good and established nations" (*Leg.* 2.35). The mixed constitution and laws to suit could be exported, and, as the best example of such a constitution, Rome should be used as a model; but this is far from saying that natural law prescribes that Roman religious rites down to every detail should be imposed on other people for their happiness. Indeed, the contingency of Rome's version of the mixed constitution provides an impediment against the simple exportation of particular Roman religious rites in the service of a wider project of nation-building.

Comparing Cicero and Rousseau's accounts of civil religion reveals an irony. Viewed from one perspective, Rousseau's civil religion is weaker than Cicero's because unlike Cicero's it lacks the sort of detailed legislation necessary to foster civic virtue and to bind citizens to one another and to the city. Rousseau omitted such details precisely because he wanted to unhitch his religious laws from the constitution in order to avoid the harmful effects of the ancient world's integration of religion and constitution; yet for Cicero it is precisely the contingency of the Roman constitution that ruled out the wholesale exportation of Roman religious rites and institutions to conquered peoples, thereby limiting religious imperialism.

Civil Religion and Universal Principles

Approximately fifty years ago, the sociologist Robert Bellah published a groundbreaking article arguing for the existence of "an elaborate and well institutionalized civil religion in America" (1970: 168). This religion is separate from and exists alongside the historic faiths and churches. Though incorporating biblical imagery, it is shaped by the American historical experience, and hence "genuinely American and genuinely new. It has its own prophets and its own martyrs, its own sacred events and sacred places, its own solemn rituals and symbols" (Bellah 1970: 186). Examples come readily to mind: martyrs like Abraham Lincoln or Martin Luther King, Jr. (also a prophet); sacred places like the national cemeteries at Arlington and Gettysburg; holidays like Memorial Day ("a rededication to the martyred dead, to the spirit of sacrifice, and to the American vision"), Thanksgiving (which "serves to integrate the family into the civil religion"), or the Fourth of July; the veneration of the American flag; patriotic songs and hymns such as "My Country, 'Tis of Thee" or "God Bless America"; and documents like the Declaration of Independence or Gettysburg Address that form the ideals and principles of the American Republic – what Kass, Kass, and Schaub (2011: xx–xxi) call "the American Creed" (other quotations from Bellah 1970: 179).

Given the great distances between the twentieth-century American landscape and that of eighteenth-century Geneva or Paris – let alone ancient Rome – Bellah understandably deals with different concerns from Cicero and Rousseau. Yet Bellah's account of civil religion shares one important problem with his predecessors: the tension within civil religion between the general and universal and the local and particular. At times Bellah can use language evocative of American exceptionalism: "[American civil religion] is concerned that America be a society as perfectly in accord with the will of God as men can make it, and a light to all the nations" (1970: 186). But for Bellah "the core of the American civil religion" is related to "higher principles," historically supplied by Christianity and Enlightenment reason, which transcend and judge national loyalty (Bellah 1968: 391). "The civil religion at its best is a genuine apprehension of universal and transcendent religious reality as seen in or, one could almost say, as revealed through the experience of the American people ... At its best, it has been neither so general that it has lacked incisive relevance to the American scene nor so particular that it has placed American society above universal human values" (1970: 179–80).

How will the American civil religion adapt as the nation's future is increasingly bound up in a global order? For Bellah this question constitutes the "third time of trial" for American civil religion. Today we remain a long way from the "genuine transnational sovereignty" and world civil religion imagined by Bellah. Yet as liberal democracies are racked by nationalist movements responding to pressures and fissures from globalization and continue to suffer from disaffected individualism (liberalism's longstanding byproduct), it remains important to consider the rituals, beliefs, and values that bind us together as citizens, how and to what extent they relate to universal principles of human flourishing, and on what grounds differences can be embraced or tolerated. Though their answers will not be ours, it is nevertheless instructive to consider the Roman experience as we contemplate these matters.

CHAPTER 7

Imperialism, Just War Theory, and Cosmopolitanism

Introduction

Throughout this book, we have seen that Roman political thinkers might at times work within categories familiar to us and think in terms amenable to analysis by contemporary concepts; at other times, Roman thought offers different ways of defining or conceiving these concepts; and at still other times, Roman analysis of political phenomena cannot adequately be captured by modern concepts. Conceptual care is always required when analyzing Roman thought, and this is especially true when we come to theories of international relations.

Consider the "slippery concept" of empire (Gruen 1984: 273). Today we typically associate the Roman Empire with a territorial entity, perhaps because of the impressive extent of Roman rule: by Marcus Aurelius' death in 180 CE, lands under Roman control stretched from central Scotland in the north to Egypt in the south, from Spain in the west to Albania in the east.[1] However, the Latin word for empire, *imperium*, did not come to indicate empire in this sense until the first century CE (Richardson 2008). *Imperium* originally and most fundamentally meant "command" or "rule." While Roman empire required Roman rule or control, there were ways for Rome to assert control other than by territorial conquest and direct government. Consider for instance the liberal extension of citizenship in the late Republic and Principate (see chapter 3). By making all peoples anywhere in the world potential Roman citizens, the Romans imposed rule in the form of a legal rather than political or moral empire (Moatti 2015). This universalizable order promotes the type of control associated with *imperium* or empire. The idea of acquiring imperial control through legal devices is not confined to Rome. A similar notion has led the French

---

[1] For historical overviews of Roman expansion, see Lintott 1993: 1–15 (a brief summary) and Harris 2016.

political philosopher Pierre Manent to suggest that the early twenty-first-century United States exercised a more "truly imperial government" than the territorial nineteenth-century British Empire (2006: 49).

Just as empire can be understood in different ways, so too imperialism has been conceived in terms of theories of economics (Lenin 2010), sociology (Schumpeter 1952), and power (Morgenthau 1985). While the Romans themselves frequently advertised to the outside world that defensive reasons caused them to undertake the wars that led to imperial expansion, their actual motives were more complex (Derow 1979; Harris 2016). From his vantage point in the first century BCE, Cicero offered a variety of reasons for Rome's imperial expansion, including concern for Rome's international reputation, glory, the defense of allies, increasing trade and tax revenue, and protecting citizens abroad (see Cic. *Man.*, with Steel 2001: 128). All of these factors have been discussed by modern historians, who disagree about the relative explanatory power for Roman imperialism of theories based on defensive wars, an aggressive political culture, economic considerations, and "organizational techniques" such as favorable treaties, colonization, citizenship, coinage, and military power. In order to let the Romans speak for themselves, we will assume a theoretically unencumbered definition of imperialism that takes the term simply to mean the conception of how empire is acquired and maintained (Erskine 2010).[2]

In addition to Roman thinking about imperialism, this chapter will also consider Rome's contribution to two related ideas with lasting influence in international relations, just war theory – the idea that armed conflict should be justified and governed by rules – and cosmopolitanism – the notion that human beings have obligations to, and should care for, other human beings beyond members of their own particular political society. In keeping with the primary emphasis of this book, the analysis here has at its center the republican tradition. The first half of the chapter will shine the spotlight on several key republican thinkers' analyses of the relationship between republican government and the acquisition, maintenance, and expansion of empire. While Polybius, Cicero, Sallust, and Tacitus made their own particular contributions to the issue, for each, Roman imperialism was connected to principles of republican government. The second half of the chapter will focus on the development of just war theory and

---

[2] Defensive wars: Badian 1968. Aggression: Harris 1979. Economic considerations: Harris 1971; 1979; Sherwin-White 1980; Gruen 1984 (downplays economic motives). Honor, status, and alliances: North 1981: 7–8; Eckstein 1995: ch. 3 (on Polybius). "Organizational techniques": Harris 2016: 44–48.

cosmopolitanism. We will conclude by comparing Roman republicanism's contributions to international relations with some important contemporary discussions in the field.

Polybius, the Mixed Constitution, and Empire

The goal of Polybius' *Histories* was "to discover by what means and by what type of constitution (*politeia*) almost the entire inhabited world was conquered and in less than fifty-three years brought under the single rule (*archē*) of the Romans, an achievement that is without historical precedent" (1.1.5). In book 6 Polybius poses this question once more (6.2.2–4), and this time he answers it with an analysis of the Roman constitution, which we examined in chapter 1. Polybius suggests that there is an intimate connection between Rome's constitution and its success as an imperial power. (*Archē*, translated "rule" above, also means "empire.") According to Polybius, the same principles that explain the success of the Roman Republican constitution also explained Rome's acquisition of empire. As Ryan Balot notes (2010: 485), "he explained imperialism as a necessary outgrowth of Roman republicanism and proposed that republican politics was the key to Rome's imperial success." An especially clear snapshot of Polybius' argument for this point is provided by his evaluation of the mixed constitutions of Sparta, Carthage, and Rome in terms of their relative imperial success.

As Polybius had explained earlier in book 6, Lycurgus, the Spartan lawgiver, had expertly designed Sparta's constitution to ensure internal harmony (see chapter 1). In addition to the checks and balances in its offices, Polybius points out how other Spartan institutions promoted the virtues of self-discipline and courage – virtues essential to a military regime that is unified within and well protected from invasion from without. Yet, as Polybius emphasizes, there was no restraint on Sparta's imperial ambitions. As the historian describes Sparta's establishment of a hegemony over its neighbors (6.48.6), he characterizes the Spartans as "supremely ambitious, eager for supremacy, and greedy" (6.48.8), covetous (6.49.1), greedy (6.49.1), and eager for supremacy (6.49.2).

Why was this ambition for empire unrestrained? Polybius' vocabulary of imperial ambition reflects his vocabulary of constitutional corruption from the earlier discussion of constitutional change, where he emphasized the increased appetitiveness of the ruling classes that could only be restrained by the presence of fear and the capacity to imagine shared suffering (see especially 6.7.7, 8.5, 9.6–7). This parallel holds the key to Sparta's overambitious foreign policy. When confronted by an external enemy of Greece – Persia – Sparta fought for the freedom of the other Greek city-states (6.49.4). Yet as soon as the threat from Persia had been thwarted, Sparta, left with nothing to fear, desired to dominate its fellow Greek city-states (6.49.5–6). Thus, Polybius identifies a problem with Sparta's constitution: while Lycurgus had successfully provided mechanisms for utilizing the restraining power of fear in Sparta's domestic relations, he failed to identify any such restraining mechanism in its foreign relations. Worse still, Polybius argues, some of the very mechanisms designed by Lycurgus to create moderation and civic harmony at home by eliminating greed and outside influences (e.g., an iron currency intended to thwart commerce) made it impossible for Sparta to manage an empire (6.50.1–4).

As for Carthage's mixed constitution, Polybius explains the superiority of Rome's constitution in the first instance by reverting to his earlier theory of cyclical constitutional change. Carthage, he argues, was already in decline during its confrontation with Rome, whereas the Roman constitution was at its peak. While both constitutions were mixed, at Rome the senate still had a predominant voice, whereas at Carthage power had already shifted in the favor of the people. In Polybius' opinion, Carthage's democratic shift put it at a distinct disadvantage against Rome, whose wise leaders among the consuls and senate guided the recovery from its defeats at the hands of its enemies (6.51). Second, Rome's empire was built not by mercenaries, as was Carthage's, but by its own citizens shaped by its own constitution to be patriotic and courageous (6.52). In particular, institutions such as the funeral oration inspired Rome's citizen-soldiers "to endure everything on behalf of the commonwealth for the sake of obtaining the glory that accompanies the good deeds of the brave" (6.54.3).

When compared to Sparta and Carthage, the specific ways in which Rome's constitution led to imperial success become clear. Rome's aristocratic honor code impelled its leaders to seek the prestige of imperial rule (6.50), which it acquired because of the excellence of its laws, customs, institutions, and way of life (Eckstein 1995: ch. 3). From religion, to the influence of the senate, to its efficient military machine (described at 6.19–42), Polybius argued that numerous aspects of the Roman *politeia* contributed to its success. As Balot (2010: 492) summarizes, "among all imperial contenders known to Polybius, Rome had the best combination of military discipline, judicious policy making, courage to pursue military victory, and patriotic involvement of all citizens in the city's future success."

While Polybius is most concerned to explain Rome's imperial success, recent studies stress that Polybius' account includes a warning to the Romans of their empire's potential downfall (Balot 2010; Baronowski 2011: 61–63, 164–75; Champion 2013). Indeed, the cases of both Sparta and Carthage may be seen as a warning and challenge to Rome. Can Rome avoid following Carthage down the natural path of constitutional degeneration and corruption that ends with mob rule (cf. 6.57.1–9 and 6.51.4–8)? And, though it is endowed with sufficient resources to manage an empire, can Rome, unlike Sparta, restrain itself from grasping after domination enough to maintain imperial rule without provoking the resentment of its subjects, which the desire for mastery naturally incites? With Carthage's powers diminished and hence also the restraining fear of the enemy that had previously mobilized Rome (6.18.3), will Rome be any more successful than previous imperial rivals like Sparta and Athens at identifying a restraining mechanism? If not, according to the logic of Polybius' theory, Rome will share their fate (36.9.3–5).

Sallust, Fear of the Enemy, Collective Action, and Empire

After returning to Rome from an embassy to Carthage in 153 BCE, Cato the Elder, impressed by the wealth, military strength, and power of Rome's greatest rival, made it his habit to conclude every speech in the senate, no matter the motion under consideration, with "Carthage must be destroyed." Each and every time, Scipio Nasica would counter: "Carthage must be spared." Why would Scipio Nasica argue for the preservation of Rome's bitterest rival at whose hands his grandfather's generation had suffered the worst military defeat thus far in Roman history? Diodorus Siculus explains:

> So long as Carthage survived, the fear that she generated compelled the Romans to live together in harmony and to rule their subjects equitably and with credit to themselves – much the best means to maintain and extend an empire; but once the rival city was destroyed, it was only too evident that there would be civil war at home, and that hatred for the governing power would spring up among all the allies because of the rapacity and lawlessness to which the Roman magistrates would subject them. All this did indeed happen to Rome after the destruction of Carthage ... (*Library of History* 34/35.33.5–6; trans. Walton, Loeb)

According to Scipio Nasica, the fear of the enemy leads to collective action and restraint, which in turn allowed Rome to maintain and extend its empire (Wood 1995; Evrigenis 2008: 36–42). Somewhat paradoxically, antagonism, conflict, and rivalry lead to cohesiveness, order, and productivity both at home and abroad.

Of course the general idea that conflict could be productive lay at the heart of Polybius' thought, and the Greek historian frequently identified the salutary effects of fear, including the fear of an external enemy (e.g., 6.10.8–9, 18.2–3, 44.4, 56.11; 36.9.3–5). However, perhaps no thinker emphasized more clearly than Sallust the capacity of the fear of an external enemy to provide internal stability. One historian of political thought has even coined the term "Sallust's theorem" for the idea that "fear of an external enemy promotes internal social unity" (Wood 1995: 181). As Sallust himself pithily puts it, "Fear of an enemy (*metus hostilis*) preserved good political conduct" (*Iug.* 41.2). In each of his surviving works, Sallust attributes moral degeneration and the lack of collective action among Romans to the peace and security experienced at Rome in the wake of Carthage's destruction (*Cat.* 10; *Iug.* 41; *Hist.* 1.11–12).

Three important points must be noted. First, Rome was not the only beneficiary of the stable international order produced by the rivalry between Rome and Carthage. *The Jugurthine War* illustrates the point negatively by highlighting the corruption that results in Africa as well as in Rome once Carthage is removed from the picture. No longer did the leaders of the Numidians perform "glorious military deeds" as did King Masinissa during the second Punic War (5.4). The end of the international order promoted by the imperial rivalry between Rome and Carthage led not only to moral declension and threats to Rome's imperial glory and liberty (39.1) but also to disorder and corruption within Africa. As Thomas Wiedemann (1993: 53) observes, "throughout the monograph, Sallust's account of the actions of Rome's African enemies emphasizes division and disorder."

Second, while Sallust pinpoints the beginning of moral and constitutional decline under the Republic to the immediate aftermath of the defeat of Carthage, he does not assign this same date to the beginning of Rome's imperial decline. In fact, according to his analysis in the *Histories*, Rome's empire did not reach its height until 51 BCE – after a full century of decline in Roman morality and political cooperation (1.11). As Sallust had argued in *Catiline's Conspiracy*, "the sheer size" of the *res publica* allowed it to endure for many years the corruption of its generals and magistrates, and to weather generations relatively barren of men great in virtue until the time when men of virtue would once again arise. (He identifies Cato and Caesar as such men in recent days (53.5–6).) Anticipating one aspect of James Madison's famous argument for large republics in *Federalist* 10, Sallust suggests that the vast size and resources of a republic-cum-empire like Rome allows it to weather political corruption and to produce the sort of virtuous or (in Madison's language) "fit men" required for republican government.

Third, like Polybius, Sallust recognizes that the salutary effects of fear may extend beyond the external fear of the enemy to the internal fear among the various components of the constitution. As he points out at *Histories* I.II, the residual fear of the royal line of Tarquins no less than wars with Etruria contributed to "the fair and orderly rule of law" that characterized the early Republic. Like Polybius, Sallust recognizes that there is a correlation between the principles that ensure external and internal stability (cf. Harris 2016: 11–12).

Cicero on Justice, Honor, Fear, and Empire

The link between republican government and empire continues to be displayed in Cicero's writings on empire – *De republica*, *De legibus*, and *De officiis* – as well as in a number of his speeches (on which, see Steel 2001). We will leave for later in the chapter discussion of the related theories of just war and cosmopolitanism that are treated alongside empire in Cicero's writings.

In *De republica* discussion of empire takes center stage – literally, as the third of the six-book work features a debate on whether justice is necessary for Rome's acquisition and maintenance of empire. One of the dialogue's characters, Philus, playing devil's advocate and professing to employ arguments used by the Academic skeptic Carneades during his famous visit to Rome in 155 BCE, argues that it is impossible for any regime to pursue justice while successfully acquiring and maintaining an empire. International relations are not matters of justice but of national interest or advantage, understood in terms of wealth, power, and rule (3.18 Powell = 3.24b Zetzel). Wise leaders, that is, those who wish to position their country to achieve its interests, will act unjustly when necessary. Rome managed to conquer the world, not by acting justly but by acting shrewdly to extend its power at the expense of the conquered.[3]

This argument against justice in international relations is countered by an argument on behalf of justice by another character, Laelius. In a famous passage, Laelius argues that all human beings, regardless of citizenship or nationality, must obey a rational, natural, eternal, and unchangeable law (3.27 Powell = 3.33 Zetzel). Laelius' argument attempts to show that the wise administration of empire in the interests of both the rulers and ruled

---

[3] Philus' speech and Carneades: Ferrary 1977; Glucker 2001; Powell 2013.

may be consistent with justice. Utilizing the analogies of the rule of the soul over the body, masters over slaves, kings and fathers over citizens and children, Laelius seeks to establish that it is natural and good for the stronger and more mature to rule over the weaker, so long as the rule is conducted with the subject's well-being in mind (Erskine 2011: 193). Natural justice in fact justifies the acquisition of empire by republics because empire brings justice and order to an otherwise chaotic world (cf. *Off.* 2.26–27). Strong republics may help the weak when they rule for the benefit (*utilitas*) of the weak. Republican empires may "remove the opportunity to do injury from wicked peoples" (August. *C.D.* 19.21.34–35 = 3.36 Zetzel).[4]

Laelius argues that it is actually in the interest of republics to conduct imperial rule justly, for Philus' argument did not account for the fact those who violate the natural law will be subject to its sanctions: individual violators find themselves exiled from their own natures as human beings (3.27 Powell = 3.33 Zetzel); nations are punished by an unnatural death (3.33 Powell = 3.34b Zetzel). Unlike in the thought of Polybius and Sallust, fear plays a destructive rather than a constructive role in international relations. Rome's empire (*imperium*) should be maintained by justice (*ius*) rather than by force (*vis*), by voluntary consent (*voluntas*) rather than by fear (*terror*; 3.34 Powell = 3.41 Zetzel).

In what way may this premature death come for republics that violate the natural law? Cicero's *De officiis* provides a possible explanation. Cicero argues that since Rome's rule has begun to rely on fear rather than on justice and benevolence, it has received its rightful punishment: the loss of its republican form of government (2.27–29; Pangle and Ahrensdorf 1999: 67). This may happen for two reasons. The first regards the influence of empire on behavior at home. Sallust, as we noted earlier, argued that empire can help a republic endure civic corruption at home, thereby preserving a republican constitution; here Cicero warns that the corrupt handling of empire may prepare the ground for civic corruption at home, thereby destroying a republican constitution.

The second reason has to do with the influence over others that an unjust imperial power forfeits by ruling blatantly in its own interest and relying solely on power and fear to maintain its empire. As is clear from other republican thinkers such as Polybius, such rule forfeits the leverage of an enhanced status or prestige derived from an honorable reputation, that is, being known in the international sphere as one who will keep

---

[4] Laelius' argument: Ferrary 1974; Zetzel 1996; J. W. Atkins 2013: 36–42. Imperialism and the analogy of master and slave: Erskine 2011: 192–200; Garnsey 1996: 40–43; Lavan 2013: 115–19.

promises and honor treaties and alliances (Eckstein 1995: 56–70; cf. Erskine 2011: 185). Cicero denies that one can realistically expect to encounter the sort of scenario sketched by Philus in *Republic* 3, where he presents advantages accruing to fundamentally unjust actors who nevertheless are held to be honorable by others (3.13 Powell = 3.27 Zetzel). To be able to attain the reputation for honorable actions, one must actually act honorably, if not always then at least consistently (*Off.* 2.43). States should try to cultivate this capital rather than relying on fear because "the force of goodwill is great, but the force of fear is feeble" (*Off.* 2.29).

Cicero uses a number of examples in *De officiis* to defend versions of this basic thesis: honor and standing are too valuable sources of agency and influence in international relations to be sacrificed in the name of a perceived short-term advantage. For example, in 278 BCE the senate refused to poison King Pyrrhus, even though his assassination would most likely have ended the war and extended Rome's power: such an action would have been rightly seen as dishonorable by others and consequently would have reduced Rome's standing in the eyes of other cities (1.40; 3.86–87). Another powerful example, also discussed to similar effect by Polybius (6.58, with Eckstein 1995: 65–67), concerns the Roman senate's decision during the second Punic War neither to condone a Roman soldier's use of a technicality to invalidate a promise to Hannibal nor to agree to a prisoner exchange at the expense of Rome's dignity (Cic. *Off.* 3.113–14). Both Polybius and Cicero stress that the Romans' adherence to their honor code under extreme pressure broke the spirit of the great Carthaginian general, Hannibal. The point: honor and the reputation and status that accompany it are important sources of influence in international relations. Cicero reaffirms the more general Roman republican perspective that the consideration of Rome's reputation for honor and good faith (*fides*) in international affairs should constrain the senate's decision-making (North 1981: 7–8; Burton 2011).

Tacitus on Empire: Liberty, Conflict, and Order

Tacitus' *Agricola* was completed in 98 BCE under the emperor Nerva, at a time when Rome was struggling to expand and maintain its empire in Britannia (England, Scotland, and Wales) and Germany beyond the Rhine and Danube. We have already encountered this text in our consideration of the virtues under the Principate (chapter 3); here we will briefly underscore its value for thinking about empire, in particular as it relates to liberty, conflict, and order (and its limits).

Consider first conflict and order. Much of the drama of the *Agricola* takes place in Britannia, at and beyond the borders of the Roman world (K. Clarke 2001). The picture of unconquered Britain is generally one of conflict and war. Though briefly united by fear of the Romans (as per Sallust's theorem), the lack of order and organization ultimately contributed to the Britons' downfall. The world outside of Rome is pictured as one of chaos, violence, and conflict between constantly warring tribes (Sailor 2012). Roman *imperium* can provide order (cf. *Hist.* 4.74; Rutherford 2010: 326–27).

Yet as the *Agricola* explores the lack of order absent Roman imperial power, it also explores the limits of order and empire. Unlike Alexander the Great who disregarded all boundaries, Agricola was constantly running up against the limits of nature in his attempt to extend Rome's empire (*Agr.* 32–34).[5] And, returning to a theme we saw in Tacitus' treatment of the Principate (chapter 1) and rhetoric (chapter 5), the *Agricola* suggests that complete peace and order may come at a heavy cost for the conquered. In a famous passage, Tacitus recounts Agricola's efforts at Romanizing the Britons as part of a nation-building project. He helped them attain peace by systematic acculturation, which Tacitus refers to as the Britons' "enslavement" (21.2).

Constructed around a powerful analogy between Principate and empire, the *Agricola* is in fact very much a work about freedom and its loss: freedom exists neither at Rome under Domitian nor for the nations subject to Rome (Liebeschuetz 1966). However, freedom does emerge at one place in the work: in an exchange between Agricola and Calgacus, the commander of the Britons, immediately before the battle of Mons Graupius in Scotland, where the Britons make their final stand (see 30–34). Calgacus delivers an admirable speech that exhibits all of the virtues of republican rhetoric. He contrasts Roman "peace" with the liberty enjoyed by the Britons. In his conclusion, he deconstructs the Roman claim to empire: "Plundering, slaughtering, and ravaging they call by the false name 'empire'; they make a wasteland and call it 'peace'" (30.5). Republican freedom and oratory flourish at the boundaries of the Roman order.[6]

Scholars debate whether Tacitus is criticizing the institution of the Principate and Roman imperial conquest. Perhaps, as Dylan Sailor (2012)

---

[5] See Bosworth (2004) for the intertextual references here to Quintus Curtius' account of Alexander the Great.

[6] Analogy between Principate and empire: Whitmarsh 2006; Sailor 2012.

has suggested, the *Agricola* presents a qualified defense of Roman imperialism on the grounds that, despite its destruction of freedom, it is better than the chaos, disorder, and violence that marked the previous state of affairs. Whatever Tacitus' stance towards the Principate, the idea that the struggle for imperial glory produces order is familiar from Polybius, Cicero, and Sallust. As for republican liberty, it turns out to be a fragile flower that blossoms most fully neither under the complete control of emperor and empire (no room to grow) nor under the complete disorder of constantly recurring skirmishes among the Britons (too chaotic and unstable to take root for long) but in a world in which Roman *imperium* has established enough order to provoke the opposition of a strong but free nation that honorably opposes it.[7]

The Roman Origins of Just War Theory

When, if ever, is armed conflict justified? Are there norms that should guide war once it begins? The United States' controversial use of military force over the past half-century, from the Vietnam War in the 1960s and 1970s to the recent wars in Iraq and Afghanistan, has repeatedly thrust "just war theory" into the American public consciousness.[8] Traditionally, the idea of a "just war" establishes conditions for armed conflict that limit both the grounds under which a state of war may be declared (*ius ad bellum*: "the justice of going to war") and particular acts of violence between combatants within a state of war (*ius in bello*: "the justice within war"). The specific conditions traditionally enumerated by modern just war theorists include the following (Johnson 1981; Orend 2008):

A. Ius ad bellum

1. Just cause: a war must be fought for a just reason such as resisting aggression. Recovering property and punishing evil are also sometimes suggested.
2. Right intention: a nation may only intend to fight a war for the sake of its just cause, not for other motives for which wars are sometimes fought, e.g., the desire for territorial expansion, hatred of the enemy, or the desire for domination.

---

[7] For the debate over Tacitus' political allegiances, see Kapust 2012.
[8] See, e.g., Walzer 1977 (prompted by Vietnam); Elshtain 2003; S. L. Carter 2011.

3. Proper authority: a war must be waged by a legitimate authority (i.e., a state).
4. Last resort: war should not be undertaken until all other avenues of redress have been exhausted.
5. Public declaration: wars should be publicly declared.
6. Reasonable probability of success: wars should not be waged if they are unlikely to bring about the objective for which they are being fought.
7. Proportionality: wars must not be waged if the universal benefit of war (i.e., the good sought) does not outweigh the universal disadvantage (i.e., the destruction likely incurred).

B. *Ius in bello*

1. Proportionality: the use of force within war must be proportional to the end sought.
2. Discrimination: soldiers are to be distinguished from civilians; only the former are proper participants in war.
3. No means of fighting that are *mala in se* ("evil in themselves"): traditional examples include mass rape, genocide, poisoning, treachery, and biological weapons.

Just war theory has a long history, which scholars often trace back to St. Augustine, "the first great formulator of the theory that war might be 'just'" (P. Ramsey 1992: 8).[9] However, just war theory owes a great debt to the Roman republican tradition. In fact, many of the individual specifications of just war theory can be found in the works of Cicero.

Let's start with the basic division of the conditions of just war into *ius ad bellum* and *ius in bello*. Cicero's law code in *De legibus* at one place reads: "Let them wage just wars justly" (*Leg.* 3.9). According to this law, there exists (a) such a thing as a just state of war (roughly corresponding to *ius ad bellum*) and (b) just ways of waging war (roughly corresponding to *ius in bello*). Cicero enumerates the conditions for such wars most systematically in *De republica* and *De officiis*.

According to Cicero, for a war to be undertaken justly, the nation must have a just cause such as protecting itself or its allies from aggression, recovering property, or punishing an enemy for injustices; its

---

[9] Johnson 1981 begins with St. Augustine but acknowledges the tradition's "earliest roots in pre-Christian cultures" (xxiv).

intentions to go to war must be formally announced and publicly declared beforehand; this declaration of war should only follow the denial of a request for satisfaction from the nation against which one has a grievance (*Rep.* 3.25 Powell = 3.35a Zetzel; *Off.* 1.36). More generally, "wars ought to be undertaken for this reason – to live in peace without injustice" (*Off.* 1.35). As far as just conduct within wars is concerned, war is to be limited between soldiers (*Off.* 1.36–37; cf. Livy 36.5.6); truces, treaties, promises, and oaths must be honored (*Off.* 1.38–40); acts bringing grave dishonor to one's country should be avoided (*Off.* 1.40; cf. 1.159; 3.86); and, once the war has concluded, the victor should spare those who were not "cruel or savage in warfare" and give refuge to those who seek it (*Off.* 1.35). Even if wars are waged for empire and glory, the just cause for which one entered into war in the first place must be "completely present" (1.38).

On one hand, Cicero's enumeration of just war principles sounds familiar: present to some degree are such key *ius ad bellum* principles as A1 just cause (resisting aggression, recovery of property, punishment of evil), A2 intentionality, A4 last resort, A5 public declaration of war, and the *ius in bello* principle of B2 discrimination. In addition to these formal principles, one can find in Cicero supporting material for A3 proper authority (*Off.* 3.107: exclusion of pirates from laws of just war), B1 proportionality (*Off.* 1.33: leniency in punishment), and B3 no means *mala in se* (*Off.* 1.40; 3.86: poisoning forbidden).

However, on closer inspection, there are important differences from modern notions associated with later just war theory. Perhaps most striking to contemporary readers is that Cicero's theory does not proscribe wars undertaken for the purpose of competing for the glory of empire (*Off.* 1.38; see Brunt 1990: 288–323). Such wars are difficult to square with a commitment to just war theory out of a concern for human rights, as assumed by modern accounts such as Michael Walzer's in his classic *Just and Unjust Wars* (1977). This difference stems from the roots of Cicero's account, deep within the Roman republican tradition (*Off.* 1.36; see J. Barnes 2015).

The traditional Roman republican just war theory is very different from modern concerns with protecting human rights and providing space for humanitarian intervention. Roman republican just war theory does not derive from abstract principles of justice; it is anchored primarily in notions of religion and honor. Key concepts include *ius* (justice, right), *maiestas* (dignity, majesty, sovereignty), *auctoritas* (reputation for leadership, prestige), *dignitas* (worthy standing), and *gloria* (glory, honor) of the Roman people and *res publica* (Drexler 1988).

Consider first just war theory's religious foundation, which is disclosed through such concepts as *maiestas*, a word that indicates the dignity or majesty of a god, and *ius*. The justice or right by which war was declared was originally the right (*ius*) of fetiales, the priests who guided and advised the senate on foreign policy. If Rome had a grievance against another regime, these priests would travel to the offending regime and request restitution. If denied, a state of war was declared, and the offending party was "unjust by right" (Plautus, *Amphitryon* 247; Harris 1979: 169). A couple of presumptions lie behind this idea. First, the gods are witnesses to treaties and value *fides*, or good faith (cf. Livy 3.2.4 and Drexler 1988: 190). Second, in international relations where there is no judge, and it was in doubt about who was at fault in breaking a contract, the outcome of a war acted as a just judge – the gods ensured it (Livy 21.10.9; cf. Cic. *Off.* 1.38 and Dante, *On Monarchy* 2). To win a war was to be proven just; to lose was to be proven to be in the wrong. If one believes that the outcome of a war vindicates one's fidelity to one's promises, one can see why the Romans included holding in good faith oaths given to enemies among the principles of just war (Cic. *Off.* 3.107).

Perhaps of even greater importance for the republican theory of just war than religion is honor, captured by the terms *auctoritas*, *dignitas*, and *gloria*. As the Rhodian embassy flatteringly reports at Livy 37.54.15–16, in contrast to those whose major motivation for war was the acquisition of territory, you Romans "have fought your wars on behalf of worthy standing (*dignitas*) and glory (*gloria*) before the entire human race, which has for a long time now viewed your name and empire (*imperium*) as next to the immortal gods." At *De legibus* 3.9, Cicero explicitly connects honor and glory with just war theory: "Let them wage just wars justly; let them be sparing of the allies; let them contain themselves and their men; let them augment the glory of their people; let them return home with honor" (trans. Zetzel). Here Cicero associates waging wars justly – justice within war, i.e., the sparing of allies and the restraint of soldiers – with the desire for glory, honor, and the status that accompanies these goods. Likewise, in *De officiis*, he suggests that wars fought for the glory of empire are contested between competitors for honor (*honor*) and worthy standing (*dignitas*) and are thus waged less bitterly. By imposing limits on what one may honorably do in combat, wars for glory limit injustice within war (*Off.* 1.38).

Some scholars have suggested that Cicero's use of the laws of just war arising from the warrior code of Republican Rome conflicts with his concept of a natural law establishing a community of justice among human beings (E. M. Atkins 1990; Brunt 1990: 307–308). While Cicero recognizes the normative force of reason behind natural law, he also acknowledges the important psychological point that human beings are powerfully motivated by the desire for honor and glory, which at Rome was traditionally achieved through military action. Because of the relative strength of the passion for honor, reason has limited effectiveness in political affairs. As Cicero makes clear, there is moral capital to be derived from the consideration of human beings as honor- and status-loving agents, even if it involves a logic that differs in some respects from that which would obtain were humans to be considered merely as rational beings inhabiting "the world community of justice and reason" (Nussbaum 1996: 8). In particular, the logic of the honor code stipulates that there are some things a warrior will not do in battle, both because such deeds are beneath his own "dignity" and because they would deny the "dignity" of his foe as a fellow contender (*competitor*) for honor (*Off.* 1.38; cf. Barton 2001: 84–86). This logic appears to assume, as recent studies have observed more generally of honor cultures, that behind the struggle for glory and status lies a deep-seated desire for recognition from one's fellow competitors.[10]

This desire for recognition has transcultural cachet, a point Cicero underscores by quoting the words of King Pyrrhus of Epirus, who in 280 BCE returned to the Romans captives without a fee, for he judged such leniency appropriate in a war contested "by manly virtue" (1.38). If the contests between republics for the glory of empire both presuppose and reinforce a mutual recognition of the "dignity" of one's opponent from the perspective of a man of honor contending for greater honor, then such contests help support a notion of "justice within war" by guarding against the dehumanization of one's opponents that leads to the greatest atrocities and injustices in combat (von Heyking 2007). In a similar way, the modern aid organization the Red Cross finds that its humanitarian mission to limit the impact of war is accomplished most effectively by communicating to warriors in the language not of human rights but of the warrior's honor code, which, once translated into different vernaculars, helps reinforce basic tenets of the rules of warfare adopted by the Geneva conventions and which constitute international humanitarian law (Ignatieff 1998: 147).[11]

---

[10] Limits of reason in human psychology and politics in Cicero's thought: J. W. Atkins 2013. Glory as a powerful motivating force in *De officiis*: Long 1995. Recognition as a fundamental value in status-seeking honor cultures: Lendon 1997; Barton 2001: 84–86; Lebow 2008.

[11] It is worth underscoring that "dignity" for Cicero is primarily an honor term related to status and as such can be enhanced, diminished, or lost rather than as (in the modern language of human rights) something indelibly and equally possessed by all as a human attribute. On "dignity" in Roman thought, see Pöschl 1989 and Griffin 2017.

"Just" Wars in Early Christian Thought

From its roots in Roman republicanism, "just war theory" entered the Christian tradition through St. Ambrose (337–97) and St. Augustine. In the three centuries prior to Constantine, prominent Christians such as Tertullian, the brilliant Greek theologian Origen (c. 185–254), and Lactantius made powerful arguments on behalf of pacifism, although Lactantius modified his views after the rise of Constantine. As Christians became more involved in the military and in civil administration, they had to grapple with how their duties to Rome fit within the context of their commitment to Christianity, especially to Christ's command to love one's neighbor (Matthew 22:39; Mark 12:31; Luke 10:27; see also chapter 3). The teachings on war by Ambrose and Augustine originated in response to this concern.[12]

Ambrose, the bishop of Milan, addresses war most extensively in his *De officiis*, his work on ethics for clergy modeled on Cicero's *De officiis*. While Ambrose transforms Cicero's ethic, the bishop draws upon his Ciceronian model for the structure, terminology, and discussion topics of his own work (J. W. Atkins 2011). Thus, it is no surprise that Ambrose treats war and violence at some length. He distinguishes between just and unjust wars (1.176), and he takes over several important aspects of Cicero's treatment of the topic. Just grounds for war include punishing evil (1.129; 3.110–11, 116) and defending one's countrymen against aggression (1.129, 176–77; 3.23). War should be fought to restore peace (3.23). Once war has begun, Ambrose stresses that promises to enemies should be kept (3.69) and mercy should be given to defeated enemies (3.87). Combatants are limited to soldiers. Clergy should not participate in war, and the church as an institution lacks the authority to wage war (*Off.* 1.175; *On Widows* 8.49, with Swift 1983: 108–109).

Ambrose differs from Cicero on some aspects of his discussion of war. Ambrose dethrones imperial glory as a licit motivation for war, though he does recognize that there is glory for those who undertake personal dangers in combat in order to preserve the peace of all (3.23). Reflecting on the Old Testament account of Israel's conquest of Canaan, he also acknowledges the justice of wars of conquest directly commanded by God (3.54–56). However, as with his virtue ethic more generally, Ambrose most fully departs from Cicero when he applies Jesus' command to love one's

---

[12] Christian attitudes towards violence before Constantine: Swift 1983: 32–79; Wynn 2013: ch. 2. On Lactantius, see also the introduction to Bowen and Garnsey 2003, esp. 50–51.

neighbor. Cicero had argued that an individual's right to self-defense was a necessary legal principle (*Pro Milone* 9–10) – a principle that the sixteenth- and seventeenth-century Dutch jurist Hugo Grotius later adopted as one of the grounds for a just war. Ambrose counters that the just Christian, out of devotion to his neighbor, should forgo using violence in self-defense against an attacker, thereby following the example of Christ (3.27–28). However, at times this same love for one's neighbor may authorize the use of violent force – to stand by passively and watch a neighbor being assaulted would be an act of injustice (cf. Cic. *Off.* 1.28). Ambrose illustrates the point by citing Moses' killing of an Egyptian who was assaulting a fellow Hebrew man (1.179). Thus, Ambrose was able to draw on the Gospel love commandment to discriminate between authorized and unauthorized uses of violent force.[13]

St. Augustine's reflections on war are scattered throughout several texts composed over three or four decades.[14] The bibliography is immense, and there is widespread disagreement, including on the fundamental question of whether the basic views of this "founding father" fit within the later just war tradition.[15] Augustine's discussion of war intersects with his treatment of broader issues, such as justice, legitimacy, and authority (see chapter 1), the nature and status of peace as a good, love and desire, the fallen human condition, and God's role as judge. These broader concerns, which lie at the center of Augustine's political thought, contribute to the distinctive elements of his discussion of war.

Like St. Ambrose before him, St. Augustine echoes several elements familiar from the Ciceronian treatment of just wars: a war must have a just cause, such as punishing the wicked, recovering stolen property, or defending one's city against foreign aggression; peace is the purpose of war; promises in war made to enemies must be kept.[16] However, Augustine's discussion reveals significant differences from the Ciceronian republican

---

[13] The previous two paragraphs on Ambrose's theory on just war are indebted to Swift 1983: 96–110 and von Heyking 2007. Glory in war: von Heyking 2007: 25. The love commandment and virtue ethics: J. W. Atkins 2011. Grotius on Cicero and self-defense: Straumann 2015: 171. The love commandment and just war: Swift 1983: 100–103.

[14] Key texts: *On the Free Choice of the Will* 1.5; *Reply to Faustus the Manichaean* 22; *Letter* 138 to Marcellinus; *Letter* 189 to Boniface; *Letter* 222 to Darius; *Questions on the Heptateuch*; *Sermon* 30; *City of God*, esp. 4.15; 18.2; 19.7, 12, 13 (list in Lenihan 1988). English translations: E. M. Atkins and Dodaro 2001; Tkacz and Kries (1994); Dyson 1998 (*City of God*).

[15] Bibliography: Markus 1983; Swift 1983; P. Ramsey 1992; Mattox 2006. Skepticism about Augustine as a just war theorist: Lenihan 1988; Holmes 1999; Wynn 2013.

[16] For discussion of these features of Augustine's thought with references, see Swift 1983: 110–49.

just war teaching, especially with respect to religion and glory. Consider four important features of Augustine's thinking on warfare.

First, Augustine emphasizes that war (and other acts of violence) must be carried out under or by a legitimate authority, a topic he discusses at length in *Against Faustus the Manichaean* (*Contra Faustum* 22.73–79; cf. *C.D.* 1.26). Soldiers, judges, military leaders, and magistrates may legitimately use force, but private individuals may not, even for the purpose of self-defense (*Ep.* 47.5). God too is a legitimate authority (hence, Augustine justifies Old Testament wars commanded by God). Citing chapter 13 of St. Paul's letter to the Romans, Augustine argues that God has delegated the authority for preserving civic peace to magistrates and other legitimate governing authorities. Thus, just men may serve even under "sacrilegious" leaders, who bear the moral responsibility for the orders they ask their subordinates to carry out (*C. Faust.* 22.75). (Augustine suggests that subordinates may be guiltless in carrying out unjust orders that do not clearly violate "the sure command of God.")

God's delegation of the authority to preserve civic peace to rulers regardless of their piety severs warfare's immediate tie to religion. War for Augustine is a feature of the *saeculum* – the present age in which human society is characterized by the intermingling of people with very different and irreconcilable beliefs about ultimate matters such as religion but who nevertheless cooperate on matters of shared interest, such as war and peace.[17] Though God oversees all events within the *saeculum*, including wars, his purposes for any given event or series of events are inscrutable (*C. Faust.* 22.78). We cannot know the "sacred" significance of a war's outcome. Thus, Augustine undermines the fundamental presupposition of Roman republican thinking on just war: victory no longer indicates that the gods have vindicated the victor's cause.

Second, Augustine increases focus on right intention. Wars must not be motivated by desire for harming, revenge, or domination (*C.D.* 4.6). Behind this lies Augustine's well-known account of human motivations in terms of ordered and disordered loves. Unjust motives for war, like all unjust desires, come from inordinately loving lower goods for their own sake rather than for the sake of enjoying God (*C. Faust.* 22.78). Much as Ambrose before him, Augustine believes that benevolence, mercy, and love for one's neighbor can properly motivate warfare (*C. Faust.* 22.79). One aids and serves the wicked by depriving them of their opportunity for continued unjust action (injustice harms the souls of those who commit

---

[17] For *saeculum*, see Markus 1970 with the qualifications of Markus 2006.

it) and by establishing a just and peaceful society where virtue can flourish (*Ep.* 138.14).[18]

Third, wars are the result of necessity (*Ep.* 189.5–6; *C.D.* 4.15; 19.7). They are an unavoidable byproduct of humankind's fallen and corrupt condition. Even in the case of "just" wars, there will be a degree of injustice on both sides (P. Ramsey 1992: 19). Whereas the wicked aim to use war to establish an unjust peace according to their base desires for conquest, those who undertake a just war seek to establish a more just peace based on an agreement of better desires (*C.D.* 19.12). However, perfect peace coming from the union of perfectly ordered desires is not possible in this mortal life (*C.D.* 19.17) and even a relatively successful temporal peace is never free from the danger of sedition, war, and bloodshed (*C.D.* 19.5). Thus, the just soldier and magistrate will wage war despite the manifold evils involved for the same reason that the just judge will take his place at the bench: he is compelled by necessity imposed by the human condition (cf. *C.D.* 19.6).

Finally, Augustine does not allow for wars waged for the glory of empire (*C.D.* 3.14). In detaching glory from warfare, Augustine, like Ambrose before him, limits the grounds of acceptable warfare (von Heyking 2007). In the process, he also drops the capacity of glory and honor to limit actions within war. Augustine's view on honor largely prevailed within the later just war tradition, and it is absent from most contemporary accounts. However, the concept never completely disappeared. It was a substantial part of reflection on just wars by the seventeenth-century legal and political philosopher Hugo Grotius – an important figure in the modern tradition. More recently, drawing on Grotius, contemporary just war theorist Larry May (2007) has attempted to reestablish honor (as part of a wider notion of "humanness") at the heart of just war thinking.

Cosmopolitanism

Writing in his *Meditations*, the Roman emperor Marcus Aurelius (ruled 161–80 CE) argues for the following set of propositions (4.4; trans. Hammond):

> If mind is common to us all, then we have reason also in common – that which makes us rational beings. If so, then common too is the reason which dictates what we should or should not do. If so, then law too is common to us all. If so, then we are citizens. If so, we share in a constitution. If so, the

---

[18] On the connection between love and war in Augustine, see P. Ramsey 1992; Holmes 1999.

universe (*kosmos*) is a kind of community (*polis*). In what else could one say that the whole human race shares a common constitution?

Though Marcus himself never explicitly self-identified as a Stoic, he was heavily influenced by Stoic thought, and in fact a similar set of propositions are found in sources that either claim or appear to reproduce Stoic arguments (Long and Sedley 67A, 67L; Cic. *Leg.* 1.23). The logic of Marcus' argument runs as follows: As rational beings all human beings share in reason. Reason prescribes how human beings should relate to one another (and in other versions, to the gods) as fellow rational beings and in particular as social and political animals. Insofar as reason prescribes and regulates human conduct, it may be understood as having the force of law. Those whose lives are regulated by a common law may be understood to be fellow citizens of a common city. And since the common law that regulates their lives is the natural and rational law of the cosmos, the entire cosmos may be seen as a city and human beings as its citizens. Hence, a human being may be rightly called a *kosmopolitês* or "cosmopolitan," a citizen of the world.

According to tradition, the term "cosmopolitan" originated with Diogenes the Cynic (D.L. 6.63), who lived in Athens and Corinth in the fourth century BCE. As a result of a radical commitment to living according to nature, Diogenes and later Cynics rejected social conventions, including conventional politics and the polis (Epict. *Discourses* 3.22.47). Given this, it is likely that Diogenes used the term "cosmopolitan" in a negative sense as a term of criticism (a "citizen of the world" rather than a citizen of the particular *polis* he happened to inhabit), though this is a matter of debate among scholars. Cynicism greatly influenced the founder of Stoicism, Zeno of Citium (a city in Cyprus) and Athens (344–262 BCE); his chief work of political philosophy, the *Republic*, infamously contained a number of unconventional proposals such as wives in common, unisex clothing, and the abolition of currency – all in the name of promoting a way of life in accordance with nature and virtue. Even when cosmopolitanism developed the positive notion of duties to other human beings beyond one's *polis*, the notion of citizenship involving commitment to the constitution of a cosmic city of justice and reason threatened the primacy of the constitution and institutions of conventional cities.[19]

---

[19] Cynic cosmopolitanism: Moles 1996; 2000 (challenges the orthodoxy of "negative cosmopolitanism"); cf. Schofield 1999a: 141–45. Zeno's *Republic* and the subsequent cosmopolitan tradition: cf. Schofield 1999a; Sellars 2007; Vogt 2008; J. W. Atkins 2015; forthcoming e.

Despite the potential of their school's philosophy for political and social corrosiveness, Roman Stoics such as Seneca and Marcus Aurelius advocated and lived lives of deep political and social engagement. As Seneca himself noted, all human beings have the potential to be citizens of two *res publicae* – the "truly common" cosmopolis of "gods and human beings" and the particular city of their birth. It is possible to serve both commonwealths at the same time, even if some people choose to commit themselves to one at the expense of the other (*De otio* 4.1). Although in *De otio* Seneca suggests that the Stoic wise person will in practice if not in principle excuse himself or herself from political involvement (8.1–4), this extreme position seems to break with the predominant attitude towards politics of other Roman Stoics and indeed of Seneca himself (Griffin 1976: ch. 10). Instead, Roman Stoics generally taught that the life lived in accordance with nature could be deeply integrated into political and social life. These Stoics believed they could best promote the universal human society by serving particular political societies and communities. Whereas Zeno had argued for the abolition of the family, Roman Stoics positively treated Romans' obligations to parents, spouses, children, and country (Reydams-Schils 2005).

Cicero was not himself a Stoic, and in his philosophical writings, he exercised a degree of independence from his sources. However, his *De officiis*, which takes as its model a lost work by the Stoic philosopher Panaetius, would become a foundational work in the later cosmopolitan tradition (Nussbaum 1997; 2000). More clearly than any surviving prior work, *De officiis* stresses the key cosmopolitan principle that every human being should be a unit of moral concern for his fellow humans solely on account of his humanity (*Off.* 3.27). (While earlier texts in the Stoic cosmopolitan tradition clearly valued the rationality of gods and sages, it is not clear that they accorded this same value to the overwhelming majority of human beings, whom they regarded as fools and slaves.) In arguing for the existence of a "fellowship of the entire human race" (*Off.* 1.50–51), Cicero draws on the Stoic idea that human beings are endowed with a natural social instinct, which is developed through a process known as *oikeiôsis*, "appropriation" or "making something one's own" (1.50–51; cf. *Off.* 1.11–12). Through *oikeiôsis* children come to recognize themselves as their own, and thus begin to care for themselves and their own welfare. As they mature, they begin to see their immediate family as their own, and so begin to care for them and their welfare. As they continue to extend this care for others outwards, it gradually encompasses more people until it covers the entire human race. (The Greek Stoic philosopher Hierocles, writing early in the second century CE, provides a particularly vivid version of this idea.) At the end of this process, human beings recognize that, inasmuch as all (mature) human beings possess reason, which constitutes their (true) selves and determines their (true) interests, they should identify with all human beings and have concern for their welfare. Cicero sometimes expresses the point by quoting a line from the Roman comic poet Terence's play *The Self-Tormentor* (line 77): "I am a human being; I think that nothing human is alien to me." (For the Stoics, "alienation" is the opposite of "appropriation.")[20]

Cicero argues that if we by nature should care for all other human beings, then we have duties or obligations towards all. Our actions towards other members of the universal human fellowship should display justice, which Cicero expresses in negative terms through a *formula* or "rule of procedure": we are to refrain from harming other human beings for the sake of our own advantage (*Off.* 3.21, 23). In addition, we have some minimal positive obligations to help strangers and foreigners – to give directions to the lost and to offer counsel, water, and fire to those in need (1.51–52). Such acts of kindness cost us little, allowing us to devote most of our resources to assist those closer to us: our family, friends, fellow citizens, and country. Articulating what we may call a "principle of proximity," Cicero contends that "human society and its union will be best preserved if your acts of kindness are conferred upon each person in proportion to the closeness of their relationship to you" (*Off.* 1.50). He strongly defends the primacy of the *res publica* over other forms of human association as the object of a citizen's greatest allegiance inasmuch as the commonwealth embraces all of its citizens' deepest loves and affections (*Off.* 1.57).[21]

Cicero's account was influential (Nussbaum 2000). For example, the eighteenth-century philosopher Adam Smith identified in *De officiis* grounds to support his own moral theory. In particular, Smith makes space for universal justice (especially in its negative sense, as the prohibition against harming others) and for beneficence towards strangers; he rejects what he sees as the impractical cosmopolitan ideal of detached impartiality,

---

[20] Scholars, working from a variety of angles, have written at length on *oikeiôsis*. Pembroke 1971 is a seminal article; Ramelli and Konstan 2009 (a translation of and commentary on Hierocles' surviving work) contains full bibliography on the topic. Cicero cites *The Self-Tormentor* 77 at *Leg.* 1.33 and *Off.* 1.30. Seneca cites the line at *Ep.* 95.53.

[21] On *Off.* 1.50–57, see E. M. Atkins 1990; Nussbaum 2000; R. Woolf 2015: 180–83; Griffin 2017: 61–62. For an account of how Cicero reconciles the patriotic and cosmopolitan strands within *De officiis*, see J. W. Atkins forthcoming b.

and he defends the modern nation-state as that which encompasses and promotes all of our strongest natural loves and affections.[22]

While Cicero's account in *De officiis* was more influential, Seneca also treated the obligations of justice and generosity towards strangers that we all possess by virtue of our common humanity (see *Letter* 95). Justice requires that we refrain from harming other human beings, and generosity, that we help the shipwrecked sailor, give directions to the lost, and provide food to the starving (95.51). His own "rule of procedure" to guide our interactions with fellow human members of the "great body" of gods and human beings echoes that of Cicero in its negative articulation of the duties of justice, but Seneca seems to have a more expansive understanding of the duties of generosity: nature decrees that we must be ready to assist all who require our help (95.52, with Griffin 2017: 62–63). Though Seneca does not explicitly say so in this passage, he most likely understood such assistance to be limited by considerations such as the giver's relative means (Griffin 2013: 250). The grounds for and limits of our obligation to provide aid to strangers continue to be matters of debate for contemporary cosmopolitans (Unger 1996; Nussbaum 2000; Appiah 2006: ch. 10).

Marcus Aurelius, the last of the so-called five good emperors, ruled when Rome's empire was at its height. One could easily imagine combining the political reality of a vast empire with the cosmopolitan unity of mankind. If human beings should be united under, and have their lives regulated by, a common set of laws, then perhaps it would be best for a common political authority to rule over all human beings and enforce these laws? Marcus himself never advocated this idea, which contemporary scholars sometimes call "political" or "legal" cosmopolitanism (Pogge 1992; Held 2010). However, a generation or two earlier, Plutarch in his *Life of Alexander* had read such aspirations into Alexander the Great's conquests, and some 1100 years later Dante Alighieri would characterize the Roman Empire in similar terms (*On Monarchy* 1.3.4; 2.8).

Contemporary cosmopolitanism takes as axiomatic the primacy of the individual as a unit of moral concern, the equal moral worth of all individuals, and the idea that human beings should generally be concerned about the welfare of other human beings regardless of regime (Pogge 1992; Nussbaum 1996; Held 2003). All three of these tenets were present to various degrees in the Roman Stoic cosmopolitan movement, but not without important qualifications. In line with the early Greek Stoics, the Romans

---

[22] Adam Smith and Cicero's *De officiis*: Forman-Barzilai 2010 (esp. 120–32). Compare Smith's defense of the nation-state at *Theory of Moral Sentiments* VI.ii.1.2 with Cic. *Off.* 1.53–57.

continued to relate individual human nature to the nature of the cosmos as part to the whole, a relation that enabled them to argue that there can be no conflict between the good of the individual and that of the community.[23] Moreover, as we have seen, Cicero, Seneca, and Marcus Aurelius all lived and taught a cosmopolitanism that was deeply embedded in particular regimes, an outlook that anticipates contemporary defenses of partial or "rooted" cosmopolitanism (Appiah 2005; 2006). Finally, while Cicero's "cosmopolitanism" emphasizes a general moral concern for all human beings, this concern is not characteristically expressed in the language of human rights or equal and inherent human dignity that is often used by modern cosmopolitans (for rights in Cicero, see chapter 2; cf. Griffin 2017 on dignity). By contrast, and in line with the rest of the Roman republican tradition, his thought gives much weight to the pursuit of the hierarchical and transient goods of honor and status.

Roman Republicanism and Realism

As this chapter has worked through Roman reflections on imperialism, just war theory, and cosmopolitanism, it has been building towards a distinctive picture of a Roman republican conception of international relations. This picture will more fully come into focus by contrasting it with an important contemporary theory of international relations – realism. While other theories could have been chosen, realism is an appropriate choice for a systematic comparison, both because some of its key tenets appear at first blush to have been embraced by Roman republican thinkers and because recent studies have utilized it as the interpretive framework through which to analyze Republican Rome's interactions with its neighbors (Eckstein 2006; 2008).

Realism in contemporary theory occupies a big tent; to focus our analysis, we will focus on the thought of two of its most influential twentieth-century theorists, Hans Morgenthau and Kenneth Walz. For Morgenthau (1985: 31), "international politics, like all politics, is a struggle for power." International relations are characterized by the subordination of justice and morality to power relations (Morgenthau 1970: 382; Art and Walz 1983: 6). In this regard, realists find inspiration in the famous line from

---

[23] See, e.g., Marcus Aurelius, *Meditations* 5.22 and 6.44. As Inwood and Donini (1999: 676) note, "nothing is more characteristic of the [Stoic] school, from the beginnings in the late fourth century to the end of antiquity, than the thesis that human and cosmic nature are related as part to whole." For this relation as it applies to the early Greek Stoic natural law tradition, see J. W. Atkins 2015.

Thucydides, "The strong do what they can and the weak suffer what they must" (5.89). In such an environment, fear and security are recognized as fundamental motivating factors.[24]

Building on and critiquing Morgenthau, Walz's "neo-realism" contends that the most salient fact to understanding state behaviors is to recognize them as actors in an anarchic international order; the lack of peace in international relations is one sign of this lack of order (1979: 161–63). In such an environment, states should seek to optimize security rather than (as in the thought of Morgenthau) to maximize power. Most fundamentally, states act to ensure their survival (Walz 1979: 91–92). Walz's focus on the international anarchic system cleaves apart international relations from domestic politics: principles that account for domestic politics cannot also explain a state's behavior in the international realm. Finally, Walz (1979: 204–206) has argued that a system in which two superpowers predominate international affairs provides the greatest order and stability.

Several of these aspects of realist thought should be familiar from Roman republicanism. Polybius and Sallust, for example, stress the stability that can arise in a bipolar world in which the fear of an enemy fosters collective action. And one can certainly find passages in which Roman writers entertain (without endorsing) the notion of an international sphere without constraints. For instance, both Julius Caesar and Livy put into the mouths of Rome's enemies the Thucydidean idea that "right" in war was a matter of the will of the strong (*Gallic War* 1.36; Livy 5.36.5). Still, on the whole, Roman republicanism deeply challenges the central tenets of realism.

Roman republicanism's departure from realism stems from the central role of honor in republican thought. As we have seen, republicanism posits that Roman actors were motivated not just by power or by the material concern for security, but even more by the non-material need for the recognition of others. The reputation of being seen to be honorable by other actors in international relations was an important source of status, prestige, and influence. As Ted Lendon (1997: 74) notes, "the city must act well: a city had a moral character just like a man, and the city's prestige rested in part upon widespread perception of that character."

The value placed on honor and the need for recognition generates order in the international sphere. It undergirds, for instance, the principles that limit and regulate war among nations. Even republican thinkers like Polybius and Sallust, who allow that fear can produce order, also

---

[24] While Thucydides is traditionally read as a "realist," some alternative interpretations move him closer to the Roman republican conception of international relations (see, e.g., Lebow 2001).

acknowledge the important order-producing role of honor. Along with Cicero, Livy, and Tacitus, these writers held that the antagonistic pursuit of goods such as glory contributes order to an international system that allows for conflict while limiting its effects. As we have seen, a similar relationship between status, honor, conflict, and order also informs republican thinking about the mixed constitution. According to Polybius and Cicero, the Roman constitution was a product of the antagonistic struggle for honor and (for Cicero) freedom that subsequently provided an order that contained and limited conflict (chapter 1). Unlike Walz, for Roman republicanism similar principles explain and produce domestic and international order, even if the latter order is necessarily thinner than the former. For Roman republicanism, the absence of peace does not necessarily signify a condition of anarchy.

The important role of honor for status and agency also explains why survival for states cannot be their most overriding and important end. Survival is something that should not be chosen if the price is the complete loss of honor and standing. Cicero points out at the end of *De officiis* book 1 (1.159) that there are some things so disgraceful that one shouldn't do them even if the survival of the *res publica* were at stake. And, what is even more significant, the *res publica* wouldn't want such disgraceful deeds to be performed on its behalf. For his part, Polybius praises wars undertaken for the sake of honor even when the outcome is disastrous (Eckstein 1995: 70). These examples from Cicero and Polybius would make no sense according to realists and other contemporary theories of international relations that place little value on the immaterial goods of recognition and honor.

This does not mean that Roman republicanism in the context of interstate relations is nonsense. In fact, the consideration of reputation and status as important sources of agency and influence in international relations continues to receive much attention from contemporary scholars (Dafoe, Renshon, and Huth 2014). Recently Richard Ned Lebow (2008) has argued that human beings have a universal drive for honor and the recognition of others; once one acknowledges this, one can explain the actions of a number of historical regimes (ranging from fifth-century Greek citystates to the United States) that would otherwise remain opaque to leading contemporary theories of international relations that focus on fear or material interests. Lebow's theory – a type of "constructivism" – shares a number of other elements with Roman republicanism and suggests that Roman republicanism still has much to offer current students of international relations.

Conclusion

In the landmark 2015 US Supreme Court case *Obergefell vs. Hodges*, the court held that the due process and equal protection clauses of the Constitution's Fourteenth Amendment granted to same-sex couples a fundamental right to marry. Affirming the centrality of marriage by turning to its "ancient origins," the majority opinion quoted Cicero's *De officiis* 1.54 (citing p. 57 of Walter Miller's translation in the Loeb edition) as follows: "The first bond of society is marriage; next, children; then, the family."[1] This quotation, however, represents only one clause of a much longer sentence in Latin – two in English following Miller's text and translation:

> For since the reproductive instinct (*libidinem procreandi*) is by Nature's gift the common possession of all living creatures, the first bond of union is that between husband and wife (*prima societas in ipso coniugio est*); the next, that between parents and children; then we find one home, with everything in common. And this is the foundation of civil government, the nursery, as it were, of the state (*seminarium rei publicae*).

The court's translation, though certainly acceptable, differs from that of the credited edition. What interests us here is what was omitted. Placed within its wider context, one can see why the court saw it "fair and necessary" to add that this and other references were "based on the understanding that marriage is a union between two persons of the opposite sex." But this acknowledgment still does not adequately capture the force of Cicero's argument, which begins by grounding the cause of marriage's status as the "first bond of union" in the "reproductive instinct" and concludes by establishing the household's importance as the foundation of the republic. Ultimately Cicero's readers' greatest love and allegiance should be to the republic, which encompasses everything else that they love as their own (1.57). For Cicero, the shape and significance of marriage is established

[1] *Obergefell v. Hodges*, 576 U.S. __. 135 S.Ct. 2584, 2594 (2015).

by natural, socially productive drives establishing a union or partnership (*societas*) that in turn has obligations to the larger society that it forms and supports.

Read with an eye to its relevance to our time and place, the court's elision of "nature" and "political society" from Cicero's argument achieves striking results: it emphasizes the shared value of marriage's importance while concealing a deep divergence over why it is important. The court begins its case by asserting, "the right to personal choice regarding marriage is inherent in the concept of individual autonomy."[2] For Cicero the significance of marriage derives from the fact that human beings are dependent and interdependent rather than autonomous. This divergence should not surprise. "The right to personal choice" and "individual autonomy" reflect modern liberal-democratic values. To our ears Cicero's radical denial of individual autonomy by redefining the interests of the individual in light of the community (see esp. 3.40) is as discordant as the patriarchal Roman household that his discussion of marriage evoked for his Roman readers.

The court's use of Cicero in its discussion of marriage well illustrates Roman political thought's general relationship to liberal democracy. On one hand, we can recognize familiar concepts and concerns. This is understandable, not least because of Rome's contribution to the history of the western world (Richard 2010). On the other hand, we find many of these same concepts and concerns to contain foreign elements. This too is understandable, for to study Roman political thought is to investigate a way of thinking that is not our own. What should one make of this combination of the familiar and the foreign?

One possibility is to treat Roman political thought in the same way as the court in *Obergefell* handled Cicero: focus on the portions that affirm what we see as central to our own history and present condition at the expense of the rest. Much recent scholarship on Roman republicanism has taken this path, putting aside the outmoded aristocratic Roman honor code and civic virtues to pursue liberal concerns with liberty, constitutionalism, and popular sovereignty or democratic concerns with structural inequality.[3] The problem is not that individual studies do this: it is extremely important to draw attention to the common concerns we

---

[2] *Obergefell*, 135 S.Ct. at 2599.
[3] Liberty: Pettit 1997; Skinner 1998; Kapust 2011b. Constitutionalism and sovereignty: Straumann 2016. Structural inequality: Connolly 2015. For Connolly our own inability to live up to our democratic ideals renders Roman inequality familiar.

share with the Romans. The problem occurs when the sum total of individual studies skews towards the familiar at the expense of the foreign. This risks distorting Roman political thought, for as we have seen in this book, Roman political culture, and the illiberal honor code at its heart, is the core that unites many of Roman republicanism's concepts, including the constitution, liberty, citizenship, virtue, corruption, religion, rhetoric, imperialism, and just war theory.

A second approach, reacting against the first, emphasizes the foreignness of Roman society at the expense of the familiar. Roman republicanism, based on illiberal and undemocratic foundations, cannot be made to serve liberal-democratic ends without anachronism and distortion (Ando 2010).

The structure and argument of this book has presupposed a third possibility, that Roman political thought is most relevant to modern readers when we take seriously both the familiar and the foreign, and indeed the very fact of the mixture of the two. We acknowledge that we can recognize at least some of our own problems and concepts in Roman political thought; at the same time, we recognize that the particular ways in which the Romans conceived of common problems and conceptualized common concepts are foreign. These twin realities make the Romans particularly worth our study. That concepts like liberty, rights, citizenship, civil religion, or imperialism are recognizable and important concepts in our world ensures an easy entry point into ideas worthy of our deep and immediate consideration; the fact that Roman thought articulates them differently guarantees that in considering the Romans we will not be entering an echo chamber in which our own assessment of these ideas and the problems surrounding them bounces back to us.

The Romans' solutions will not, and cannot, be our solutions – at least, not beyond the most general levels of principle. And where general principles offered by Roman thinkers differ from the presuppositions of our own times, we will have to adjudicate between the two. As leading political philosophers from very different traditions have taught, we must do our own thinking for ourselves (Strauss 1968: 8; Skinner 1998: 118). But our thinking will be greatly impoverished if it is done in isolation from the political thought of other times and places.

In conclusion, let's reflect on how some of the familiar and foreign aspects of Roman political thought explored in this book work together to make Roman republicanism relevant for citizens of modern liberal democracies at a time in which an increasing number of people feel that recent political events in the west have revealed the "metacrisis of liberalism," an ideology unraveling before our eyes from internal tensions that its critics have long been pointing out.[4]

Of course liberalism has its variants, and an enormous body of literature has defended the philosophy against its critics.[5] The details need not detain us here. The following reflections assume only that there are legitimate areas of concern attending many of the core concepts typically, if not necessarily, associated with liberalism – ideas such as individual autonomy, rights, capitalism, materialism, universalism, tolerance, and rationalism. Perhaps some form of liberalism can adequately address these concerns. Perhaps the weaknesses of liberalism are fatal, and we must look to a post-liberal future. Or perhaps the way forward is to adjust liberalism so that it less profoundly affects practices to which it may be hostile but on which it nevertheless must depend. I will leave it to the reader to ruminate on which of these options is preferable.

Let's begin with the book's final chapter. Sometimes the search for a relevant republicanism has purged Roman republicanism of its predisposition to militarism and national glory (Nederman 2000). Yet to bracket Roman imperialism on this ground removes from consideration potentially important Roman contributions to modern international relations theory, for it is precisely through considering Rome's (to us) illiberal honor code that Roman republicans raise important concerns related to the desire for recognition as a motivating force. Critics of liberalism have argued that, because liberalism mistakenly assumes that "the majority of people in the modern world have material well-being as their primary goal," it gives insufficient weight to the immaterial desire for recognition that also deeply motivates human beings.[6] Insofar as Roman republicanism treats concerns with status, honor, and recognition alongside such influential concepts as imperialism, just war theory, and cosmopolitanism, it provides an excellent resource for exploring the nature, logic, and implications of such concerns for international relations.

Another element of Roman republicanism sometimes purged by modern theorists is religion. In the place of the central Roman republican virtue of *pietas* – devotion to the gods and country – we are offered a patriotism duly

[4] The "metacrisis of liberalism": Milbank and Pabst 2016. For some influential academic critiques of liberalism, see MacIntyre 1984; Sandel 1996; 1998; Taylor 1989; Walzer 1983; 1994.
[5] One strategy of liberalism's defenders has been to try to adapt liberal democracy to accommodate civic virtue: see, e.g., Dagger 1997; Spragens 1999; Gregory 2008.
[6] Quote from Lebow 2008: 159 (made in the context of liberalism as a theory of international relations). For recognition as an important value in domestic politics, see Taylor 1994 (a seminal essay).

cleansed of ugly nationalistic impulses (Viroli 1995; 2002). Yet to remove devotion to the gods from its place alongside devotion to country is to miss an opportunity to see the relevance of both aspects of civil religion to our contemporary world. We might benefit from reflection on Rome, not only as we consider how to cultivate a particular devotion to country within the wider framework of larger universal loyalties and values, but also as we reckon with how regimes should treat those citizens whose religious devotion challenges the predominant and definitive values of a given political society.

Toleration is regarded as a "quintessentially liberal value" (Mendus 1988: 5), and one that liberals frequently anchor in assumptions regarding the nature and role of religious belief that are often incompatible with the views of those religious adherents who see religion as constitutive of a way of life rather than as an expression of private personal beliefs. Given the large numbers of people from many religious traditions living both inside and outside liberal democracies, the following question remains important for the future of liberalism: can liberal democracies permit citizens to exercise toleration grounded in something other than the religious skepticism or individual autonomy that many liberal accounts of toleration presuppose and that many believers distrust?[7] Viewed with this question in mind, Lactantius' "familiar" proto-Lockean account of toleration as a function of the individual's private will is perhaps less interesting than his "foreign" illiberal theological argument for toleration from divine punishment. No doubt conflict will arise, not least because, as Steven L. Carter (2004) has argued, religion and liberal democracy both offer competing claims on the allegiances of citizens. Still, there is a better chance to establish a workable "peace treaty" (to use Carter's language) if we are not distracted from where the conflict really lies by unnecessarily coupling theological and civic tolerance.

Treatments of toleration in the Roman world also have a more positive contribution to make to current discussions of the topic. In his recent book *Confident Pluralism*, John Inazu argues that thriving in a deeply divided, pluralistic society such as the present-day United States requires a commitment not only to certain legal protections but also to the character traits of tolerance, patience, and humility. For Inazu, tolerance recognizes the freedom of others to pursue beliefs and practices we believe are wrong; patience involves restraint and endurance in the face of our differences; humility requires us to accept that we don't always need to "prove" that our beliefs and practices are correct and that those who find them objectionable are wrong (2016: ch. 5). The early discussions of toleration by

---

[7] Grounds for toleration: Mendus 1988.

Stoics and Christians suggest that Inazu is right to group these virtues together. Indeed, both the Stoics Epictetus and Marcus Aurelius and the Carthaginian bishop Cyprian, working from within two different frameworks, suggest that tolerance in fact requires patient endurance and the recognition of the limits of our responsibility to correct or punish the incorrect views of others. These ancient authors prompt us to ask ourselves whether a "liberal" commitment to toleration might be enhanced by a recommitment to other virtues that liberalism has long obscured.

A core value of both modern liberal democracy and Roman republicanism is liberty. Another is the concept of individual rights, which, as I argued in chapter 2, is just one place at which Constant's dichotomy between the ancients and moderns breaks down. Roman republicanism reveals that the concept of individual rights, demarcating a notion of ownership in a world where many people were property, is ipso facto neither liberal nor democratic.

Of course the modern liberal notion of human rights based on individual human autonomy proscribes slavery, which was left largely untouched by the republican notion of citizens' rights based on custom and constitution. And indeed providing a vocabulary that recognizes the dignity of all human beings is one of liberalism's greatest achievements. Yet by itself this liberal notion of rights is inadequate. For one thing, rights, whether construed positively as entitlements to certain goods or negatively as "the 'right' to be left alone" (Hauerwas 1987: 238), ensure neither the necessary agency for political action nor the sphere in which to act. According to Roman republicanism, honor and the *res publica* provided the agency and space for action. Liberalism has been searching for its own resources for agency and public action since Constant. That autocracy arose at Rome by eliminating both political space and agency suggests why this search should continue to merit our attention.

Historically the liberal conception of liberty as autonomy has been accompanied and supported by at least one set of assumptions about the human relationship to nature. Beginning with the thought of Francis Bacon, René Descartes, and Thomas Hobbes, human beings came to be regarded as separate from an unintelligible and hostile nature that they must strive to master and control. As nature increasingly succumbs to human control through scientific and technological progress, the sphere of human autonomy expands. As a result, liberal technologically progressive societies have increasingly altered the environment and depleted natural resources, to name just one problem related to technology and liberalism.[8]

---

[8] For the problem of technology and liberalism, see the essays in Melzer, Weinberger, and Zinman (1993).

In an important recent book about environmental politics, Jedidiah Purdy has suggested that we might develop a new virtue ethic to help us respond to our natural world in a way that recognizes sublimity and beauty, human finitude and frailty. He writes, "both treasuring beauty and feeling awe at sublimity are ways of respecting an order of things, and of valuing motives to act so as to uphold it, to recognize the limits it might enforce" (2015: 253). We have already encountered the most suitable word for the virtue that produces such limit-respecting feelings of awe in our discussion of Lucretius: "reverence." In contrast to Hobbes and his heirs within the liberal tradition, for Lucretius happiness lies not in fulfilling infinite, limitless desires through the conquest of nature but in experiencing the blessings that come from embracing human finitude and accepting our own natural limits within a sublime if hostile world (cf. Strauss 1968: ch. 5; Nichols 1976). Lucretius thus invites us to re-examine deeper philosophical presuppositions about human life and our relationship to our world as we consider how to cultivate a healthy attitude towards our natural environment.

Throughout this book we have observed the importance of noting differences between Roman and modern liberal notions of political concepts. In some cases, the unfamiliar Roman concepts may actually provide a richer vocabulary for capturing familiar modern political experiences. For instance, in the weeks following the 2016 presidential elections, Americans across the political spectrum were concerned with the deep divisions within their polity revealed by an ugly and contentious campaign. In such times when the sense of civic wholeness is lost, the Roman republican conception of corruption, which directs us to ask questions about the overall health of the body politic, seems to bring us far nearer to the heart of the matter than the more familiar liberal idea of corruption, which focuses more narrowly on politicians' use of their authority for personal material gain.

Cicero conceived of a political society as a cooperative enterprise (J. W. Atkins 2013: 144–52). In a liberal democracy, rights tend to "underwrite a view of human relations as exchanges rather than cooperative endeavors" (Hauerwas 1987: 238). A social economy whose chief virtue is justice, consisting of respecting rights and contracts, means that getting what we deserve is paramount. If what we receive is primarily what we deserve, we can lose the capacity for thankfulness for undeserved favors, and the notion of interdependence and mutual recognition that such gratitude nourishes. Philosophers like Lucretius, Plutarch, and Seneca remind us of the power of gratitude to counteract the individualism, greed, envy, fear, and passion for power that lead to civic corruption. Though liberalism provides rocky soil for gratitude to grow, the virtue may provide an important antidote to the endless quest to fulfill an ever-expanding cascade of needs and desires through technology and the market, a malady that, in Alexis de Tocqueville's words, leaves liberal-democratic citizens "restless in the midst of abundance" (*Democracy in America*, part 2, ch. 13; trans. Lawrence).

But there is a deeper point to make. Recent psychological studies demonstrate that a deep relationship obtains between gratitude and human happiness (Watkins 2007). Gratitude is a human virtue. This fact joined with the observation that liberalism undermines gratitude suggests that liberalism does not tell the whole truth about human beings. Liberalism is at best a partial truth; at worst, a lie that distorts and disfigures humanity. However, for all liberalism's faults, I suspect that, if given a choice, the vast majority of the readers of this book would choose to live in some version of a liberal democracy over the Roman Republic or Empire. And they would be able to make a good case for their choice. But in making their case against Rome, defenders of liberal democracy would have to recognize, in light of the material presented in this book, that their case is a relative one: liberal democracy has its weaknesses, and the extent to which it is a superior regime is merely one of degree. Conversely, there is a challenge for liberalism's critics. When measured against a highly socially stratified, restrictive, politically turbulent, violent, slave-owning ancient regime, liberal democracy will have its virtues, even in the eyes of contemporary detractors. If liberalism is a lie, perhaps it is at least in part a noble one.

Bibliographical Essay

This essay indicates readily accessible works that map a way into the topics treated in this book. I have also included readily available or preferred translations of major works treated in each chapter for those who wish to read or teach these works in English translation.

Introduction

Hammer 2014 provides an introduction to Roman political thought that proceeds author-by-author from Cicero to St. Augustine. It engages major authors' texts at a more advanced level than my book and contains an extensive recent bibliography. *The Cambridge History of Greek and Roman Political Thought* (C. J. Rowe and Schofield 2000) also proceeds author-by-author and is still excellent value. Another more recent multi-author volume, *A Companion to Greek and Roman Political Thought* (Balot 2009), proceeds thematically and contains recent bibliography. Hammer 2008 pairs four Romans with later theorists: Cicero and Arendt; Livy and Machiavelli; Tacitus and Montesquieu; Seneca and Foucault. Oxford Bibliographies Online provides a helpful guide to key bibliography for most of the authors, texts, and themes discussed in this book. J. W. Atkins 2012 (revised 2015) covers bibliography for Greek and Roman political philosophy. Black 2009 treats Greek, Roman, and early Christian political thought alongside that of ancient China, Israel, India, Iran, Egypt, and Mesopotamia.

Important treatments of republicanism by political theorists include Pettit 1997; Skinner 1998; Viroli 1995; 2002. Kapust 2011b approaches Roman republican thought through a study of the major Roman historians. Connolly 2015 provides a literary and theoretical approach to key authors, including some (e.g., Horace) not usually associated with republicanism. For Roman political culture, see especially Hölkeskamp 2010 and Arena and Prag forthcoming. Hammer 2015 offers a comparative approach to the Roman Republic and Greek democracy, covering many features of the political culture of the Roman *politeia*. For Rome's intellectual culture during the crucial last century of the Republic, see Rawson 1985 and Moatti 2015.

Chapter 1

Straumann 2016 argues for the emergence of a first-century BCE constitutionalism at Rome; Lintott 1999 provides a helpful overview of the Roman "constitution." Millar's various essays (culminating in Millar 1998) sparked a major debate by arguing that Rome is a democracy, a view also assumed in his study of the reception of Rome in the later history of political thought (2002a). Strong critiques of Millar are found in Mouritsen 2001 and Cartledge 2016. Morstein-Marx 2004 contributes to this debate through a detailed study of the popular assembly (*contio*). Mouritsen 2017 provides an overview of Roman political institutions and practices in the late Republic in greater detail and with a far more extensive bibliography than I can provide. For Polybius' thought, see von Fritz 1954; Hahm 1995; and Walbank's commentary (1957–79), monograph (1972), and essays (2002). Waterfield 2010 provides an accessible translation of the *Histories'* first six books. For the mixed constitution, see Nippel 1980; Lintott 1997; Hahm 2009; J. W. Atkins 2013: ch. 3 (which focuses mainly on Cicero and Polybius). Schofield 1995 is a classic article arguing for the notion of political legitimacy in Cicero's *De republica*. Zetzel 1999 (second edn. 2017) provides an accurate translation and useful introduction to *Rep.* The classic work on Seneca's political thought is Griffin 1976. Braund (2009) provides text, translation, and useful commentary for Seneca, *De clementia*. Further analysis of the constitutional theory of *De clementia* can be found in Stacey 2007: ch. 1. Text and translation for Dio Chrysostom can be found in the Loeb Classical Library.

Chapter 2

The classic modern essay on different concepts of liberty is Berlin 1969. For the neo-republican (or neo-Roman) idea of liberty, see Pettit 1997 and Skinner 1998; 2002. For slavery in ancient political thought (Greek, Roman, Christian, and Stoic), see Garnsey 1996. For Roman liberty, the classic works are the long essay "*Libertas*" in Brunt 1988 and the somewhat dated but still valuable monograph, Wirszubski 1950. Arena 2012 is an important recent monograph devoted to liberty in the Roman Republic indebted to Skinner's approach to intellectual history. For property in Roman political thought and the later tradition, see Garnsey 2007. For citizens' rights in Cicero and Roman law, see J. W. Atkins 2013: ch. 4. A translation for the *Digest* of Justinian is provided by Watson 1985. Warrior 2006a offers a useful translation of the first five books of Livy; Hard 2014 is the most recent translation of Epictetus' works.

Chapter 3

For the history of the concept of citizenship, see Walzer 1989 and Pocock 1995. The classic treatment of Roman citizenship is Sherwin-White 1973, which examines the political development of citizenship from our earliest evidence to the fourth century CE. Nicolet 1980 examines citizenship in Republican Rome, especially as it pertains to voting, military service, and economic life. Boatwright 2012 covers Rome's assimilation of key peoples. Earl 1967 approaches the Roman political tradition through analysis of virtue and the Roman honor code. For ancient republican virtues, see Schofield 2009 and Hellegouarc'h 1972. Kaster 2005 discusses virtues leading to emotional responses that promote community. For the virtues in Cicero's *De officiis*, see the introduction to Griffin and E. M. Atkins 1991 (which also provides a very good translation), E. M. Atkins 1990 (justice), and Long 1995 (the virtues and the Roman honor code). For virtues communicated by emperors, see Wallace-Hadrill 1981 and Noreña 2001; 2011. Kapust 2011b: ch. 5 looks at the virtue of prudence in the *Agricola*. Translations for the elder and younger Pliny may be found in the Loeb Classical Library. Mattingly and Rives 2009 provides an accessible translation of the *Agricola*. For Augustine's political thought, see the translation of the *City of God* by Dyson 1998 and the translation of politically relevant letters and sermons by E. M. Atkins and Dodaro 2001. The bibliography for Augustine's political thought is immense. A good place to begin is Bruno 2014, a guide to twentieth- and twenty-first-century interpretations of Augustine's political thought.

Chapter 4

For a historically informed analysis of the idea of corruption, see Euben 1989. For intellectual histories of reverence and gratitude, see respectively Woodruff 2001 and Leithart 2014. For corruption in Sallust, see Connolly 2015: ch. 2. A good recent translation of Sallust's writings is Batstone 2010. For an analysis of Lucretius' political thought that pays attention to the poet's concern with the background of Roman politics, see the classic article by Fowler 1989. Smith 2001 is an excellent prose translation. For Lucretius' concern with power and limits, see Hammer 2014: ch. 2 (which includes recent bibliography). Nichols 1976 and Colman 2012 discuss Lucretius' relationship with modern political thought. Strauss's "Notes on Lucretius" (Strauss 1968: ch. 5) is an interpretation by an important twentieth-century political theorist. For Lucretius' relationship to Epicurus, see Clay 1983 and Sedley 1998. A translation of Seneca's *De beneficiis* can be found in Cooper and Procopé 1995; the authoritative study of the work, including Seneca's insights on gift exchange, is Griffin 2013. For the political psychology of Plutarch's *Lives*, see Duff 1999; for their political thought, see Liebert 2016; for English translations of the *Marius* and *Pyrrhus*, consult the Loeb Classical Library. For gratitude, see Scruton 2010a; Ceaser 2011; and Leithart 2014. See also the psychological study of the virtue of gratitude by Watkins 2007.

Chapter 5

Garsten 2006 provides a defense of rhetoric and judgment rooted in an analysis of major texts in the history of political philosophy (chapter 5 is devoted to Cicero); Remer 2017 defends the morality of rhetoric through a study of Cicero and "the Ciceronian tradition" (Quintilian, John of Salisbury, Justus Lipsius, Edmund

Burke, the authors of the *Federalist Papers*, and J. S. Mill). Beiner 1983 is a provoca-tive account of judgment by a political philosopher drawing on Aristotle, Arendt, and Kant. Connolly 2007 explores some of this chapter's major concerns in Roman rhetoric, especially in Cicero. Steel and van der Blom 2013 is a valuable collec-tion of essays on rhetoric in the Republic. Kapust 2011b focuses on rhetoric as it relates to republican thought in Sallust, Livy, and Tacitus (with several substantive glances at Cicero). Kennedy 1972 is the standard history of rhetoric in the Roman world. J. May and Wisse 2001 provide a good English translation of Cicero's *De oratore*. Serviceable translations of Cicero's other rhetorical works, the *Rhetorica ad Herennium*, Quintilian's *Institutes*, and Tacitus' *Dialogus de oratoribus* can be found in the Loeb Classical Library. Skinner 1996 provides a useful survey of Quintilian's thought as a background to rhetoric in Hobbes. For the themes of this chapter in the *Dialogus*, see especially Saxonhouse 1975; Bartsch 1994: 98–147; van den Berg 2014. Woodman 2010 and Pagán 2012 are guides to Tacitus and his reception.

Chapter 6

Beard, North, and Price 1998 is a two-volume commentary (vol. 1) and sourcebook of texts in translation (vol. 2) that covers religion at Rome from early Rome to the empire of the fifth century CE. Rüpke 2007 provides a broad, accessible treatment of Roman religion. For an English translation of Cicero, *De legibus*, see Zetzel 1999 (sec-ond edn. 2017). Garnsey 1984 is a short treatment of toleration from classical Athens to the Roman Empire that includes both pagan and Christian writings. North 2003 looks at toleration through a study of Rome's treatment of the Bacchanalia. de Ste. Croix 1963 examines the persecution of early Christians. C. K. Rowe 2009 deals with questions of tolerance and polytheism in the context of the early Christian commu-nity as described in the New Testament book of Acts. Bowen and Garnsey 2003 offers a good translation with introduction of Lactantius' *Divine Institutes*. Streeter 2006 provides helpful context for discussions of toleration by Tertullian and Lactantius. As for writing on toleration by contemporary political theorists, Walzer 1997 engages the topic through a historical case-study approach. Forst 2013 combines a philosophical account of toleration with a rich historical treatment of the topic (including in early Christianity). Mendus 1988 offers a collection of ways modern and contemporary philosophers and philosophies justify toleration. For the classic study of the contem-porary notion of civil religion in America, see Bellah 1970.

Chapter 7

Erskine 2010 provides an accessible overview of Roman imperialism and supplies key texts. Another accessible introductory text is G. Woolf 2012. Champion 2004 provides a thematically organized sourcebook containing both primary sources and excerpts from the work of key contributors. Harris 2016 traces the rise and fall of Roman imperial power from the fifth century BCE to the seventh century CE. The foundational modern realist text in international relations is Morgenthau

1985 (first published in 1948). For neo-realism, see Walz 1979. Lebow 2008 critiques realism in part by drawing on ancient Greek thought. Eckstein 2006 and 2008 apply realism to the interactions among states within the Roman world, an approach usefully qualified by Burton 2011. Harris 1979, arguing against the defensive war theory (e.g., Badian 1968), approaches Roman expansion through Roman attitudes towards glory, honor, and war; North 1981 provides important qualifications. The classic modern work on just war theory is Walzer 1977. The standard historical treatment of the topic is Johnson 1981. Important works by contemporary cosmopolitan theorists include Pogge 1992; Nussbaum 1996; 2002; Held 2003. Recent studies of Polybius on empire include Balot 2010 and Baronowski 2011; for external fear leading to collective action, see Wood 1995 and Evrigenis 2008; for Cicero on just war, empire, and cosmopolitanism, see J. W. Atkins forthcoming b. Swift 1983 discusses the major authors in early Christian treatments of warfare. For the integration of Roman Stoicism and social life, see Reydams-Schils 2005. Cooper and Procopé 1995 provide an accessible translation for Seneca, *De otio*; Hammond 2006, for Marcus Aurelius' *Meditations*. For Roman Stoic cosmopolitanism, see Nussbaum 1996; 1997; 2002; Long 2008; Schofield 2013; Griffin 2017. For the contribution of Cicero's *De officiis* and Stoic texts to the later cosmopolitan tradition, see Nussbaum 1997; 2000; for the later republican tradition, see Viroli 1995.

Bibliography

Adcock, F. E. (1959) *Roman Political Ideas and Practice*. Ann Arbor, MI.

Alexander, M. (2006) "Law in the Roman Republic," in Rosenstein and Morstein-Marx (2006), 236–55.

Algra, K. A., J. Barnes, J. Mansfeld, and M. Schofield (eds.) (1999) *The Cambridge History of Hellenistic Philosophy*. Cambridge.

Allen, D. (2014) *Our Declaration: A Reading of the Declaration of Independence in Defense of Equality*. New York and London.

Ando, C. (2010) "'A dwelling beyond violence': on the uses and disadvantages of history for contemporary republicans," *HPT* 31 (2): 183–220.

   (2011) *Law, Language, and Empire in the Roman Tradition: Empire and After*. Philadelphia.

   (2012) *Imperial Rome AD 193 to 284: The Critical Century*. Edinburgh.

Annas, J. (2013) "Plato's *Laws* and Cicero's *De legibus*," in M. Schofield (ed.), *Aristotle, Plato and Pythagoreanism in the First Century BC: New Directions for Philosophy*, 206–24. Cambridge.

Appiah, K. A. (2005) *The Ethics of Identity*. Princeton.

   (2006) *Cosmopolitanism: Ethics in a World of Strangers*. New York.

Arena, V. (2011) "Roman sumptuary legislation: three concepts of liberty," *European Journal of Political Theory* 10 (4): 463–89.

   (2012) *Libertas and the Practice of Politics in the Late Roman Republic*. Cambridge.

   (2015) "Informal norms, values, and social control in the Roman participatory context," in Hammer (2015), 217–38.

   (2016) "Popular sovereignty in the late Roman Republic: Cicero and the will of the people," in R. Bourke and Q. Skinner (eds.), *Popular Sovereignty in Historical Perspective*, 73–95. Cambridge.

Arena, V., and J. Prag (eds.) (forthcoming) *A Companion to Roman Political Culture*. Malden, MA.

Arendt, H. (1958) *The Human Condition*. Chicago.

   (1968) *Between Past and Future: Eight Exercises in Political Thought*, revised edn. New York.

   (1973) *The Origins of Totalitarianism*, third edn. New York.

   (2006 [1963]) *On Revolution*. New York.

205

Art, R. J., and K. N. Waltz (1983) "Technology, strategy, and the uses of force," in R. J. Art and K. N. Waltz (eds.), *The Use of Force*, 1–32. Lanham, MD.

Asmis, E. (2004) "The state as a partnership: Cicero's definition of *res publica* in his work *On the State*," *HPT* 25 (4): 569–99.

(2005) "A new kind of model: Cicero's Roman constitution in *De Republica*," *AJPh* 126 (3): 377–416.

(2008a) "Cicero on natural law and the laws of the state," *ClAnt* 27 (1): 1–33.

(2008b) "Lucretius' new world order: making a pact with nature," *CQ* 58 (1): 141–57.

Astin, A. E. (1988) "*Regimen morum*," *JRS* 78: 14–34.

Atkins, E. M. (1990) " '*Domina et regina virtutum*': justice and *societas* in *De officiis*," *Phronesis* 35 (1): 258–89.

Atkins, E. M., and R. Dodaro (eds.) (2001) *Augustine: Political Writings*. Cambridge.

Atkins, J. W. (2011) "The *Officia* of St. Ambrose's *De officiis*," *Journal of Early Christian Studies* 19 (1): 49–77.

(2012) "Greek and Roman political philosophy," in D. Clayman (ed.), *Oxford Bibliographies in "Classics."* Oxford [online; updated 2015].

(2013) *Cicero on Politics and the Limits of Reason: The Republic and Laws*. Cambridge.

(2014) "A revolutionary doctrine? Cicero's natural right teaching in Mably and Burke," *Classical Receptions Journal* 6 (2): 177–97.

(2015) "Zeno's *Republic*, Plato's *Laws*, and the early development of Stoic natural law theory," *Polis* 32 (1): 166–90.

(2016) "Classic Communication," *Duke Magazine*, Special Issue 2016, 14–15, http://dukemagazine.duke.edu/article/classic-communication.

(2017) "Natural law and civil religion: *De legibus* book II," in O. Höffe (ed.), *Ciceros Staatsphilosophie: Ein Kooperativer Kommentar zu De re publica und De legibus*, 167–86. Klassiker Auslegen 64. Berlin.

(forthcoming a) "Constitution and empire in Roman republican thought," in *Museum and Ancient Roman Civilization*. Beijing. [English title of Chinese text.]

(forthcoming b) "Cosmopolitanism, just wars, and empire," in J. W. Atkins and T. Bénatouïl (eds.), *Cambridge Companion to Cicero's Philosophy*. Cambridge.

(forthcoming c) "Leo Strauss's Lucretius and the art of writing," in P. Burian, G. Davis, and J. Strauss Clay (eds.), *Beiträge zur Altertumswissenschaft*, Special issue edition. Berlin.

(forthcoming d) "Non-domination and the *libera res publica* in Cicero's republicanism," in V. Arena (ed.), *Liberty: An Ancient Concept for the Contemporary World, History of European Ideas*, Special issue edition.

(forthcoming e) "Politics, *politeia*, and rational control," in G. Cambiano and A. Lianeri (eds.), *The Edinburgh Critical History of Greek and Roman Philosophy*. Edinburgh.

Badian, E. (1958) *Foreign Clientelae 264–70 B.C.* Oxford.

(1968) *Roman Imperialism in the Late Republic*. Ithaca, NY.

Ball, T., J. Farr, and R. Hanson (eds.) (1989) *Political Innovation and Conceptual Change*. Cambridge.

Balot, R. (2001) *Greed and Injustice in Classical Athens*. Princeton.

(2010) "Polybius' advice to the Imperial Republic," *Political Theory* 38 (4): 483–509.

Balot, R. (ed.) (2009) *A Companion to Greek and Roman Political Thought*. Malden, MA.

Baraz, Y. (2012) *A Written Republic: Cicero's Philosophical Politics*. Princeton.

Barlow, J. J. (2012) "Cicero on property and the state," in Nicgorski (2012), 212–41.

Barnes, J. (2015) "Cicero and the just war," in J. Barnes, *Mantissa: Essays in Ancient Philosophy IV*, M. Bonelli (ed.), 56–79. Oxford.

Barnes, T. D. (1968) "Legislation against the Christians," *JRS* 58: 32–50.

(1985) *Tertullian: A Historical and Literary Study, reissued with corrections and a postscript*. Oxford.

Baronowski, D. (2011) *Polybius and Roman Imperialism*. London.

Barton, C. (2001) *Roman Honor: The Fire in the Bones*. Berkeley.

Bartsch, S. (1994) *Actors in the Audience: Theatricality and Doublespeak from Nero to Hadrian*. Cambridge, MA.

Batstone, W. W. (2010) (ed. and trans.) *Sallust: Catiline's Conspiracy; The Jugurthine War; Histories*. Oxford.

Bauman, R. (2000) *Human Rights in Ancient Rome*. London.

Beard, M. (1986) "Cicero and divinization: the formation of a Latin discourse," *JRS* 76: 33–46.

(2015) *SPQR: A History of Ancient Rome*. London.

Beard, M., J. North, and S. Price (1998) *Religions of Rome*, 2 vols. Cambridge.

Beck, H. (2011) "Consular power and the Roman constitution: the case of *imperium* reconsidered," in H. Beck et al. (eds.), *Consuls and the Res Publica: Holding High Office in the Roman Republic*, 77–96. Cambridge.

Bederman, D. (2008) *The Classical Foundations of the American Constitution: Prevailing Wisdom*. Cambridge.

Beiner, R. (1983) *Political Judgment*. Chicago.

(ed.) (1995) *Theorizing Citizenship*. Albany.

(2011) *Civil Religion: A Dialogue in the History of Political Philosophy*. Cambridge.

Bélanger, R. (1985) "Le plaidoyer de Tertullien pour la liberté religieuse," *Studies in Religion* 14 (3): 281–91.

Bell, P. (ed. and trans.) (2009) *Three Political Voices from the Age of Justinian: Agapetus, "Advice to the Emperor"; Dialogue on Political Science; Paul the Silentiary, "Description of Hagia Sophia."* Liverpool.

Bellah, R. (1968) "Response," in D. R. Cutler (ed.), *The Religious Situation: 1968*, 388–93. Boston.

(1970 [1967]) "Civil religion in America," in *Beyond Belief: Essays on Religion in a Post-Traditional World*, 168–89. New York.

Berlin, I. (1969) *Four Essays on Liberty*. Oxford.

Black, A. (2009) *A World History of Ancient Political Thought*. Oxford.

Blits, J. H. (2014) *The Heart of Rome: Ancient Rome's Political Culture*. Lanham, MD.

Boatwright, M. T. (2012) *Peoples of the Roman World.* Cambridge.

Boesche, R. (1987) "The politics of pretence: Tacitus and the political theory of despotism," *HPT* 8 (2): 189–210.

Bohman, J., and W. Rehg (eds.) (1997) *Deliberative Democracy: Essays on Reason and Politics.* Cambridge, MA.

Bosworth, A. B. (2004) "'Mountain and molehill?' Cornelius Tacitus and Quintus Curtius," *CQ* 54 (2): 551–67.

Bowen, A., and P. Garnsey (eds. and trans.) (2003) *Lactantius: Divine Institutes.* Liverpool.

Bradley, K. (2011) "Slavery in the Roman Republic," in K. Bradley and P. Cartledge (eds.), *The Cambridge World History of Slavery*, Volume 1: *The Ancient Mediterranean World*, 241–64. Cambridge.

Braund, S. (ed. and trans.) (2009) *Seneca, De Clementia: Edited with Text, Translation and Commentary.* Oxford.

Brennan, T. C. (2004) "Power and process under the Republican 'constitution'," in H. I. Flower (ed.), *The Cambridge Companion to the Roman Republic*, 31–65. Cambridge. [Second edn. published in 2014.]

Brink, C. O., and F. W. Walbank (1954) "The construction of the sixth book of Polybius," *CQ* 4 (3–4): 97–122.

Brooks, D. (2015) "The structure of gratitude," *New York Times*, July 28, 2015, www.nytimes.com/2015/07/28/opinion/david-brooks-the-structure-of-gratitude.html.

Brouwer, R. (2011) "Polybius and Stoic *tyche*," *GRBS* 51: 111–32.

Brown, P. (1967) *Augustine of Hippo.* London. [Revised edn. published in 2000.]

Bruno, M. J. S. (2014) *Political Augustinianism: Modern Interpretations of Augustine's Political Thought.* Minneapolis, MN.

Brunt, P. A. (1988) *The Fall of the Roman Republic and Related Essays.* Oxford.

(1990) *Roman Imperial Themes.* Oxford.

(2013) *Studies in Stoicism.* Oxford.

Buckland, W. W. (1908) *The Roman Law of Slavery: The Condition of the Slave in Private Law from Augustus to Justinian.* Cambridge. [Reprinted 1970.]

(1963) *A Textbook of Roman Law from Augustus to Justinian*, third edn., revised by P. G. Stein. Cambridge.

Burton, P. J. (2011) *Friendship and Empire: Roman Diplomacy and Imperialism in the Middle Republic (353–146 B.C.).* Cambridge.

Cammack, D. (2013) "Rethinking Athenian Democracy," PhD diss., Harvard University.

Carter, D. (2013) "Republicanism, rights and democratic Athens," *Polis* 30 (1): 73–91.

Carter, S. L. (2004) 'Can religion tolerate democracy? (and vice versa?)," in J. Purdy, A. Kronman, and C. Farrar (eds.), *Democratic Vistas: Reflections on the Life of American Democracy*, ch. 4. New Haven. Published online: DOI: 10.12987/yale/9780300102567.003.0005.

(2011) *The Violence of Peace: America's Wars in the Age of Obama.* New York.

Cartledge, P. (2009) *Ancient Greek Political Thought in Practice.* Cambridge.

(2016) *Democracy: A Life.* Oxford.

Cartledge, P., and M. Edge (2009) "'Rights', individuals, and communities in ancient Greece," in Balot (2009), 149–63.

Castner, C. (1988) *Prosopography of Roman Epicureans from the Second Century B. C. to the Second Century A. D.* Studien zur klassischen Philologie 34. New York.

Ceaser, J. (2011) "No thanks to gratitude," *Policy Review* 170: 59–73, www.hoover .org/research/no-thanks-gratitude.

Champion, C. B. (ed.) (2004) *Roman Imperialism: Readings and Sources.* Oxford.
   (2013) "Polybius on political constitutions, interstate relations, and imperial expansion," in H. Beck (ed.), *Blackwell's Companion to Ancient Greek Government*, 119–30. Malden, MA.

Clair, J. (2016) *Discerning the Good in the Letters and Sermons of Augustine.* Oxford.

Clarke, G. (2005) "Third-century Christianity," in A. Bowman, A. Cameron, and P. D. A. Garnsey (eds.), *The Cambridge Ancient History*, Volume 12: *The Crisis of Empire, A. D. 193–337*, second edn., 589–671. Cambridge.

Clarke, K. (2001) "An island nation: re-reading Tacitus' '*Agricola*'," *JRS* 91: 94–112.

Clarke, M. T. (2014) "Doing violence to the Roman idea of liberty? Freedom as bodily integrity in Roman political thought," *HPT* 35 (2): 211–33.

Clay, D. (1983) *Lucretius and Epicurus.* Ithaca, NY.

Colman, J. (2012) *Lucretius as Theorist of Political Life.* New York.

Connolly, J. (2007) *The State of Speech: Rhetoric and Political Thought in Ancient Rome.* Princeton.
   (2015) *The Life of Roman Republicanism.* Princeton.

Connor, W. R. (1984) *Thucydides.* Princeton.

Cooper, J. M., and J. F. Procopé (eds. and trans.) (1995) *Seneca: Moral and Political Essays.* Cambridge.

Crawford, M. H. (1996) *Roman Statutes*, 2 vols. BICS Supp. 64. London.

Cress, D. A. (ed. and trans.) (1987) *Jean-Jacques Rousseau: The Basic Political Writings.* Indianapolis, IN.

Crook, J. A. (1955) *Consilium Principis: Imperial Councils and Counsellors from Augustus to Diocletian.* Cambridge.
   (1995) *Legal Advocacy in the Roman World.* Ithaca, NY.

Dafoe, A., J. Renshon, and P. Huth (2014) "Reputation and status as motives for war," *Annual Review of Political Science* 17: 371–93.

Dagger, R. (1997) *Civic Virtues: Rights, Citizenship, and Republican Liberalism.* Oxford.

Deane, H. A. (1963) *The Political and Social Ideas of St. Augustine.* New York.

De Blois, L., J. Bons, T. Kessels, and D. M. Schenkeveld (eds.) (2005) *The Statesman in Plutarch's Works*, Volume 2: *The Statesman in Plutarch's Greek and Roman Lives.* Leiden.

Derow, P. S. (1979) "Polybius, Rome, and the East," *JRS* 69: 1–15.

De Ste. Croix, G. E. M. (1954) "*Suffragium*: from vote to patronage," *The British Journal of Sociology* 5 (1): 33–48.
   (1963) "Why were the early Christians persecuted?," *Past and Present* 26: 6–38. [Reprinted in de Ste. Croix (2006) *Christian Persecution, Martyrdom, and Orthodoxy*, M. Whitby and J. Streeter (eds.), ch. 3. Oxford.]

Dodaro, R. (2004a) *Christ and the Just Society in the Thought of Augustine.* Cambridge.

(2004b) "Political and theological virtues in Augustine, *Letter* 155 to Macedonius," *Augustiniana* 54: 431–74.

Dowling, M. B. (2006) *Clemency and Cruelty in the Roman World.* Ann Arbor, MI.

Drexler, H. (1988) *Politische Grundbegriffe der Römer.* Darmstadt.

Duff, T. (1999) *Plutarch's Lives: Exploring Virtue and Vice.* Oxford.

Dyck, A. R. (2004) *A Commentary on Cicero, De legibus.* Ann Arbor, MI.

Dyson, R. W. (ed. and trans.) (1998) *Augustine: The City of God against the Pagans.* Cambridge.

Earl, D. C. (1961) *The Political Thought of Sallust.* Cambridge.

(1967) *The Moral and Political Tradition of Rome.* Ithaca, NY.

Eckstein, A. M. (1995) *Moral Vision in the Histories of Polybius.* Berkeley.

(2006) *Mediterranean Anarchy, Interstate War, and the Rise of Rome.* Berkeley.

(2008) *Rome Enters the Greek East: From Anarchy to Hierarchy in the Hellenistic Mediterranean, 230–170 BC.* Malden, MA.

Edge, M. (2009) "Athens and the spectrum of liberty," *HPT* 30 (1): 1–45.

Elshtain, J. B. (1995) *Augustine and the Limits of Politics.* Notre Dame, IN.

(2003) *Just War against Terror: The Burden of American Power in a Violent World.* New York.

Erskine, A. (2010) *Roman Imperialism.* Edinburgh.

(2011) *The Hellenistic Stoa: Political Thought and Action*, second edn. London.

(2013) "How to rule the world: Polybius book 6 reconsidered," in B. Gibson and T. Harrison (eds.), *Polybius and His World: Essays in Memory of F. W. Walbank*, 231–45. Oxford.

Euben, J. P. (1986) "Political corruption in Euripides' *Orestes*," in J. P. Euben (ed.), *Greek Tragedy and Political Theory*, 222–51. Berkeley.

(1989) "Corruption," in Ball, Farr, and Hanson (1989), 220–46.

(1990) *The Tragedy of Political Theory: The Road Not Taken.* Princeton.

Evrigenis, I. D. (2008) *Fear of Enemies and Collective Action.* Cambridge.

Fantham, E. (1995) "Rewriting and rereading the *Fasti*: Augustus, Ovid and recent classical scholarship," *Antichthon* 29: 57–84.

(1998) (ed.) *Ovid: Fasti Book IV.* Cambridge.

(2004) *The Roman World of Cicero's De Oratore.* Oxford.

Feig Vishnia, R. (2012) *Roman Elections in the Age of Cicero: Society, Government, and Voting.* New York and London.

Ferrary, J.-L. (1974) "Le discours de Laelius dans le troisième livre du *De Re Publica* de Cicéron," *MEFRA* 86 (2): 745–71.

(1977) "Le discours de Philus (Cicéron, *De Re Publica* III, 8–31) et la philosophie de Carnéade," *REL* 55: 128–56.

(1984) "L'archéologie du *De Re Publica* (2, 2, 4–37, 63): Cicéron entre Polybe et Platon," *JRS* 74: 87–98.

Ferry, L., and R. Kingston (2008) "Introduction: the emotions and the history of political thought," in L. Ferry and R. Kingston (eds.), *Bringing the Passions Back In: The Emotions in Political Philosophy*, 3–18. Vancouver and Toronto.

Fish, J. (2011) "Not all politicians are Sisyphus: what Roman Epicureans were taught about politics," in J. Fish and K. R. Sanders (eds.), *Epicurus and the Epicurean Tradition*, 72–104. Cambridge.

Fitzgerald, W. H. (1951) "*Pietas epicurea*," *CJ* 46: 195–99.

Flower, H. I. (1996) *Ancestor Masks and Aristocratic Power in Roman Culture*. Oxford.

Fontana, B. [Benedetto] (1993) "Tacitus on empire and republic," *HPT* 14 (1): 27–40.

Fontana, B. [Biancamaria] (ed. and trans.) (1988) *Constant: Political Writings*. Cambridge.

Forman-Barzilai, F. (2010) *Adam Smith and the Circles of Sympathy: Cosmopolitanism and Moral Theory*. Cambridge.

Forst, R. (2013) *Toleration in Conflict: Past and Present*, trans. Ciaran Cronin. Cambridge.

Fowler, D. (1989) "Lucretius and politics," in M. Griffin and J. Barnes (eds.), *Philosophia Togata I: Essays on Philosophy and Roman Society*, 120–50. Oxford.

Galinsky, K. (1996) *Augustan Culture: An Interpretive Introduction*. Princeton.

Gardner, J. (1993) *Being a Roman Citizen*. London and New York.

Garnsey, P. (1970) *Social Status and Legal Privilege in the Roman Empire*. Oxford.

  (1984) "Religious toleration in classical antiquity," in W. J. Sheils (ed.), *Persecution and Toleration*, 1–27. Studies in Church History 21. Oxford.

  (1996) *Ideas of Slavery from Aristotle to Augustine*. Cambridge.

  (2007) *Thinking about Property: From Antiquity to the Age of Revolution*. Cambridge.

  (2017) "Property and its limits: historical analysis," in B. Winiger, M. Mahlmann, S. Clément, and A. Kühler (eds.), *La propriété et ses limites/Das Eigentum und seine Grenzen*, 13–38. Stuttgart.

Garsten, B. (2006) *Saving Persuasion: A Defense of Rhetoric and Judgment*. Cambridge, MA.

Garver, E. (2004) *For the Sake of Argument: Practical Reasoning, Character, and the Ethics of Belief*. Chicago.

Gelzer, M. (1969 [1912]) *The Roman Nobility*, trans. R. Seager. Oxford.

Gill, C. (2000) "Stoic writers of the Imperial era," in C. J. Rowe and Schofield (2000), 597–615.

Girardet, K. (1983) *Die Ordnung der Welt: Ein Beitrag zur philosophischen und politischen Interpretation von Ciceros Schrift De Legibus*. Wiesbaden.

Glucker, J. (2001) "Carneades in Rome: some unsolved problems," in J. G. F. Powell and J. A. North (eds.), *Cicero's Republic*. BICS Supplement 76, 57–82. London.

Goldie, M. (2010) "Introduction," in M. Goldie (ed.), *John Locke: A Letter Concerning Toleration and Other Writings*, ix–xxiii. Indianapolis, IN.

Goodin, R. E. (2000) "Democratic deliberation within," *Philosophy and Public Affairs* 29: 81–109.

Goodman, M. (2008 [2007]) *Rome and Jerusalem: The Clash of Ancient Civilizations*, paperback edn. New York.

Gowing, A. (2005) *Empire and Memory: The Representation of the Roman Republic in Imperial Culture*. Cambridge.

Gregory, E. (2008) *Politics and the Order of Love: An Augustinian Ethic of Democratic Citizenship*. Chicago.

Griffin, M. T. (1976) *Seneca: A Philosopher in Politics*. Oxford.

(2000) "Seneca and Pliny," in C. J. Rowe and Schofield (2000), 532–58.

(2003) "*De beneficiis* and Roman society," *JRS* 93: 92–113.

(2013) *Seneca on Society: A Guide to De beneficiis*. Oxford.

(2017) "Dignity in Roman and Stoic thought," in R. Debes (ed.), *Dignity: A History*, ch. 2. Oxford. Published online: DOI: 10.1093/acprof:oso/9780199385997.003.0003.

Griffin, M. T., and E. M. Atkins (eds. and trans.) (1991) *Cicero: On Duties*. Cambridge.

Griswold, C. L. (1986) "The Vietnam veterans memorial and the Washington Mall: philosophical thoughts on political iconography," *Critical Inquiry* 12 (4): 688–719.

Grodzinski, D. (1974) "*Superstitio*," *REA* 76: 36–60.

Gruen, E. (1984) *The Hellenistic World and the Coming of Rome*, 2 vols. Berkeley.

Gutmann, A., and D. Thompson (2004) *Why Deliberative Democracy?* Princeton.

Habermas, J. (1995) "Citizenship and national identity: some reflections on the future of Europe," in Beiner (1995), 255–81.

Hahm, D. (1995) "Polybius' applied political theory," in Laks and Schofield (1995), 7–47.

(2009) "The mixed constitution in Greek thought," in Balot (2009), 178–98.

Hammer, D. (2008) *Roman Political Thought and the Modern Theoretical Imagination*. Norman, OK.

(2014) *Roman Political Thought: From Cicero to Augustine*. Cambridge.

(ed.) (2015) *A Companion to Greek Democracy and the Roman Republic*. Malden, MA.

Hammond, M. (ed. and trans.) (2006) *Marcus Aurelius: Meditations*. London.

Hansen, M. (1999) *The Athenian Democracy in the Age of Demosthenes: Structure, Principles, and Ideology*, trans. J. A. Crook, second edn. London.

Hard, R. (2014) *Epictetus: Discourses, Fragments, Handbook*. Oxford.

Harries, J. (2007) *Law and Crime in the Roman World*. Cambridge.

Harris, W. V. (1971) "On war and greed in the second-century BC," *American Historical Review* 76: 1,371–85.

(1979) *War and Imperialism in Republican Rome, 327–70 BC*. Oxford. [Paperback edn. with new preface published in 1984.]

(2001) *Restraining Rage: The Ideology of Anger Control in Classical Antiquity*. Cambridge, MA.

(2016) *Roman Power: A Thousand Years of Empire*. Cambridge.

Hauerwas, S. (1987) "On the 'right' to be tribal," *Christian Scholar's Review* 16 (3): 238–41.

Held, D. (2003) "Cosmopolitanism: globalism tamed?," *Review of International Studies* 29 (4): 465–80.

(2010) *Cosmopolitanism: Ideals and Realities*. Cambridge.

Hellegouarc'h, J. (1972) *Le vocabulaire Latin des relations et des partis politiques sous la République*. Paris.

Hodgson, L. (2017) *Res Publica and the Roman Republic: "Without Body or Form."* Oxford.

Hohfeld, W. N. (1919) *Fundamental Legal Conceptions*. New Haven.

Hölkeskamp, K.-J. (1993) "Conquest, competition, and consensus: Roman expansion in Italy and the rise of the *nobilitas*," *Historia* 42: 12–39.

(2010) *Reconstructing the Roman Republic: An Ancient Political Culture and Modern Research*. Princeton.

Holmes, R. L. (1999) "St. Augustine and the just war theory," in Matthews (1999), 323–44.

Honoré, T. (2002) *Ulpian: Pioneer of Human Rights*, second edn. Oxford.

(2010) "Ulpian, natural law and Stoic influence," *The Legal History Review* 78: 199–208.

Ignatieff, M. (1998) *The Warrior's Honor: Ethnic War and the Modern Conscience*. New York.

Inazu, J. (2016) *Confident Pluralism: Surviving and Thriving through Deep Difference*. Chicago.

Inwood, B. (1995) "Politics and paradox in Seneca's *De beneficiis*," in Laks and Schofield (1995), 241–65. [Reprinted in Inwood (2005), 65–94.]

(2005) *Reading Seneca: Stoic Philosophy at Rome*. Oxford.

Inwood, B., and P. L. Donini (1999), "Stoic ethics," in Algra, Barnes, Mansfeld, and Schofield (1999), 675–758.

Inwood, B., and L. P. Gerson (eds. and trans.) (1994) *The Epicurus Reader: Selected Writings and Testimonia*. Indianapolis, IN.

Inwood, B., and F. D. Miller, Jr. (2007) "Law in Roman philosophy," in F. D. Miller, Jr. and C. A. Biondi (eds.), *A Treatise of Legal Philosophy and General Jurisprudence*, Volume 6: *A History of the Philosophy of Law from the Ancient Greeks to the Scholastics*, 133–65. Dordrecht.

Johnson, J. T. (1981) *Just War Tradition and the Restraint of War: A Moral and Historical Inquiry*. Princeton.

Johnston, D. (1999) *Roman Law in Context*. Cambridge.

(2000) "The jurists," in C. J. Rowe and Schofield (2000), 616–34.

Jones, C. P. (1971) *Plutarch and Rome*. Oxford.

Kahlos, M. (2007) *Debate and Dialogue: Christian and Pagan Cultures c. 360–430*. Aldershot.

Kapust, D. J. (2004) "Skinner, Pettit and Livy: the conflict of the orders and the ambiguity of republican liberty," *HPT* 25 (3): 377–401.

(2011a) "Cicero on *decorum* and the morality of rhetoric," *European Journal of Political Theory* 10 (1): 92–113.

(2011b) *Republicanism, Rhetoric, and Roman Political Thought: Sallust, Livy, and Tacitus*. Cambridge.

(2012) "Tacitus and political thought," in Pagán (2012), 504–28.

Kapust, D. J., and B. P. Turner (2013) "Democratic gentlemen and the lust for mastery: status, ambition, and the language of liberty in Hobbes' political thought," *Political Theory* 41 (4): 648–75.

Kass, A. A., L. R. Kass, and D. Schaub (eds.) (2011) *What So Proudly We Hail: The American Soul in Story, Speech, and Song*. Wilmington, DE.

Kass, L. R. (2002) *Life, Liberty, and the Defense of Dignity: The Challenge for Bioethics*. San Francisco.

Kaster, R. (2005) *Emotion, Restraint and Community in Ancient Rome*. Oxford.

Kennedy, G. (1972) *History of Rhetoric*, Volume 2: *The Art of Rhetoric in the Roman World, 300 B.C.–A.D. 300*. Princeton.

Kenney, E. J. (ed.) (2014) *Lucretius: De rerum natura Book III*, second edn. Cambridge.

Kindt, J. (2012) *Rethinking Greek Religion*. Cambridge.

Konstan, D. (2005) "Clemency as a virtue," *CP* 100 (4): 337–46.

  (2015) "Reading the past (on comparison)," in Hammer (2015), 8–19.

Köstermann, E. (1930) "Der Taciteische *Dialogus* und Ciceros Schrift *de Re Publica*," *Hermes* 65: 396–421.

Krause, S. R. (2002) *Liberalism with Honor*. Cambridge, MA.

Laks, A., and M. Schofield (eds.) (1995) *Justice and Generosity: Studies in Hellenistic Social and Political Philosophy*. Cambridge.

Lasch, C. (1991) *The True and Only Heaven: Progress and Its Critics*. New York.

Lavan, M. (2013) *Slaves to Rome: Paradigms of Empire in Roman Culture*. Cambridge.

  (2016) "The spread of Roman citizenship, 14–212 CE: quantification in the face of high uncertainty," *Past and Present* 230 (1): 3–46.

Lawrence, G. (trans.) and J. P. Mayer (ed.) (1969) *Alexis de Tocqueville: Democracy in America*. New York.

Lebow, R. N. (2001) "Thucydides the constructivist," *American Political Science Review* 95 (3): 547–60.

  (2008) *A Cultural Theory of International Relations*. Cambridge.

Leithart, P. J. (2014) *Gratitude: An Intellectual History*. Waco, TX.

Lendon, J. E. (1997) *Empire of Honour: The Art of Government in the Roman World*. Oxford.

Lenihan, D. (1988) "The just war theory in the work of Saint Augustine," *Augustinian Studies* 19: 37–70.

Lenin, V. I. (2010 [1917]) *Imperialism: The Highest Stage of Capitalism*. London.

Leydet, D. (2014) "Citizenship," in E. N. Zalta (ed.), *The Stanford Encyclopedia of Philosophy* (Spring 2014 Edition), http://plato.stanford.edu/archives/spr2014/entries/citizenship/.

Liebert, H. (2016) *Plutarch's Politics: Between City and Empire*. New York and Cambridge.

Liebeschuetz, W. (1966) "The theme of liberty in the *Agricola* of Tacitus," *CQ* 16: 126–39.

Linderski, J. (1985) "Buying the vote: electoral corruption in the late Republic," *Ancient World* 11: 87–94.

  (1986) "The augural law," *ANRW* 2.16.3: 2,146–312.

  (1995) "Cicero and Roman divination," in *Roman Questions: Selected Papers*, 458–84. Stuttgart.

Lintott, A. W. (1972) "*Provocatio*: from the struggle of the orders to the Principate," *ANRW* I.2: 226–67.

  (1990) "Electoral bribery in the Roman Republic," *JRS* 80: 1–16.

(1993) *Imperium Romanum: Politics and Administration*. London.

(1997) "The theory of the mixed constitution at Rome," in J. Barnes and M. T. Griffin (eds.), *Philosophia Togata II: Plato and Aristotle at Rome*, 70–85. Oxford.

(1999) *The Constitution of the Roman Republic*. Oxford.

Lombardini, J. (2015) "Stoicism and the virtue of toleration," *HPT* 36 (4): 643–69.

Long, A. A. (1995) "Cicero's politics in *De officiis*," in Laks and Schofield (1995), 213–40.

(2002) *Epictetus: A Stoic and Socratic Guide to Life*. Oxford.

(2008) "The concept of the cosmopolitan in Greek and Roman thought," *Daedalus* 137 (3): 50–58.

Long, A. A., and D. N. Sedley (eds.) (1987) *The Hellenistic Philosophers*, 2 vols. Cambridge.

Loraux, N. (2000) *Born of the Earth: Myth and Politics in Athens*, trans. S. Stewart. Ithaca, NY.

MacCoull, L. S. B. (2006) "Menas and Thomas: notes on the '*Dialogus de Scientia Politica*'," *GRBS* 46: 301–13.

Macedo, S. (1990) *Liberal Virtues: Citizenship, Virtue and Community in Liberal Constitutionalism*. Oxford.

Macintyre, A. (1984 [1981]) *After Virtue: A Study in Moral Theory*. Notre Dame, IN.

MacMullen, R. (1981) *Paganism in the Roman Empire*. New Haven.

Maier, P. (2010) *Ratification: The People Debate the Constitution, 1787–1788*. New York.

Manent, P. A. (2006) *A World Beyond Politics? A Defense of the Nation-State*, trans. Marc LePain. Princeton.

(2013) *Metamorphoses of the City*, trans. Marc LePain. Cambridge, MA.

Markus, R. A. (1970) *Saeculum: History and Society in the Theology of St. Augustine*. Cambridge. [Second edn. published in 1988.]

(1983) "St. Augustine's views on the 'just war'," in W. J. Sheils (ed.), *The Church and War*, 1–13. Studies in Church History 20. London.

(2006) *Christianity and the Secular*. Notre Dame, IN.

Markell, P. (2008) "The insufficiency of non-domination," *Political Theory* 36 (1): 9–36.

Matthews, G. B. (1999) *The Augustinian Tradition*. Berkeley.

Mattingly, H. B., and J. B. Rives (eds. and trans.) (2009) *Tacitus: Agricola, Germania*. London.

Mattox, J. M. (2006) *St. Augustine and the Theory of Just War*. New York.

May, J. (1988) *Trials of Character: The Eloquence of Ciceronian Ethos*. Chapel Hill, NC.

May, J., and J. Wisse (eds. and trans.) (2001) *Cicero: On the Ideal Orator*. Oxford.

May, L. (2007) *War Crimes and Just War*. Cambridge.

Mayer, R. (ed.) (2001) *Tacitus: Dialogus de oratoribus*. Cambridge.

McConnell, S. (2012) "Lucretius and civil strife," *Phoenix* 66 (1): 97–121.

McGing, B. C. (2010) *Polybius' Histories*. Oxford.

Melzer, A. M., J. Weinberger, and M. R. Zinman (eds.) (1993) *Technology in the Western Political Tradition*. Ithaca, NY.

Mendus, S. (ed.) (1988) *Justifying Toleration: Conceptual and Historical Perspectives.* Cambridge.

Milbank, J., and A. Pabst (2016) *The Politics of Virtue: Post-Liberalism and the Human Future.* London and New York.

Millar, F. G. B. (1984) "The political character of the Classical Roman Republic, 200–151 B.C.," *JRS* 74: 1–19.

(1986) "Politics, persuasion, and the people before the Social War, 150–90 B.C.," *JRS* 76: 1–11.

(1995) "Popular politics at Rome in the late Republic," in I. Malkin and Z. Rubinsohn (eds.), *Leaders and Masses in the Roman World: Studies in Honor of Zvi Yavetz,* 91–113. New York. [Reprinted in Millar (2002b), 162–82.]

(1998) *The Crowd in Rome in the Late Republic.* Ann Arbor, MI.

(2002a) *The Roman Republic in Political Thought.* Hanover, NH.

(2002b) *Rome, The Greek World, and the East,* Volume 1: *The Roman Republic and the Augustan Revolution,* H. M. Cotton and G. M. Rogers (eds.). Chapel Hill, NC.

Miller, F. D., Jr. (1995) *Nature, Justice, and Rights in Aristotle's Politics.* Oxford.

Minyard, J. D. (1985) *Lucretius and the Late Republic: An Essay in Roman Intellectual History.* Leiden.

Moatti, C. (2015) *The Birth of Critical Thinking in Republican Rome,* trans. J. Lloyd, foreward by M. Schofield. Cambridge. [English translation of Moatti (1997) *La raison de Rome: Naissance de l'esprit critique à la fin de la République.* Paris.]

Moles, J. L. (1996) "Cynic cosmopolitanism," in R. B. Branham and M.-O. Goulet-Cazé (eds.), *The Cynics: The Cynic Movement in Antiquity and its Legacy,* 105–20. Berkeley.

(2000) "The Cynics," in C. J. Rowe and M. Schofield (2000), 415–34.

Momigliano, A. (1987) *On Pagans, Jews, and Christians.* Middletown, CT.

Morgan, T. (1998) "A good man skilled in politics: Quintilian's political theory," in Y. L. Too and N. Livingstone (eds.), *Pedagogy and Power: Rhetorics of Classical Learning,* 245–62. Cambridge.

Morgenthau, H. (1970) *Truth and Power: Essays of a Decade, 1960–70.* New York.

(1985 [1948]) *Politics among Nations: The Struggle for Power and Peace,* sixth edn., rev. K. W. Thompson. New York.

Morstein-Marx, R. (2004) *Mass Oratory and Political Power in the Late Roman Republic.* Cambridge.

Mouritsen, H. (2001) *Plebs and Politics in the Late Roman Republic.* Cambridge.

(2015) "The incongruence of power: the Roman constitution in theory and practice," in Hammer (2015), 146–63.

(2017) *Politics in the Roman Republic.* Cambridge.

Nederman, C. (2000) "War, peace, and republican virtue: patriotism and the neglected legacy of Cicero," in N. Thompson (ed.), *Instilling Ethics,* 17–29. Lanham, MD.

Nicgorski, W. (ed.) (2012) *Cicero's Practical Philosophy.* Notre Dame, IN.

(2016) *Cicero's Skepticism and His Recovery of Political Philosophy.* New York.

Nichols, J. H., Jr. (1976) *Epicurean Political Philosophy: The De rerum natura of Lucretius.* Ithaca, NY.

Nicolet, C. (1980) *The World of the Citizen in Republican Rome*, trans. P. S. Falla. Berkeley.

Niebuhr, R. (1953) *Christian Realism and Political Problems*. New York.

Nippel, W. (1980) *Mischverfassungstheorie und Verfassungsrealität in Antike und früher Neuzeit*. Stuttgart.

Noreña, C. F. (2001) "The communication of the emperor's virtues," *JRS* 91: 146–68.

  (2011) *Imperial Ideals in the Roman West: Representation, Circulation, Power*. Cambridge.

North, J. A. (1981) "The development of Roman imperialism," *JRS* 71: 1–9.

  (1990) "Democratic politics in Republican Rome," *Past and Present* 126: 3–21.

  (2003) "Religious toleration in Republican Rome," in C. Ando (ed.), *Roman Religion*, 199–219. Edinburgh.

  (2006) "The constitution of the Roman Republic," in Rosenstein and Morstein-Marx (2006), 256–77.

Nussbaum, M. (1994) *The Therapy of Desire: Theory and Practice in Hellenistic Ethics*. Princeton.

  (1996) "Patriotism and cosmopolitanism," in J. Cohen (ed.), *For Love of Country: Debating the Limits of Patriotism*, 2–17. Boston.

  (1997) "Kant and Stoic cosmopolitanism," *The Journal of Political Philosophy* 5 (1): 1–25.

  (2000) "Duties of justice, duties of material aid: Cicero's problematic legacy," *The Journal of Political Philosophy* 8 (2): 176–206.

  (2002) "The worth of human dignity: two tensions in Stoic cosmopolitanism," in G. Clark and T. Rajak (eds.), *Philosophy and Power in the Greco-Roman World*, 31–49. Oxford.

  (2013) *Political Emotions: Why Love Matters for Justice*. Cambridge, MA.

Oakeshott, M. (2006) *Lectures in the History of Political Thought*. Exeter.

Ober, J. (2000) "Quasi-rights: political boundaries and social diversity in democratic Athens," *Social Philosophy and Policy* 17 (1): 27–61.

Obergefell v. Hodges, 576 U.S. __. 135 S.Ct. 2584 (2015).

O'Donovan, O. (2004) "The political thought of *City of God* 19," in O. O'Donovan and J. L. O'Donovan (eds.), *Bonds of Imperfection: Christian Politics, Past and Present*, 48–72. Grand Rapids, MI.

Ogilvie, R. M. (1970) *A Commentary on Livy: Books 1–5*, corrected edn. Oxford.

Oliver, J. H. (1953) "The ruling power: a study of the Roman Empire in the second century after Christ through the 'Roman Oration' of Aelius Aristides," *TAPhS* 43: 871–1,003.

O'Meara, D. (2002) "The Justinianic Dialogue *On Political Science* and its Neoplatonic Sources," in K. Ierodiakonou (ed.), *Byzantine Philosophy and Its Ancient Sources*, 49–62. Oxford.

Orend, B. (2008) "War," in E. N. Zalta (ed.), *The Stanford Encyclopedia of Philosophy* (Fall 2008 edition), http://plato.stanford.edu/archives/fall2008/entries/war/.

Osborn, E. (1997) *Tertullian, First Theologian of the West*. Cambridge.

Ostwald, M. (1996) "Shares and rights: 'citizenship' Greek style and American style," in J. Ober and C. Hedrick (eds.), *Dêmokratia: a Conversation on Democracies, Ancient and Modern*, 49–61. Princeton.

Pagán, V. (ed.) (2012) *A Companion to Tacitus*. Malden, MA.

Pagels, E. (2012) *Revelations: Visions, Prophecy, and Politics in the Book of Revelation*. New York.

Pangle, T. (1973) *Montesquieu's Philosophy of Liberalism: A Commentary on The Spirit of the Laws*. Chicago.

Pangle, T., and P. Ahrensdorf (1999) *Justice among Nations: On the Moral Basis of Power and Peace*. Lawrence, KS.

Pembroke, S. G. (1971) "*Oikeiôsis*," in A. A. Long (ed.), *Problems in Stoicism*, 114–49. London.

Pettit, P. (1997) *Republicanism: A Theory of Freedom and Government*. Oxford.
  (2012) *On the People's Terms: A Republican Theory and Model of Democracy*. Cambridge.

Philpott, D. (2011) "Sovereignty," in G. Klosko (ed.), *The Oxford Handbook of the History of Political Philosophy*, 561–72. Oxford and New York.

Pina Polo, F. (1996) *Contra arma verbis: Der Redner vor dem Volk in der späten römischen Republik*. Stuttgart.
  (2011a) *The Consul at Rome: The Civil Functions of the Consuls in the Roman Republic*. Cambridge.
  (2011b) "Public speaking in Rome: a question of *auctoritas*," in M. Peachin (ed.), *The Oxford Handbook of Social Relations in the Roman World*, 286–303. Oxford.

Pocock, J. G. A. (1975) *The Machiavellian Moment: Florentine Political Thought and the Atlantic Republican Tradition*. Princeton.
  (1995) "The ideal of citizenship since classical times," in Beiner (1995), 29–52.

Pogge, T. (1992) "Cosmopolitanism and sovereignty," *Ethics* 103 (1): 48–75.

Pöschl, V. (1989) *Der Begriff der Würde im antiken Rom und Später*. Heidelberg.

Powell, J. G. F. (2013) "The embassy of the three philosophers to Rome in 155 B.C.," in C. Kremmydas and K. Tempest (eds.), *Hellenistic Oratory: Continuity and Change*, 219–47. Oxford.

Purdy, J. (2015) *After Nature: A Politics for the Anthropocene*. Cambridge, MA.

Raaflaub, K. A. (1984) "Freiheit in Athen und Rom: Ein Beispiel divergierender politischer Begriffsentwicklung in der Antike," *Historische Zeitschrift* 238 (3): 529–67.
  (2004) *The Discovery of Freedom in Ancient Greece*, trans. Renate Franciscono. Chicago.
  (2005) "From protection and defense to offense and participation: stages in the conflict of the orders," in K. A. Raaflaub (ed.), *Social Struggles in Archaic Rome: New Perspectives on the Conflict of the Orders*, second edn., 185–222. Malden, MA and London.

Rahe, P. (1992) *Republics Ancient and Modern*. Chapel Hill, NC.

Ramelli, I., and D. Konstan (eds. and trans.) (2009) *Hierocles the Stoic: Elements of Ethics, Fragments, and Excerpts*. Leiden and Boston.

Ramsey, J. T. (2007) "Roman senatorial oratory," in W. Dominik and J. Hall (eds.), *A Companion to Roman Rhetoric*, 122–35. Malden, MA.

Ramsey, P. (1992) "The just war according to St. Augustine," in J. B. Elshtain (ed.), *Just War Theory*, 8–22. New York.

Randall, M. H. (2013) "The history of international human rights law," in R. Kolb and G. Gaggioli (eds.), *Research Handbook on Human Rights and Humanitarian Law*, 3–34. Cheltenham, UK and Northampton, MA.

Rawson, E. (1983 [1975]) *Cicero: A Portrait*. Ithaca, NY.

(1985) *Intellectual Life in the Late Roman Republic*. Baltimore, MD.

Remer, G. (1996) *Humanism and the Rhetoric of Toleration*. University Park, PA.

(1999) "Political oratory and conversation: Cicero versus deliberative democracy," *Political Theory* 27 (1): 39–64.

(2005) "Cicero and the ethics of deliberative rhetoric," in B. Fontana, C. Nederman, and G. Remer (eds.), *Talking Democracy: Historical Perspectives on Rhetoric and Democracy*, 135–61. University Park, PA.

(2017) *Ethics and the Orator: The Ciceronian Tradition of Political Morality*. Chicago.

Reydams-Schils, G. (2005) *The Roman Stoics: Self, Responsibility, and Affection*. Chicago.

Richard, C. (1994) *The Founders and the Classics: Greece, Rome, and the American Enlightenment*. Cambridge, MA.

(2008) *Greeks and Romans Bearing Gifts: How the Ancients Inspired the Founding Fathers*. Lanham, MD.

(2010) *Why We're All Romans: The Roman Contribution to the Western World*. Lanham, MD.

Richardson, J. (2008) *The Language of Empire: Rome and the Idea of Empire from the Third Century B.C. to the Second Century A.D.* Cambridge.

Riedl, M. (2010) "Truth versus utility: the debate on civil religion in the Roman Empire of the third and fourth centuries," in R. Weed and J. von Heyking (eds.), *Civil Religion in Political Thought: Its Perennial Questions and Enduring Relevance in North America*, 47–65. Washington, DC.

Rist, J. (1982) *Human Value: A Study in Ancient Philosophical Ethics*. Leiden.

(1994) *Augustine: Ancient Thought Baptized*. Cambridge.

Rives, J. B. (1999) "The decree of Decius and the religion of empire," *JRS* 89: 135–54.

Roller, M. (2001) *Constructing Autocracy: Aristocrats and Emperors in Julio-Claudian Rome*. Princeton.

Ronson, J. (2015) *So You've Been Publicly Shamed*. New York.

Rosenstein, N., and R. Morstein-Marx (eds.) (2006) *A Companion to the Roman Republic*. Malden, MA.

Roskam, G. (2007) *Live Unnoticed (Λάθε Βιώσας): On the Vicissitudes of an Epicurean Doctrine*. Leiden.

Rowe, C. J. (2000) "Introduction," in C. J. Rowe and Schofield (2000), 1–6.

Rowe, C. J., and M. Schofield (eds.) (2000) *The Cambridge History of Greek and Roman Political Thought*. Cambridge.

Rowe, C. K. (2009) *World Upside Down: Reading Acts in the Graeco-Roman Age*. Oxford.

Rüpke, J. (2007) *Religion of the Romans*, trans. R. Gordon. Cambridge.

Rutherford, R. B. (2010) "Voices of resistance," in C. S. Kraus, J. Marincola, and C. Pelling (eds.), *Ancient Historiography and Its Contexts: Studies in Honour of A. J. Woodman*, 312–30. Oxford.

Ryan, F. (1998) *Rank and Participation in the Republican Senate*. Stuttgart.

Sailor, D. (2008) *Writing and Empire in Tacitus*. Cambridge.

(2012) "The *Agricola*," in Pagán (ed.), 23–44.

Sandel, M. (1996) *Democracy's Discontent: America in Search of a Public Philosophy*. Cambridge, MA.

(1998 [1982]) *Liberalism and the Limits of Justice*, second edn. Cambridge.

Sauer, J. (2015) "Dichotomy in the conception of natural law in Cicero's *De legibus?*," trans. A. Lewis., in T. Vesting (ed.), *Gesetz-Rhetorik-Gewalt*, 125–53. Special issue of *Ancilla Iuris*.

Saxonhouse, A. (1975) "Tacitus' *Dialogue on Oratory*: political activity under a tyrant," *Political Theory* 3 (1): 53–68.

Schäfer, P. (1997) *Judeophobia: Attitudes towards the Jews in the Ancient World*. Cambridge, MA.

Scheid, J. (2005) "Augustus and Roman religion: continuity, conservatism, and innovation," in K. Galinsky (ed.), *The Cambridge Companion to the Age of Augustus*, 175–93. Cambridge.

Scheidel, W. (2011) "The Roman slave supply," in K. Bradley and P. Cartledge (eds.), *The Cambridge World History of Slavery*, Volume 1: *The Ancient Mediterranean World*, 287–310. Cambridge.

Schiesaro, A. (2007) "Lucretius and Roman politics and history," in S. Gillespie and P. R. Hardie (eds.), *The Cambridge Companion to Lucretius*, 41–58. Cambridge.

Schlosser, J. A. (2013) " 'Hope, danger's comforter': Thucydides' *History* and the politics of hope," *The Journal of Politics* 75 (1): 169–82.

Schofield, M. (1986) "Cicero for and against divination," *JRS* 76: 47–65.

(1995) "Cicero's definition of *res publica*," in J. G. F. Powell (ed.), *Cicero the Philosopher: Twelve Papers*, 63–83. Oxford.

(1999a [1991]) *The Stoic Idea of the City*. Chicago.

(1999b) "Social and political thought," in Algra, Barnes, Mansfeld, and Schofield (1999), 739–70.

(2000) "Epicurean and Stoic political thought," in C. J. Rowe and Schofield (2000), 435–56.

(2009) "Republican virtues," in Balot (2009), 199–213.

(2012) "The fourth virtue," in Nicgorski (2012), 43–57.

(2013) "Cosmopolitanism, imperialism, and justice in Cicero's *Republic* and *Laws*," *Intellectual History and Political Thought* 2 (1): 5–34.

(2015) "Liberty, equality, and authority: a political discourse in the later Roman Republic," in Hammer (2015), 113–27.

Schrijvers, P. H. (1996) "Lucretius on the origin and development of political life (*De rerum natura* 5.1105–1160)," in K. A. Algra, P. W. van der Horst, and

D. T. Runia (eds.), *Polyhistor: Studies in the History and Historiography of Ancient Philosophy*, 220–30. Leiden.

Schumpeter, J. (1952 [1919]) *The Sociology of Imperialism*. New York.

Schwartz, S. (2014) *The Ancient Jews from Alexander to Muhammad*. Cambridge.

Scruton, R. (2010a) "Gratitude and grace," *The American Spectator*, April 2010, http://spectator.org/39831_gratitude-and-grace.

(2010b) *The Uses of Pessimism and the Danger of False Hope*. Oxford.

Sedley, D. N. (1998) *Lucretius and the Transformation of Greek Wisdom*. Cambridge.

Segal, C. (1990) *Lucretius on Death and Anxiety: Poetry and Philosophy in De rerum natura*. Princeton.

Sellars, J. (2007) "Stoic cosmopolitanism and Zeno's *Republic*," *HPT* 28 (1): 1–29.

Shah, T. S. (2016a) "Introduction: Christianity and freedom: ancient roots and historical innovations," in Shah and Hertzke (2016), 1–32.

(2016b) "The roots of religious freedom in early Christian thought," in Shah and Hertzke (2016), 33–61.

Shah, T. S., and A. D. Hertzke (eds.) (2016) *Christianity and Freedom*, Volume 1: *Historical Perspectives*. Cambridge.

Sherwin-White, A. N. (1966) *The Letters of Pliny: A Historical and Social Commentary*. Oxford.

(1973) *The Roman Citizenship*, second edn. Oxford.

(1980) "Rome the aggressor?" *JRS* 70: 177–81.

Skinner, Q. (1978) *The Foundations of Modern Political Thought*, 2 vols. Cambridge.

(1996) *Reason and Rhetoric in the Philosophy of Hobbes*. Cambridge.

(1998) *Liberty before Liberalism*. Cambridge.

(2002) "A third concept of liberty," *Proceedings of the British Academy* 117: 237–68.

Smith, M. F. (ed. and trans.) (2001) *Lucretius: On the Nature of Things*. Indianapolis, IN.

Snyder, J., and A. Khalid (2016) "The rise of 'bias response teams' on campus," *New Republic*, published online March 30, 2016; accessed March 24, 2017, https://newrepublic.com/article/132195/rise-bias-response-teams-campus.

Sourvinou-Inwood, C. (1990) "What is *polis* religion?," in O. Murray and S. R. F. Price (eds.), *The Greek City: from Homer to Alexander*, 295–322. Oxford.

Spragens, T. (1999) *Civic Liberalism: Reflections on Our Democratic Ideals*. Lanham, MD.

Stacey, P. (2007) *Roman Monarchy and the Renaissance Prince*. Cambridge.

(2014) "The princely republic," *JRS* 104: 133–54.

Stadter, P. (2014) "Plutarch and Rome," in M. Beck (ed.), *A Companion to Plutarch*, 13–31. Malden, MA.

Steel, C. E. W. (2001) *Cicero, Rhetoric, and Empire*. Oxford.

Steel, C. E. W., and H. Van Der Blom (2013) *Community and Communication: Oratory and Politics in Republican Rome*. Oxford.

Stockdale, J. B. (1993) *Courage under Fire: Testing Epictetus' Doctrines in a Laboratory of Human Behavior*. Stanford.

Straumann, B. (2015) *Roman Law in the State of Nature: The Classical Foundations of Hugo Grotius' Natural Law Theory*. Cambridge.

    (2016) *Crisis and Constitutionalism: Roman Political Thought from the Fall of the Republic to the Age of Revolution*. Oxford.

Strauss, L. (1965 [1953]) *Natural Right and History*, paperback edn. Chicago.

    (1968) *Liberalism Ancient and Modern*. Chicago.

Streeter, J. (2006) "Appendix to chapter 5: religious toleration in classical antiquity and early Christianity," in G. E. M. De Ste. Croix, *Christian Persecution, Martyrdom, and Orthodoxy*, M. Whitby and J. Streeter (eds.), 229–51. Oxford.

Stroumsa, G. G. (1998) "Tertullian on idolatry and the limits of tolerance," in G. N. Stanton and G. G. Stroumsa (eds.), *Tolerance and Intolerance in Early Judaism and Christianity*, 173–84. Cambridge.

Strunk, T. E. (2017) *History after Liberty: Tacitus on Tyrants, Sycophants, and Republicans*. Ann Arbor, MI.

Swaminathan, S. (2009) *Debating the Slave Trade: Rhetoric of British National Identity, 1759–1815*. Burlington, VT.

Swift, L. J. (1983) *The Early Fathers on War and Military Service*. Wilmington, DE.

Syme, R. (1939) *The Roman Revolution*. Oxford.

    (1964) *Sallust*. Berkeley.

Taylor, C. (1989) *Sources of the Self: The Making of Modern Identity*. Cambridge, MA.

    (1994) "The politics of recognition," in A. Gutmann (ed.), *Multiculturalism: Examining the Politics of Recognition*, 25–73. Princeton.

Tierney, B. (1996) "Religious rights: an historical perspective," in J. Witte, Jr. and J. D. van der Vyver (eds.), *Religious Human Rights in Global Perspective: Religious Perspectives*, 17–45. The Hague, Boston, and London.

Tkacz, M. W., and D. Kries (trans. and eds.) (1994) *Augustine: Political Writings*, introduction by E. L. Fortin. Indianapolis, IN.

Trompf, G. W. (1979) *The Idea of Historical Recurrence in Western Thought: From Antiquity to the Reformation*. Berkeley.

Tully, J. H. (ed.) (1983) *John Locke: A Letter Concerning Toleration*. Indianapolis, IN.

Unger, P. (1996) *Living High and Letting Die: Our Illusion of Innocence*. Oxford.

Van Den Berg, C. (2014) *The World of Tacitus' 'Dialogus de Oratoribus': Aesthetics and Empire in Ancient Rome*. Cambridge and New York.

Van Oort, J. (1991) *Jerusalem and Babylon: A Study into Augustine's City of God and the Sources of His Doctrine of the Two Cities*. Leiden and New York.

Vasaly, A. (2015) *Livy's Political Philosophy: Power and Personality in Early Rome*. Cambridge and New York.

Veyne, P. (1990) *Bread and Circuses: Historical Sociology and Political Pluralism*, trans. B. Pearce. London.

Villey, M. (1946) "L' idée du droit subjectif et les systèmes juridiques romains," *Revue historique de droit français et étranger*, fourth series, 24–25: 201–28. [Reprinted as "Les instituts de Gaius et l'idée du droit subjectif," in M. Villey (1962), *Leçons d'histoire de la philosophie du droit*, second edn., 169–88. Paris.]

    (1964) "Le genèse du droit subjectif chez Guillaume d'Occam," *Archives de philosophie du droit* 9: 97–127.

Viroli, M. (1995) *For Love of Country: An Essay on Patriotism and Nationalism.* Oxford.

(2002) *Republicanism*, trans. A. Shugaar. New York.

Vogt, K. (2008) *Law, Reason, and the Cosmic City: Political Philosophy in the Early Stoa.* Oxford.

Von Fritz, K. (1954) *The Theory of the Mixed Constitution in Antiquity: A Critical Analysis of Polybius' Political Ideas.* New York.

Von Heyking, J. (2001) *Augustine and Politics as Longing in the World.* Columbia, MO.

(2007) "Taming warriors in classical and early medieval political theory," in H. Syse and G. M. Reichberg (eds.), *Ethics, Nationalism, and Just War: Medieval and Contemporary Perspectives,* 11–35. Washington, D.C.

Walbank, F. W. (1957–79) *A Historical Commentary on Polybius,* 3 vols. Oxford.

(1972) *Polybius.* Berkeley.

(1998) "A Greek looks at Rome: Polybius VI revisited," *Scripta Classica Israelica* 17: 45–59. [Reprinted in Walbank (2002), 277–92.]

(2002) *Polybius, Rome and the Hellenistic World: Essays and Reflections.* Cambridge.

Walker, W. (2006) "Sallust and Skinner on civil liberty," *European Journal of Political Theory* 5 (3): 237–59.

Wallace, R. W. (2009) "Personal freedom in Greek democracies, Republican Rome, and modern liberal states," in Balot (2009), 164–77.

Wallace-Hadrill, A. (1981) "The emperor and his virtues," *Historia* 30 (3): 298–323.

(1993) *Augustan Rome.* Bristol.

Walz, K. N. (1979) *Theory of International Politics.* New York.

Walzer, M. (1977) *Just and Unjust Wars: A Moral Argument with Historical Illustrations.* New York.

(1983) *Spheres of Justice: A Defense of Pluralism and Equality.* Oxford.

(1989) "Citizenship," in Ball, Farr, and Hanson (1989), 211–19.

(1994) *Thick and Thin: Moral Argument at Home and Abroad.* Notre Dame, IN.

(1997) *On Toleration.* New Haven.

Warrior, V. M. (ed. and trans.) (2006a) *Livy: The History of Rome Books 1–5.* Indianapolis, IN.

(2006b) *Roman Religion.* Cambridge.

Waterfield, R. (ed. and trans.) (2010) *Polybius: The Histories.* Oxford.

Watkins, P. (2007) *Gratitude and the Good Life: Toward a Psychology of Appreciation.* Dordrecht.

Watson, A. (trans.) (1985) *The Digest of Justinian,* Latin text ed. T. Mommsen and P. Krueger. Philadelphia.

(1987) *Roman Slave Law.* Baltimore, MD.

Watts, E. (2014) "Freedom of speech and self-censorship in the Roman Empire," *Revue Belge de philologie et d'histoire* 92 (1): 157–66.

Weithman, P. J. (1999), "Toward an Augustinian liberalism," in Matthews (1999), 304–22.

West, C. (1999) "The moral obligations of living in a democratic society," in D. Batstone and E. Mendieta (eds.), *The Good Citizen,* 5–12. New York.

Wetzel, J. (1992) *Augustine and the Limits of Virtue*. Cambridge.

Whitmarsh, T. (2006) " 'This in-between book': language, politics and genre in the *Agricola*," in B. McGing and J. Mossman (eds.), *The Limits of Ancient Biography*, 305–33. Swansea.

Wiedemann, T. (1993) "Sallust's *Jugurtha*: concord, discord and the digression," *G&R second series* 40 (1): 48–57.

Wilken, R. L. (2003) *The Christians as the Romans Saw Them*, second edn. New Haven.

(2014) *The Christian Roots of Religious Freedom*. Milwaukee, WI.

(2016) "The Christian roots of religious freedom," in Shah and Hertzke (2016), 62–89.

Wilkinson, S. (2012) *Republicanism during the Early Roman Empire*. London and New York.

Williams, R. (1987) "Politics and the soul: a reading of the *City of God*," *Milltown Studies* 19/20: 55–72.

Williamson, C. (2016) "Crimes against the state," in P. J. du Plessis, C. Ando, and K. Tuori (eds.), *The Oxford Handbook of Roman Law and Society*, 333–44. Oxford.

Wirszubski, C. (1950) *Libertas as a Political Idea at Rome during the Late Republic and Early Principate*. Cambridge.

Wirzba, N. (2002) (ed.) *The Art of the Commonplace: The Agrarian Essays of Wendell Berry*. Berkeley.

Wiseman, P. (2009) *Remembering the Roman People: Essays on Late-Republican Politics and Literature*. Oxford.

Wood, N. (1988) *Cicero's Social and Political Thought*. Berkeley.

(1995) "Sallust's theorem: a comment on 'fear' in western political thought," *HPT* 16 (2): 174–89.

Woodman, A. J. (2010) *The Cambridge Companion to Tacitus*. Cambridge.

Woodruff, P. (2001) *Reverence: Renewing a Forgotten Virtue*. Oxford.

Woolf, G. (1998) *Becoming Roman: The Origins of Provincial Civilization in Gaul*. Cambridge.

(2012) *Rome: An Empire's Story*. Oxford.

Woolf, R. (2015) *Cicero: The Philosophy of a Roman Sceptic*. London and New York.

Wynn, P. (2013) *Augustine on War and Military Service*. Minneapolis, MN.

Yakobson, A. (1999) *Elections and Electioneering in Rome: A Study in the Political System of the Late Republic*. Stuttgart.

Yardley, J. C. (trans.) (2008) *Tacitus, The Annals: The Reigns of Tiberius, Claudius, and Nero*. Oxford.

Young, F. (2000) "Christianity," in C. J. Rowe and Schofield (2000), 635–60.

Zanker, P. (1988) *The Power of Images in the Age of Augustus*, trans. A. Shapiro. Ann Arbor, MI.

Zarecki, J. (2014) *Cicero's Ideal Statesman in Theory and Practice*. New York and London.

Zetzel, J. E. G. (ed.) (1995) *Cicero, De republica: Selections*. Cambridge.

(1996) "Natural law and poetic justice: a Carneadean debate in Cicero and Vergil," *CPh* 91 (4): 297–319.

(ed. and trans.) (1999) *Cicero: On the Commonwealth and On the Laws.* Cambridge. [Second edn. published in 2017.]

Zuckert, M. (1996) *The Natural Rights Republic: Studies in the Foundation of the American Political Tradition.* Notre Dame, IN.

Index

Adams, John, 74
Adams, Samuel, 74
Aelius Aristides, 65–66
Aeneas, Roman foundation myth of, 70, 142, 144, 160
Agamemnon, 101
agonistic nature of Roman political culture, 24, 28
Agricola and Tacitus' *Agricola*
    civic virtue and, 82–84
    composition of text, 128
    on imperialism, 174–76
    liberty under empire and, 59
agriculture versus commerce in Roman republican ideology, 74–75
Agrippa I (king of Judea), 149
Alcibiades, 107
Alexander the Great, 31, 33, 175, 188
ambition (*philotimia*), 106, 107
ambitus laws, 91
Ambrose of Milan
    Augustine compared, 182, 183, 184
    De officiis, on just war, 181–82
American civil religion, argument for existence of, 164–65
American Founders
    Cincinnatus as hero of, 74
    Declaration of Independence, 37, 44
    Federalist Papers, 36, 131, 171
    large republics, Madison's argument for, 171
    liberty and faction, Madison on, 131
    Polybius, framers of American constitution influenced by, 36
    religious freedom, Jefferson on, 155–58
American presidential elections (2016), 198
anakuklôsis (cyclical political change), Polybius' theory of, 22–24
Ando, Clifford, 42

Antipater of Tarsus, 108
Antonine Constitution (extension of citizenship to all free persons in Roman world), 65–67, 69, 166
Antoninus Pius (Roman emperor), 65
Apollo and Vesta cults moved to home of Augustus Caesar, 59, 142
appellatio (right to ask tribunes for help or *auxilium*), as citizens' right, 47
Appius Claudius, 47, 48
Arena, Valentina, 54
Arendt, Hannah, 38
aristocracy (rule by the few), Polybius on, 15
aristocrats (*optimates*), 4, 36, 48, 93, 117
Aristotle
    on belief engendered by emotion, 119
    chance, political change dependent on, 22
    on character (*êthos*), 119, 122
    on citizenship and civic virtue, 65, 73, 85
    compared to Roman political thought, 7
    on equality, 51
    harmony as goal of politics for, 24
    ideal, rational rule, interest in, 22, 26
    on individual rights, 27
    on liberty, 38
    "mixed constitution," model of, 23, 28
    philosophical method of being able to argue both sides of question, 124
    Politics, 73, 99
    on study of *politeia*, 6
assemblies, Roman, *see also* Centuriate Assembly; *contio*; senate, Roman
    augurs' powers over, 20, 141
    civil religion and, 139
    Curiate Assembly, 16
    plebeian assemblies, 17
    Polybius on, 15–18, 19–22
    Tribal Assembly, 16

Athenian democracy and Roman republicanism
  citizenship, 70
  constitutional differences, 20–22
  deliberative oratory, 117
  equality and liberty in, 49–50
  hasty decisions, dangers of, 141
  on individual rights, 49
  on liberty, 39, 60
  relationship between, 6–8
  religious tolerance, 146
auctoritas (authority), 27, 140
augurs and auspices, 20, 139, 140–41
Augustine of Hippo (St. Augustine)
  Ambrose compared, 182, 183, 184
  biographical information, 85
  Cicero and, 35, 87, 88
  on citizenship and civic virtue, 84–90
  City of God, 35, 85–88
  Confessions, 85
  Contra Faustum, 183
  on honor code, 87–88
  on Jews and Judaism, 148
  on just war, 177, 182–84
  Letters, 88–89
  on political legitimacy, 35
  political writings of, 6
  on religious tolerance, 159
  Sallust influenced, 87, 88
Augustus Caesar (Gaius Octavius)
  on civic virtue, 79
  civil religion under, 59, 141–42
  contio abolished by, 124
  liberty and rule of, 58–59
  Res Gestae, 29, 30, 79
  rhetoric under, 124, 131
  Roman constitution under, 29–30
  Vesta and Apollo cults moved to home of,
    59, 142
auxilium (right of tribune to grant help
    to citizens in response to their appeal), 47

Bacchanalia, senate regulation of, 145–46
Bacon, Francis, 197
balance of powers, *see* separation and balance
    of powers
Balbus, 70
Balot, Ryan, 168, 169
Barton, C., 55
Bartsch, S., 129
Beard, M., 139
Beiner, Ronald, 123
Bellah, Robert, 164–65
Berlin, Isaiah, "Two Concepts of Liberty"
    (1969), 38, 39, 45, 50

Berry, Wendell, 75
Bodin, Jean, 19
Brexit, 63
Britain, Agricola in, *see* Agricola and Tacitus'
    Agricola
Brutus (abolisher of Tarquinian monarchy), 13
Brutus (assassin of Julius Caesar), 33

Calgacus (British commander), 175
Camillus, 144
Cammack, Daniela, 117
Cannae, battle of (216 BCE), 14
Canuleius (tribune), 48, 51, 52
Caracalla (Roman emperor), 66
cardinal virtues, as civic virtues, 76–78,
    80, 83, 89
Carneades, 172
Carter, Steven L., 196
Carthage
  health of Roman state and survival/defeat of,
    170, 171
  Polybius on mixed constitution of, 169
  Punic War, second, 171, 174
Cartledge, P., 7
Cassius Dio (Dio Cassius)
  on *auctoritas*, 28
  on Augustus Caesar, 29
  politeia, use of Greek concept of, 3
Catiline, 24, 56, 93, 126, 132
Cato the Elder
  on citizenship and civic virtue, 72, 73, 74
  imperialism and, 170
  on liberty, 50, 55
  rhetoric and, 112, 125
Cato the Younger, 87, 93, 129, 132
Ceaser, J., 109
Centuriate Assembly
  Cicero on, 20, 28
  Polybius on, 16
  senate ratification required for votes of, 20
character (*êthos*) and rhetoric, 119, 122
Christianity
  citizenship and civic virtue transformed
    by, 84–90
  civil religion, Rousseau on Christianity
    as, 136
  constitution and, 35
  importance of, 5
  Judaism and, 150
  on just war theory, 181–84
  on pacifism, 181
  persecution of, 143, 150–52, 158
  Roman understanding of Judaism versus, 149
  on tolerance, 153–60

Cicero (Marcus Tullius Cicero)
  on *auctoritas*, 27
  on augur's powers over popular assemblies, 20, 141
  Augustine and, 35, 87, 88
  biographical information, 1
  on Centuriate Assembly, 20, 28
  on chance in political evolution, 26
  on citizens' rights, 46, 47–49, 52–54
  on citizenship, 65, 67, 70–71, 72
  on civic virtue, 73, 76–78, 81, 83
  on civil religion, 137–38, 144, 145, 161–64
  on class dynamics, 28
  on constitution, 11, 13, 24–28
  consulship, campaign for, 1–2, 24
  on *contio*, 17
  cooperative enterprise, on society as, 198
  on corruption, 91–92
  death of, 29
  decline narratives of rhetoric and, 124
  Dialogue on Political Science citing, 36
  Dio Chrysostom compared, 34
  on Epicureanism, 97
  on equality, 51–54
  exile of, 44
  on gratitude, 103
  on honor and order, 191
  on human nature, 25
  ideal, rational rule, interest in, 26
  on imperialism, 167, 172–74
  on individual rights, 45
  on Jews and Judaism, 148
  on just war, 177–78
  justification of literary efforts by, 56
  on liberty, 5, 40, 43, 55, 57–58, 61
  on natural law, 13, 41, 156, 161–64, 179
  politeia, use of Greek concept of, 3
  on political conflict, 28
  Polybius compared, 25–28, 173, 174
  on popular sovereignty, 7, 26–27
  on property rights, 43–44
  Quintilian and, 125–27
  realism and, 191
  on rhetoric, deliberation, and judgment, 112, 116, 118–24
  Sallust compared, 173
  Seneca the Younger compared, 31–32
  on separation/balance of powers, 27
  significance of political writings of, 5
  Tacitus and, 129, 131–32, 133, 176
  on tolerance, 153
  transformation of Rome from republic to form of monarchy (Empire) and, 8
Cicero (Marcus Tullius Cicero), works, *see also De officiis; De republica*
  Ad Quintum fratrum, 55

  Brutus, 118, 124, 132, 133
  De divinatione, 137
  De domo sua, 44
  De inventione, 113, 118, 121, 124
  De lege agraria, 45
  De legibus, 13, 41, 92, 93, 118, 137, 140, 161–64, 177, 179
  De natura deorum, 137
  De oratore, 118, 119, 120, 121, 124, 125, 129
  Epistulae ad familiares, 56
  Orator, 118, 120
  Paradoxa Stoicorum, 153
  Philippics, 5
  Pro Balbo, 70–71
  Pro Flacco, 17
  Pro Marcello, 31
  Pro Plancio, 103
Cincinnatus (Lucius Quinctius Cincinnatus), 74–75
Cineas (Thessalian orator), 107
citizenship, 63–90, *see also* civic virtue
  Christian transformation of, 84–90
  civitas sine suffragio (citizenship without the vote), 71
  colonies and, 71
  dual citizenship, 70
  extension of citizenship by Republic, 69–73
  extension of citizenship to all free persons in Roman world (Antonine Constitution), 65–67, 69, 166
  identity and sense of status deriving from, 68
  liberal versus republican approaches to, 64–65, 67–68
  military service and, 68
  modern concepts of citizenship, 63–65
  political participation and Roman citizenship, 68
  private individuals in *res publica*, imperial citizens as, 59–60
  rights of citizens, 46–49, 68, (*see also appellatio; auxilium; conubium; provocatio; suffragium*)
  Roman foundation myths and extension of citizenship, 70
  Roman Republic, citizenship under, 67–73
  taxation and Roman citizenship, 66, 68
civic virtue, *see also specific virtues*
  agriculture versus commerce in Roman republican ideology, 74–75
  cardinal virtues, 76–78, 80, 83, 89
  Christian transformation of, 84–90
  of elites under imperial rule, 81–84
  of emperor, 79–80
  honor code and, 73, 76, 81–84

under Principate, 79–84
regime determining, 73
in Roman Republic, 73–79
civil law (*ius civile*), 41
civil religion in Rome, 136–65, *see also*
  Christianity; Jews and Judaism; *pietas*;
  tolerance, religious
  augurs and auspices, 20, 139, 140–41
  Bellah's American civil religion and, 164–65
  Cicero on, 137–38, 144, 145, 161–64
  concept of, Rousseau versus Cicero on,
    136–38, 145
  constitution, relationship to, 138,
    139–41, 163–64
  decentralized nature before Decius, 143
  Decius' edict centralizing and enforcing
    practices, 143
  imperial cult, 142–43
  imperialistic exportation of, 160–64
  just war theory and, 179
  magistrates and, 139
  modern liberal democracy and, 137,
    164–65, 195
  mystery religions, 145
  Polybius on, 21, 100
  pontifex maximus, emperor as, 142
  priests and priesthoods, 139–40, 142
  under Principate, 141–44
  reverence, corruption, and the passions,
    101–2, 109
  Rousseau on, 136–38, 145, 160, 162, 163, 164
  universal principles and particular practices,
    tension between, 138, 143, 160, 161–62,
    163, 164–65
  Vesta and Apollo cults moved to home of
    Augustus Caesar, 59, 142
civil wars in Rome, 24, 29, 118, 128
class and status, *see also* honor code
  aristocracy (rule by the few), Polybius on, 15
  citizenship, identity and sense of status
    deriving from, 68
  civic virtues of elites, under imperial
    rule, 81–84
  civil religion and, 139–40
  conflict of the orders, 17
  constitution and class dynamics, 28
  corruption of elites and, 91–96
  desire for security/fear of death at root of, 100
  dignitas, importance of, 55–56
  populares (men of the people) versus *optimates*
    (aristocrats), 4, 36, 48, 93, 117
  Roman concern with, 4
  struggle for status ameliorated by honor, 191
Claudius (Roman emperor), 149
Cleopatra, 29

Clodius, 44
coins, civic virtues personified on, 79
colonies and citizenship, 71
Columella, 148
commerce versus agriculture in Roman
  republican ideology, 74–75
commercium (right to conduct business), 71
competitive nature of Roman political
  culture, 24, 28
conflict of the orders, 17
Connolly, Joy, 28, 57, 93, 127
consilium (judgment)
  civil religion and, 140
  rhetoric and (*see* rhetoric, deliberation, and
    judgment)
Constant, Benjamin, "The Liberty of the
  Ancients Compared with that of the
  Moderns" (1819), 8, 37–38, 39, 49,
  60, 197
Constantine I the Great (Roman emperor), 34,
  35, 85, 149, 152, 181
constitution, Roman, 11–36, *see also* mixed
  constitutions
  Christianity and, 35
  Cicero on late Republican, 11, 13, 24–28
  civil religion, relationship to, 138,
    139–41, 163–64
  concept of, 11–13
  customary rights and institutions, force
    of, 12–13
  Dio Chrysostom on, 33–34
  imperial transformation of Rome
    and, 29–34
  interaction between different
    institutions of, 18
  Latin terms for, 11
  natural law and, 13
  Pliny the Younger on, 33
  political legitimacy and, 16, 20, 27, 34–36
  Polybius on Republican, 13–24, 36
  Seneca the Younger on *princeps*, 31–33
  Spartan and Carthaginian constitutions
    compared, 168–70
  written constitution, lack of, 11
consulship
  Augustus Caesar's hold on, 29
  Cicero's campaign for consulship against
    Catiline, 1–2, 24
  Polybius on, 14
contio
  abolished by Augustus, 124
  Polybius on, 17
  rhetoric in, 114, 115–17, 119, 122, 127
control/ownership and liberty, 40, 43, 45,
  47, 58, 61

conubium (right to marry), as citizens' right, 47, 48, 68, 71
Corpus Iuris Civilis, 35
corruption and the passions, 91–111
  Cicero on, 91–96
  finitude (death), fear of/acceptance of, 100–1, 102, 103, 198
  gratitude, importance of, 102–6, 108, 109–11, 198–99
  honor code and, 92, 94
  hope, 108–9, 110
  Lucretius and Epicureanism on, 95, 96–102
  modern concepts of, 91, 95, 109–11, 198–99
  philotimia (ambition or love of honor), 106, 107
  Plutarch on, 95, 106–9
  reverence and *pietas*, 101–2, 109
  Roman Republic's concept of, 91–96
  Sallust on, 92–95, 102
  Seneca the Younger on, 95, 103–6
cosmopolitanism, 84, 167, 184–89
courage, as civic virtue, 76, 77, 83
Crassus (Lucius Crassus), 1
Crassus (Marcus Licinius Crassus), 25, 55, 70
Curiate Assembly, 16
Curtius Rufus, 148
Cynicism, as philosophical school, 185
Cyprian of Carthage, *De bono patientiae,* on religious tolerance, 153–54, 197

Dante Alighieri, *On Monarchy,* 188
De officiis (Cicero)
  Ambrose of Milan, on just war, compared, 181–82
  on citizenship and civic virtue, 76–78, 81
  on cosmopolitanism, 186–88
  on honor code, 191
  imperialism in, 173–74
  just war theory in, 177, 179
  on liberty, 44, 48, 58
  Obergefell vs. Hodges (U.S. Supreme Court, 2015) citing, 192–93
  on rhetoric, 118, 120
De republica (Cicero)
  as Platonic-style dialogue, 118
  on civil religion, 140
  on imperialism, 172–73
  on importance of Roman political culture, 4
  on just war, 177
  on liberty, 46, 52, 53, 54, 57
  on Roman constitution, 11, 20, 25, 26, 27, 28, 36
  Scipio Africanus in, 25, 26, 28, 52, 54
  Tacitus and, 129, 133
death (finitude), fear of/acceptance of, 100–1, 102, 103, 198

Decius (Trajan Decius; Roman emperor), 143, 152
Declaration of Independence, 37, 44
decline narratives, Roman attraction to, 124
deliberation (generally), *see* rhetoric, deliberation, and judgment
deliberative democracy, 113, 120
deliberative rhetoric, 114, 115–18, 126
democracy, *see also* Athenian democracy and Roman republicanism; modern liberal democracy and Roman republicanism
  hasty decisions in, 141
  in Polybius' account of Roman constitution, 19–22
Democritus, 98
Descartes, René, 197
Dialogue on Political Science, 35
Digest, 35, 41
dignitas and liberty, 55–56, 58
Dio Cassius, *see* Cassius Dio
Dio Chrysostom
  on civic virtue, 79–80
  on constitution and monarchy, 33–34
  Orationes, 79, 80
  "Roman" nature of political writings of, 5
  Seneca compared, 33
Diocletian (Roman emperor), 34, 124, 152, 158
Diodorus Siculus, 170
Diodotus, 109
Diogenes the Cynic, 185
Dionysius of Halicarnassus, 3, 55
Dominate, 34
Domitian (Roman emperor), 59, 82, 84, 125, 128, 175
Donatists, 159
dual citizenship, 70
duoviri, 139

Earl, Donald, 82
Edge, Matt, 50
elites, Roman, *see* class and status; honor code; senate, Roman
emotion
  corruption and (*see* corruption and the passions)
  rhetoric and, 119–21, 126
emperor *see also specific emperors*
  as *paterfamilias,* 30, 59
  as *pontifex maximus,* 142
  civic virtue of, 79–80
Empire, *see specific entries at* imperial
Ennius, 56
environment and nature, human relationship to, 197–98
Epictetus, 148, 153, 197
  Discourses, 59–60

Epicureanism
  compared to Roman political thought, 7
  Epicurus and founding principles of, 96–97,
      98, 99, 100, 101, 102, 103
  gratitude in, 103, 105, 110
  Lucretius on corruption, 95, 96–102
epideictic rhetoric, 114, 123
Eprius Marcellus, 131, 133
equality
  equal rights, 53
  isonomia (political equality), 50, 53
  before the law, 48, 51, 52, 53
  of political participation, 49–54
Erotianus, 148
êthos and rhetoric, 119, 122
evocatio, 144
extortion (*repetundae*), 91

faithfulness or trustworthiness (*fides*), as civic
    virtue, 77
Fannius (C. Fannius), 72
fathers, *see paterfamilias*
fear
  Cicero on imperialism and, 173
  of death (finitude), 100–1, 102, 103, 198
  of external enemy, 170–72, 175
Federalist Papers, 36, 131, 171
fetiales, 139
few, rule by (aristocracy), Polybius on, 15
fides (faithfulness or trustworthiness), as civic
    virtue, 77
finitude (death), fear of/acceptance of, 100–1,
    102, 103, 198
Flaccus (Lucius Valerius Flaccus), 148
Forst, Rainer, 145, 147
foundation myths, Roman, 70, 142, 160
freedom, *see* liberty

Gaius (Roman emperor), 149
Gaius Gracchus, 71
Gaius Memmius, 57
Gaius Octavius, *see* Augustus Caesar
Gallio (proconsul of Achaea), 150
Gallus (Trebonianus Gallus; Roman emperor), 152
Garnsey, Peter, 45, 144
gender, *see* women
Geneva Conventions, 180
Gibbon, Edward, 59
gift economy, Roman, 104
"good life," Roman concept of, 75, 78, 84,
    90, 123
gratitude, corruption, and the passions, 102–6,
    108, 109–11, 198–99
greatness of spirit (*magnitudo animi*), as civic
    virtue, 77
Grotius, Hugo, 182, 184

Habermas, Jürgen, 63, 117, 119
Hammer, D., 7
Hannibal of Carthage, 14, 174
happiness and gratitude, 199
heads of household, *see paterfamilias*
Helvidius Priscus, 83, 129
Henry, Patrick, 74
Hermarchus, 99
Herodotus, 14, 22
Hierocles, 186
Hobbes, Thomas, 19, 38, 113, 118, 124, 132, 197
honor code
  Augustine on, 87–88
  Cicero on imperialism and, 173–74
  civic virtue and, 73, 76, 81–84
  corruption and, 92, 94
  "good life" promoted by, 75, 78, 84, 90, 123
  importance in Roman political culture, 9
  just war theory and, 179–80
  liberty and, 55, 57
  modern sense of, 191
  order, generation of, 190
  political participation and, 40, 54–57
  struggle for status ameliorated by, 191
Honoré, Tony, 41
hope, corruption, and the passions, 108–9, 110
Horace, 82, 148
horizontal and vertical toleration, 149, 152
human nature
  Cicero on, 25
  Polybius on, 22–23
human or natural rights, Roman lack of concept
    of, 43, 45
Hume, David, *The Natural History of Religion*
    (1757), 145

immigration, modern concerns about, 63–65
imperial cult, 142–43
imperial transformation of Rome, *see also*
    Principate
  citizenship extended to all free persons in
      Roman world (Antonine Constitution),
      65–67, 69, 166
  civic virtue, 79–84
  civil religion and, 141–44
  constitution and, 29–34
  Dominate, 34
  liberty under, 57–60, 130
  political legitimacy and residual
      republicanism, 34–36
  private individuals in *res publica,* imperial
      citizens as, 59–60
  from republic to form of monarchy, 7–8
  rhetoric, Quintilian and decline narratives
      of, 124–28
  tetrarchy, 34

imperialism, 168–76
  Cicero on, 172–74
  as concept, 166–67
  defined, 167
  justice and, 172–74
  Polybius on, 168–70
  Sallust on productive nature of fear of
    external enemy, 170–72
  Tacitus' *Agricola* on, 174–76
imperialistic exportation of religion, 160–64
Inazu, John, *Confident Pluralism* (2016), 196
individual rights
  Aristotle and Plato on, 27
  in Athens versus Rome, 49
  citizens' rights and liberties, 46–49
  liberty and, 44–46
  ownership and control demarcated by, 45
interdependence and gratitude, 105
international relations, 166–91, *see also*
  imperialism; just war theory
  cosmopolitanism, 84, 167, 184–89
  ius gentium (law of nations), 41
  modern concepts of, 166, 195
  realism, 189–91
Iphigenia, sacrifice of, 101
isonomia (political equality), 50, 53
ius ad bellum (justice of going to war), 176–78
ius civile (civil law), 41
ius gentium (law of nations), 41
ius in bello (justice of waging war), 176–78
ius naturale, *see* natural law

Jefferson, Thomas, *Notes on the State of Virginia*
  (1785), on religious freedom, 155–58
Jews and Judaism
  Christianity and, 150
  Jewish rebellions of 66-70, 115-117, and 132-
    135, 148, 149
  Roman tolerance of, 147–50, 152
Johnston, D., 31
Josephus
  politeia, use of Greek concept of, 3
  on Roman tolerance of Judaism, 149
judgment (*consilium*)
  civil religion and, 140
  rhetoric and (*see* rhetoric, deliberation, and
    judgment)
judicial rhetoric, 114–15
Julius Caesar
  Cato the Younger and, 129
  citizenship and, 70, 78
  constitution and, 25, 31
  corruption and, 93, 97, 107
  divinization of, 142
  as Epicurean, 97

liberty, Roman ideas about, 55, 58
  Marius as model for, 107
  realism and, 190
just war theory, 176–84
  Ambrose of Milan on, 181–82
  of Augustine of Hippo, 177, 182–84
  in Christian thought, 181–84
  Cicero on, 177–78
  defined, 167
  of Grotius, 182, 184
  honor code and, 179–80
  ius ad bellum (justice of going to war), 176–78
  ius in bello (justice of waging war), 176–78
  modern expressions of, 176–77, 178, 180, 184
  religion and, 179
  Roman republican origins of, 177–80
justice
  as civic virtue, 77, 83, 88
  imperialism and, 172–74
  social economy and, 198
Justinian I (Roman emperor), 35
Juvenal, 148

Kass, A. A., 164
Kass, Leon R., 101, 164
Kaster, R., 78
Kennedy, G., 127
Kenney, E. J., 100
King, Martin Luther, Jr., 164
kingship, *see* monarchy

Lactantius, *The Divine Institutes*
  on pacifism, 181
  on religious tolerance, 158–60
Latin versus Roman colonies, 71
Lebow, Richard Ned, 191
legitimacy, political
  constitution and, 16, 20, 27, 34–36
  deliberative democrats on, 113, 117, 119
  religious toleration and, 155–58
Lendon, Ted, 190
Lex Aquilia, 43
Lex Hortensia, 17
Lex Iulia maiestatis, 130
lex maiestatis, 130
Lex Ogulnia, 140
Lex Oppia, 50
liberty, 37–62, *see also* equality
  ancient versus modern concepts of, 37–40, 42,
    60–62, 197–98
  Athenian versus Roman, 39, 60
  citizens' rights and, 46–49 (*see also*
    appellatio; *auxilium*; *conubium*;
    provocatio; *suffragium*)
  dignitas, importance of, 55–56, 58

environment and nature, human relationship
    to, 197–98
    under imperial transformation of Rome,
    57–60, 130
    individual rights and, 44–46
    license versus, 132
    magistrates, restraints on, 54–55, 58
    negative and positive, 38, 39, 50, 197
    neo-republican analysis of, 38–39, 42, 61
    ownership/control central to ideas of, 40, 43,
    45, 47, 58, 61
    paterfamilias, power of, 42
    political participation central to ideas of, 40,
    49–50, 54–57, 58–59, 60, 61
    private individuals in *res publica*, imperial
    citizens as, 59–60
    property and, 43–44, 45
    public versus private, 42, 54–55, 58, 60
    religion, Jefferson and Tertullian on freedom
    of, 154–58 (*see also* tolerance, religious)
    rhetoric and, 130–32
    slavery and Roman law of persons, 40–43
    women, restrictions on, 42
license versus liberty, 132
Licinius (Roman emperor), 152
Lincoln, Abraham, 164
    "The Perpetuation of our Political
    Institutions" (1838), 109
Livy
    Ab urbe condita, 13, 46
    on Cincinnatus, 74–75
    on citizens' rights, 46–48
    on civil religion, 139, 145
    on consulship, 29
    on equality, 50–51, 52
    on honor and order, 191
    on Jews and Judaism, 148
    on liberty, 40, 43, 57
    political writings of, 2, 6
    realism and, 190
    on republicanism, 2
Locke, John, 27, 38, 43, 155
    A Letter Concerning Toleration (1689), 160
Lombardini, John, 153
Longinus, 124
Lucan, 148
Lucretia, rape of, 13, 29, 47
Lucretius
    biographical information, 96
    on corruption and the passions, 95, 96–102
    De rerum natura, 96, 97, 98, 103
    finitude (death), fear of/acceptance of, 100–1,
    102, 103, 198
    on gratitude, 103, 198
    on Jews and Judaism, 148

political writings of, 6
    on reverence and *pietas*, 101–2
    Sallust compared, 97, 98
Luke (evangelist), 150, 151
Lycurgus, 23, 168

Macedonius, Letter of Augustine to, 89
Macer (C. Licinius Macer), 46, 57
Machiavelli, Niccolò, 160
    Discourses on the First Decade of Livy (1531), 46
    The Prince (1532), 32, 36
MacIntyre, Alasdair, 45
Madison, James, 131, 171
magistrates
    civil religion and, 139
    liberty and powers of, 54–55, 58
magnitudo animi (greatness of spirit), as civic
    virtue, 77
Manent, Pierre, 167
many, rule by, *see* popular sovereignty
Marcellinus, Letter of Augustine to, 88
Marcus Aurelius (Roman emperor), 153, 166,
    184–85, 186, 188, 197
    Meditations, 184
Marcus Lepidus, 29
Marcus Regulus, 87
Marcus Terentius, 84
Marius, in Plutarch's *Lives*, 106–8
Marius Priscus, 128
Mark Antony, 29
Markus, R. A., 86
Masinissa (Numidian king), 171
May, Larry, 184
Melians, 108
Memmius (dedicatee of Lucretius' *De rerum
    natura*), 97, 98
memory and gratitude, 105, 110
men of the people (*populares*), 48, 93, 117
mercy and related civic virtues, 78
Metellus (Quintus Metellus), funeral eulogy for
    Lucius Metellus, 76, 77
Milan, Edict of (313), 35, 85
military service and Roman citizenship, 68
Millar, Fergus, 19
Miller, Fred, Jr., 27
mixed constitutions
    of Carthage, 169
    Ciceronian versus Polybian models of, 25–28
    civil religion and, 139–41, 163
    Greek models of, 23
    of Sparta, 168–69
    Rome's compared to Sparta and
    Carthage, 168–70
Moatti, Claudia, 67
moderation, *see* temperance

modern liberal democracy and Roman
  republicanism, 8–10, 192–99
  American civil religion, argument for
    existence of, 164–65
  caution in comparing, 166
  citizenship, modern concepts of, 63–65
  constitution and, 11, 36
  corruption and the passions, 91, 95,
    109–11, 198–99
  cosmopolitanism, 188
  gift economy of Rome compared to capitalist
    meritocracies, 104
  gratitude and, 198–99
  honor code, modern sense of, 191
  international relations and, 166, 195
  just war theory, 176–77, 178, 180, 184
  liberty, ancient versus modern concepts of,
    37–40, 42, 60–62, 197–98
  methods for approaching, 193–95
  realism, 189–91
  relationship between, 8–10
  religion and, 137, 164–65, 195
  rhetoric, deliberation, and judgment, 112,
    113, 134–35
  Rockefeller vs. Hodges (U.S. Supreme Court,
    2015), 192–93
  tolerance, religious, and, 196–97
monarchy
  Dio Chrysostom on, 33–34
  imperial transformation of Rome from
    republic to form of, *see* imperial
    transformation of Rome
  Polybius on consular rule and, 14
  Seneca the Younger on *princeps*, 31–33
  Tarquinian rulers, move of Rome to republic
    from, 13, 47
Montesquieu, 36
Morgenthau, Hans, 189, 190
Morstein-Marx, Robert, 116, 117, 122
mystery religions, 145
Mytilenaean debate, 109

natural law (*ius naturale*)
  Cicero on, 13, 41, 156, 161–64, 179
  defined, 41
  Polybius on, 22–23
  Roman constitution and, 13
  in Stoicism, 162
  Tertullian on, 156
natural or human rights, Roman lack of concept
  of, 43, 45
nature and environment, human relationship
  to, 197–98
negative liberty, 38, 39, 50, 197
neo-realism, 190
neo-republican analysis of liberty, 38–39, 42, 61

Nero (Roman emperor), 31, 32, 59, 80, 125,
  128, 150
Nerva (Roman emperor), 82, 128, 174
Nicias, 108
Nietzsche, Friedrich, 101
9/11, 103
Nixon, Richard M., 91
Noreña, Carlos, 79
North, John, 139, 145

Obergefell vs. Hodges (U.S. Supreme Court,
  2015), 192–93
obsequium (compliance), as imperial civic
  virtue, 83, 84
one, rule by, *see* monarchy
optimates (aristocrats), 4, 36, 48, 93, 117
oratory, *see* rhetoric, deliberation, and
  judgment
Origen, on pacifism, 181
Ovid
  Fasti, 142
  on Jews and Judaism, 148
  Tristia, 30
ownership/control and liberty, 40, 43, 45,
  47, 58, 61

pacifism, Christian arguments for, 181
Panaetius, 186
paradiastolē (rhetorical redescription), 126, 127
the passions
  corruption and (*see* corruption and the
    passions)
  rhetoric and, 119–21, 126
paterfamilias
  citizenship of adult children and, 68
  emperor as, 30, 59
  liberty of adult children restricted by, 42
patriotism, as civic virtue, 78, 110–11, 164–65
Paul of Tarsus (St. Paul), 67, 84, 86, 150,
  153, 183
Peloponnesian War, 102, 126
Penn, William, 155
Persius, 148
Petronius, 124, 148
Philo of Alexandria, 149
Philo of Larissa, 1
philotimia (ambition or love of honor), 106, 107
pietas
  Augustus known for, 141
  as civic virtue, 78, 80, 88
  Epicurus on, 102
  Lucretius on, 101–2
  Tertullian on, 154
  Thucydides on, 102
Piso (consul and proconsul), 96
plague of Athens, 102

Plato and Platonism
    Alcibiades, 107
    chance, political change dependent on, 22
    Cicero's Platonic-style dialogues, 118
    compared to Roman political thought, 7
    Gorgias, 112, 119, 129
    harmony as goal of politics for, 24
    ideal, rational rule, interest in, 22, 26
    on individual rights, 27
    Laws, 137, 163
    Menexenus, 112
    "mixed constitution," model of, 23
    Phaedrus, 119
    philosophical method of being able to argue
        both sides of question, 124
    Plutarch as Platonist, 95
    Plutarch on death of, 108
    Republic, 4, 26, 132
    on rhetoric, 112, 117, 119, 123
    Tacitus and, 129
plebeian assemblies, 17
Pliny the Elder, 128, 148
Pliny the Younger
    on Christianity, 150–51
    on civic virtue, 79–80, 81–82, 84
    on constitution, 33
    Letters, 81–82
    Panegyricus, 33, 79–80
Plutarch
    biographical information, 106
    on corruption and the passions, 95, 106–9,
        110, 198
    on hope, 108–9, 110
    Parallel Lives, 96, 106–8, 188
    on *philotimia* (ambition or love of honor),
        106, 107
    political writings of, 6
    "Roman" nature of political writings of, 5
Pocock, J. G. A., 69
political corruption, *see* corruption and the
    passions
political culture of Rome
    agonistic nature of, 24, 28
    civic virtue and, 78
    importance of, 4–5, 9
    public speaking, importance of capacity for, 112
    Roman constitution regulated by, 12
political legitimacy, *see* legitimacy, political
political participation
    civic virtue in Roman Republic related
        to, 73
    liberty and, 40, 49–50, 54–57,
        58–59, 60, 61
    Roman citizenship and, 68
political rhetoric, *see* rhetoric, deliberation, and
    judgment

political thought, Roman, *see* Roman political
    thought
Polybius, *Histories*
    anakuklôsis (cyclical political change), theory
        of, 22–24
    on aristocracy and the senate, 15
    biographical information, 13
    Cicero compared, 25–28, 173, 174
    on civil religion in Rome, 21, 100
    on constitution, 13–24, 36
    Dio Chrysostom compared, 33
    framers of American constitution
        influenced by, 36
    on honor and order, 190
    on imperialism, 168–70
    on monarchy and consular rule, 14
    on natural law, 22–23
    politeia, use of Greek concept of, 3, 14
    political writings of, 2, 6
    on popular sovereignty, democracy, and
        assemblies, 15–18, 19–22
    pragmatic approach of, 26
    on productive nature of fear and
        conflict, 23–24, 171
    realism and, 190, 191
    "Roman" nature of political writings of, 5
    Sallust compared, 171
    on separation/balance of powers, 23
    Tacitus compared, 176
Pompey the Great, 25, 55, 70
pontifex maximus, emperor as, 142
pontifices, 139
popular assemblies, *see* assemblies, Roman
popular sovereignty
    Cicero on, 7, 26–27
    imperial transformation of Rome and, 30
    importance to *res publica*, 7
    Polybius on Roman assemblies and
        democracy, 15–18, 19–22
populares (men of the people), 48, 93, 117
positive liberty, 38, 197
power, love of (*philarchia*), 106, 107
powers, separation and balance of, *see* separation
    and balance of powers
presidential elections (2016), 198
Price, S., 139
priests and priesthoods, 139–40, 142
Principate
    civic virtue under, 79–84
    civil religion under, 141–44
    constitution under, 30–34
    defined, 30
    rhetoric, Quintilian and decline narratives
        of, 124–28
    rhetoric under, Tacitus on, 128–33
privacy, Roman lack of right of, 55

private individuals in *res publica,* imperial
    citizens as, 59–60
private versus public, *see* public versus private
property and property rights
    citizens' rights and, 49
    liberty and, 43–44, 45, 49
provocatio (right of appeal), as citizens' right, 49,
    54, 57, 67, 68, 71
public gratitude, 110, 111
public speaking *see* rhetoric, deliberation, and
    judgment
public versus private
    liberty, 42, 54–55, 58, 60
    religion and, 158
Punic War, second, 171, 174
Purdy, Jedidiah, 198
Pyrrhus (king of Epirus)
    Cicero on, 174, 180
    in Plutarch's *Lives,* 106–8

Quintilian
    Cicero and, 125–27
    Institutio oratoria, 125
    on Jews and Judaism, 148
    political writings of, 6
    on rhetoric, 124–28, 134
Quintus (brother of Cicero)
    Cicero, *Ad Quintum fratrum,* 55
    Commentariolum petitionis, 1–2

Rawls, John, 86
realism, 189–91
Red Cross, 180
Reidl, Matthias, 146
religion, *see* Christianity; civil religion in Rome;
    Jews and Judaism; *pietas*
religious tolerance, *see* tolerance, religious
Remer, Gary, 117
repetundae (extortion), 91
republicanism, Roman, *see* Roman political
    thought
restraint, *see* temperance
reverence, corruption, and the passions,
    101–2, 109, *see also* civil religion in
    Rome; *pietas*
rhetoric, deliberation, and judgment,
    112–35
    in Athens, 117
    character (*êthos*), role of, 119, 122
    Cicero on, 112, 116, 118–24
    in *contiones,* 114, 115–17, 119, 122, 127
    critical approaches to, 112–13, 118, 119
    definition of rhetoric, 112, 125
    deliberative oratory, 114, 115–18, 126
    epideictic oratory, 114, 123
    judicial oratory, 114–15

lex maiestatis, effects of, 130
liberty and, 130–32
modern approaches to, 112, 113, 134–35
paradiastolê (rhetorical rediscription),
    126, 127
passions, significance of, 119–21, 126
philosophical method of being able to argue
    both sides of question, 124
Quintilian and decline narrative of rhetoric
    under Principate, 124–28, 134
in Roman forum, 117–18
in Roman Republic, 113–18
in senate, 114, 115
Tacitus on rhetoric under the Principate,
    128–33, 134
Rhetorica ad Herennium, 114, 121, 126
rights, *see also* individual rights; property and
    property rights
    of citizens, 46–49, 68 (*see also appellatio;*
        auxilium; conubium; provocatio;
        suffragium)
    customary rights and institutions, force
        of, 12–13
    equal rights, 53
    natural or human rights, Roman lack of
        concept of, 43, 44–45
    privacy, Roman lack of right of, 55
Roman assemblies, *see* assemblies, Roman
Roman colonies versus Latin colonies, 71
Roman constitution, *see* constitution,
    Roman
Roman emperor, *see* emperor; *specific emperors*
Roman Empire, *see specific entries at* imperial
Roman forum, oratory in, 117–18
Roman foundation myths, 70, 142, 160
Roman political thought, 1–10
    Athenian democracy compared, 6–8
        (*see also* Athenian democracy and Roman
        republicanism)
    Christianity and, 5 (*see also* Christianity)
    Cicero's consulship campaign and Quintus's
        Commentariolum petitionis, 1–2
    citizenship, 63–90 (*see also* citizenship)
    civic virtue, 73–90 (*see also* civic virtue)
    civil religion, 136–65 (*see also* civil religion
        in Rome)
    constitution, 11–36 (*see also*
        constitution, Roman)
    on corruption and the passions, 91–111
        (*see also* corruption and the passions)
    imperial transformation of Rome from
        republic to form of monarchy, 7–8
    on international relations, 166–91 (*see also*
        international relations)
    liberty, 37–62 (*see also* liberty)
    methodology and approach, 5–6

modern liberal democracy and, 8–10, 192–99
  (*see also* modern liberal democracy and
  Roman republicanism)
political culture as well as formal institutions,
  importance of, 4–5, 9 (*see also* political
  culture of Rome)
"political," defined, 3–5
republicanism, concept of, 2–3
rhetoric, deliberation, and judgment,
  112–35 (*see also* rhetoric, deliberation, and
  judgment)
"Roman," defined, 5
"thought," defined, 3
timeline, xii, 5
Roman senate, *see* senate, Roman
Rome, sack of (410), 35, 86
Romulus Augustus (Roman emperor), 34
Romulus, Roman foundation myth of, 70, 142
Roskam, Geert, 97
Rousseau, Jean-Jacques
  on civil religion, 136–38, 145, 160, 162, 163, 164
  On the Social Contract (1762), 136–38
  Second Discourse on the Origins of Inequality
    (1755), 99

sack of Rome (410), 35, 86
Sailor, Dylan, 175
Sallust
  Augustine influenced by, 87, 88
  biographical information, 92
  Catiline's Conspiracy, 56, 76–78, 92, 93, 126, 171
  Cicero compared, 173
  on citizens' rights, 46
  on civic virtue, 73, 76–78, 83
  on corruption and the passions, 92–95, 102
  on fear of external enemy, 170–72, 175
  Histories, 171
  on honor and order, 190
  on imperialism, 170–72
  on individual rights, 46
  The Jugurthine War, 57, 92, 171
  justification of literary efforts by, 56
  on liberty, 40, 43, 57
  Lucretius compared, 97, 98
  on political participation, 56–57
  political writings of, 2, 6
  Polybius compared, 171
  realism and, 190
  on rhetoric, 126, 127
  Tacitus compared, 176
Scapula (African proconsul), 154, 157
Schaub, D., 164
Scheidel, Walter, 40
Scipio Africanus
  in Cicero's *De republica*, 25, 26, 28, 52, 54
  on *dignitas* and liberty, 56

Scipio Nasica, 25, 170
Scruton, Roger, 109
Second Sophistic, 66
senate, Roman
  Augustus Caesar and, 30
  Bacchanalia, regulation of, 145–46
  Centuriate Assembly votes requiring
    ratification by, 20
  civil religion and, 139
  Polybius on, 15
  rhetoric in, 114, 115
Seneca the Younger
  Cicero compared, 31–32
  on civic virtue, 79–80, 81
  on constitution, 31–33
  on corruption and the passions, 95, 103–6
  on cosmopolitanism, 188
  De beneficiis, 33, 81, 104–6
  De clementia, 31–33, 79,
  De otio, 186
  on decline of rhetoric, 124
  Dio Chrysostom compared, 33
  on gratitude, 103–6, 110, 198
  on Jews and Judaism, 148
  Stoicism of, 31, 32, 95, 104, 186
  on tolerance, 153
separation and balance of powers
  Cicero on, 27
  Montesquieu's development of idea of, 36
  Polybius on, 23
September 11, 2001 terrorist attacks, 103
Sextus Tarquinis, 13
Sibylline Books, 139, 142
Sisyphus, 97
Skinner, Quentin, 38, 50
slavery
  liberty versus, 40–43
  property rights and, 43
Smith, Adam, 187
social contract theory, 99–100
Social War, 72, 118
Socrates, 107, 112, 129, 132, 146
Sparta, Polybius on mixed constitution
  of, 168–69
status, *see* class and status
Stockdale, James Bond, 60
Stoicism
  compared to Roman political thought, 7
  cosmopolitanism, 84, 167, 184–89
  Dio Chrysostom and, 33
  Epictetus, *Discourses*, 59–60
  gratitude in, 104, 105
  natural law in, 162
  Seneca the Younger and, 31, 32, 95, 104, 186
  tolerance as virtue for, 153, 154
Straumann, Benjamin, 12

Strauss, Leo, 45
Suetonius, 141
suffragium (right to vote), as citizens' right, 47,
    48, 50, 54, 68, 69
Sulla, 24, 108, 115, 118
sumptuary laws for women, 50–51
superstitio, belief systems classified as, 147,
    150, 151
supremacy clause, 71

Tacitus, *see also* Agricola
    Annals, 30, 83, 84, 128
    biographical information, 128
    on Christianity, 150
    Cicero and, 129, 131–32, 133
    on civic virtue, 82–84
    Dialogus de oratoribus, 128–29, 131
    on funeral of Augustus Caesar, 30
    Germania, 128
    Histories, 128, 131
    on honor and order, 191
    on Jews and Judaism, 148, 150
    on liberty, 43, 59, 130
    political writings of, 2, 6
    Polybius compared, 176
    on republicanism, 2
    on rhetoric under the Principate, 128–33, 134
    Sallust compared, 176
Tarquinian monarchy, 13, 47
taxation and Roman citizenship, 66, 68
temperance, as civic virtue, 77, 83
Terence, *The Self-Tormentor,* 187
Tertullian
    Ad Scapulam, 154–55, 156, 157
    Apologeticum, 154
    De anima, 156
    on natural law, 156
    on pacifism, 181
    political writings of, 6
    on toleration, 154–59
tetrarchy, 34
Theodosius I (Roman emperor), 34, 35
Thomas Aquinas, 41
Thrasea Paetus, 83
Thucydides, *History*
    compared to Roman political thought, 7
    on hasty decisions by democratic bodies, 141
    on hope, 108, 110
    "mixed constitution," model of, 23
    on plague of Athens and lack of
        reverence, 102
    realism and, 190
    on rhetoric, 126
Tiberius (Roman emperor), 84, 124, 130, 149
Tiberius Gracchus, 25

Tibullus, 148
Tocqueville, Alexis de, 199
tolerance, religious, 144–60
    Bacchanalia, senate regulation of, 145–46
    centralization of Roman civil religion by
        Decius' edict, effects of, 143, 152
    Christianity, arguments for tolerance
        in, 153–60
    Christianity, Roman treatment of, 143,
        150–52, 158
    civic/political order and, 146–47, 151–52
    defining, 144
    horizontal and vertical toleration, 149, 152
    Jefferson, Thomas, *Notes on the State of
        Virginia* (1785), 155–58
    Jews and Judaism, treatment of, 147–50, 152
    limits of, 146
    Locke on, 160
    modern liberal democracy and, 196–97
    openness of Rome to foreign religions
        and, 144
    political legitimacy and, 155–58
    polytheism and, 145
    public versus private aspects of religion and, 158
    Roman arguments in favor of, 152–60
    Rousseau's efforts to promote, 138
    Socrates, execution of, 146
    superstitio, belief systems classified as, 147,
        150, 151
Torquatus, 96
Trajan (Roman emperor), 33, 80, 128, 150–51
Tribal Assembly, 16
tribunate, 17
Trump, Donald, 63
trustworthiness or faithfulness (*fides*), as civic
    virtue, 77
Twelve Tables, 40, 43, 48, 121

Ulpian, 12, 41, 66
    Regulae, 12
United States, *see specific entries at* American
Universal Declaration of Human Rights, 37, 44
universal principles and particular religious
    practices, tension between, 138, 143, 160,
    161–62, 163, 164–65
Urso (Spanish colony), 161

Valerian (Roman emperor), 152, 154
Varro (Marcus Terentius Varro), 12, 136, 141,
    148, 161
Vasaly, Ann, 51
Vergil, 82, 148
    Aeneid, 160
vertical and horizontal toleration, 149, 152
Vespasian (Roman emperor), 83, 149

Vesta (goddess)
    Aeneas, Roman foundation myth of, 142, 144
    Augustus Caesar, Vesta and Apollo cults
        moved to home of, 59, 142
Vibius Crispus, 131, 133
Vietnam War, 60, 176
Villey, Michel, 45
virtue, civic, *see* civic virtue
Visigoths, sack of Rome (410) by, 35, 86

Walz, Kenneth, 189, 190, 191
Walzer, Michael, 69
    Just and Unjust Wars (1977), 178
    On Toleration (1997), 147, 152

Washington, George, 74
Watergate, 91
West, Cornel, 110
Wiedemann, Thomas, 171
Wilken, Robert Louis, 155
wisdom, as civic virtue, 76, 77, 83
women
    citizenship and, 68
    liberty, restrictions on, 42
    sumptuary laws for, 50–51
Woodruff, Paul, 102, 109

Zeno of Citium, *Republic*, 185, 186

CPSIA information can be obtained
at www.ICGtesting.com
Printed in the USA
LVHW011153290721
693967LV00011B/869